LANGUAGE UNIVERSALS
AND LINGUISTIC TYPOLOGY

Language Universals and Linguistic Typology

SYNTAX AND MORPHOLOGY

Bernard Comrie

University of Chicago Press

The University of Chicago Press, Chicago 60637

Basil Blackwell Publisher Limited, Oxford

© 1981 by Bernard Comrie
All rights reserved. Published 1981

ISBN 0-226-11434-1 (cloth)
ISBN 0-226-11436-8 (paper)

Library of Congress Card Number 81-52478

Reprinted in Great Britain

88   87   86   85   5432

CONTENTS

PREFACE

After a period when the frontiers of linguistic research seemed to be concerned primarily with the analysis of English syntax, the last decade has seen a remarkable upsurge of interest in problems of language universals and linguistic typology using data from a wide range of languages. Despite the vast amount of work that has been carried out within this framework, there has been, to date, no general introductory work that has attempted to synthesize the main characteristics of this approach for the student of linguistics, who has had to turn almost from the very beginning to specialist literature on individual topics in article form. This book aims to fill this gap, to provide the advanced undergraduate and graduate student with an overview of the major current approaches to language universals and typology, with illustrations of the successes of this method – and also warnings about some of the dangers.

In a field where so much literature has arisen in a relatively short period, this book is necessarily very selective in the range of topics chosen, with preference for going into certain topics in depth rather than giving a superficial overview of the whole field. I have also restricted coverage, for the most part, to recent work on universals and typology, rather than try to give a historical account of earlier work in this area, although earlier work is mentioned, especially to the extent that it has not been subsumed by more recent research. Some of the selectivity necessarily reflects my own biases, towards those areas where I have worked myself or where I feel the most exciting results have been forthcoming. The book is concerned almost entirely with syntactico-semantic universals, although on occasion phonological universals are also used as illustrative material. I believe that critical discussion of work in a few areas is more valuable than an unannotated listing, however comprehensive, of claims that have been made about universals and typology.

The first two chapters are general in nature, presenting and arguing my view that the study of language universals can proceed most fruitfully on the basis of consideration of data from a wide range of languages, and embedding the study of syntactico-semantic universals within an integrative approach to language in which explanations for universals are sought not so much within the formal properties of language, but rather by relating formal properties of language, at various levels (including syntactic and phonological), to the extra-linguistic context within which language functions. Later chapters, for the most part, look at individual construction types or other syntactic phenomena, such as word order, relative clauses, causative constructions, case marking, from the viewpoint of universals and typological research that uses data from a wide range of languages within an integrative approach. The particular choice of topics is to a large extent arbitrary, reflecting my own interests, but if this choice is no better than some others, I would argue that it is also no worse.

It is difficult for me to give a comprehensive list of acknowledgements to all those who have contributed to the development of this book and the ideas contained in it: study of universals and typology necessarily interrelates with work on just about every other aspect of language and linguistics, and I must with regret refrain from a list of everyone who has influenced my thinking on language. The following acknowledgements therefore relate to those, in addition to linguists acknowledged specifically in the notes to the various chapters, who have influenced my thinking on universals and typology and who have influenced the particular mode of presentation adopted in this book.

My debt to Joseph H. Greenberg (Stanford University) will be apparent on almost every page: it is he, more than any other single linguist, who initiated the present interest in working on language universals on the basis of a wide range of languages, and who persisted in advocating this approach even in periods when it was far from fashionable. Edward L. Keenan (University of California at Los Angeles) helped me to see that interest in a wide range of languages is not incompatible with interests in theoretical and formal issues. My colleagues in the Department of Linguistics at the University of Southern California, sensing early on my conversion to an integrative approach to language in context, have provided an environment full of stimuli to the development of this interest.

Although at times I am necessarily critical, in this book, of the approach to language universals adopted within mainstream transformational-generative grammar, and especially by Noam Chomsky, I cannot and would not want to deny my indebtedness to my training within this model and to those who trained me in it. Whatever disagreements I have since developed with some of the tenets of the descriptive model and its ideological underpinnings, it has clearly raised syntactic analysis to a level of rigour and insightfulness without which this book would not have been possible. Similar remarks apply to the model of syntax proposed by relational grammar: although I disagree with the emphasis on structure-internal explanations of syntactic generalizations, and on many other specific and general issues, this approach to syntax has provided me with a vast number of insights into syntactic structure that would otherwise probably have escaped me, and it is with genuine, not damning, praise that I would acknowledge that, as far as formal models of syntax go, relational grammar seems to me to go the furthest.

I have also benefited considerably from discussions with linguists at various institutions engaged in research into language universals and typology, to whom I have been able to present parts of my own work and who have in turn presented some of their work to me. In particular, I would mention the participants in the Linguistic Society of America Linguistic Institute at the State University of New York at Oswego (1976), with typology as one of its foci; the Stanford Universals Project; the Universals Project (Universalien-Projekt) of the Department of Linguistics of the University of Cologne; and the Structural Typology Group of the Leningrad Section of the Linguistics Institute of the Academy of Sciences of the USSR.

The materials contained in this book derive in large part from materials tested out on students who attended my courses and seminars on language universals and typology. I would therefore like also to thank all the students, faculty members, and visitors who attended these courses at the University of Cambridge, the Linguistic Society of America Linguistic Institute at the University of Illinois at Urbana-Champaign (1978), the University of Southern California, and the Australian National University. This book has, in addition, benefited from the comments of anonymous readers for Basil Blackwell and the University of Chicago Press.

Finally, I wish to express my gratitude to the many fieldworkers and native-speaker linguists, often working well away from the beaten track and well away from mainstream theoretical linguistics, who have both provided me with invaluable material for my work and encouraged me in this work by their interest in it and the possibility of a constructive dialogue between us. I hope they realize that my aim has not been to steal a relative clause or a causative construction from their language, but rather to put into practice my belief that the maximum benefit both to general linguistics and to the description of individual languages will develop from the maximum integration of these two approaches – the one cannot flourish without the other. Or more generally: linguistics is about languages; and languages are spoken by people.

Los Angeles, January 1981   Bernard Comrie

I

LANGUAGE UNIVERSALS

1.1 APPROACHES TO LANGUAGE UNIVERSALS

1.1.1 TWO MAJOR APPROACHES

In this section, we will contrast two major methodological approaches to language universals that have been adopted in recent linguistic work. The two approaches can be contrasted on a number of parameters, the most important of these being the following: the data base for research on language universals (a wide range of languages, or just a single language); the degree of abstractness of analysis that is required in order to state language universals (for instance, in terms of surface syntactic structures or in terms of deep syntactic structures); and the kinds of explanations advanced for the existence of language universals. The individual parameters, and others, will be taken up again in subsequent sections. Although each of these parameters is logically independent of the others, in fact the two major recent approaches each represent a coherent clustering of these parameters. On the one hand, some linguists have argued that in order to carry out research on language universals, it is necessary to have data from a wide range of languages; linguists advocating this approach have tended to concentrate on universals stable in terms of relatively concrete rather than very abstract analyses, and have tended to be open, or at least eclectic, in the kinds of explanations that may be advanced for the existence of language universals. On the other hand, some linguists have argued that the best way to learn about language univer-sals is by the detailed study of an individual language; such linguists have also advocated stating language universals in terms of abstract structures (such as deep syntactic structures within transformational-generative syntax), and have tended to favour innateness as the explanation for language univer-sals. The first of these two approaches is perhaps most closely associated with the work of Joseph H. Greenberg and of those inspired by his work, and also reflects the orientation of the present book. The second is most closely associated with the work of Noam Chomsky and those most directly influenced by him, and might be regarded as the orthodox transformational position.

At first sight, at least with regard to the data base for work on language universals, it might seem that Greenberg's approach is necessarily correct, since surely in order to establish that something is universal in language one would need to look at a wide range of languages – if not, indeed, at all languages. However, the argumentation is by no means so simple as this, a point to which we will return in section 1.1.2. For the remainder of this section, we will outline the motivation for adopting Chomsky's approach to language universals. Although this argumentation is, as the subsequent discussion will show, vulnerable on a number of points, both conceptual and empirical, it does represent a coherent position with regard to language universals research which cannot simply be ignored.

A transformational-generative description of a language, or more specifically of the syntax of a language (although similar arguments could be transferred, say, to a generative-phonological description), maintains that, in addition to relatively concrete (close-to-surface) levels of syntactic representation, there are also levels of representation that are considerably more abstract, considerably removed from the surface-structure analysis: these are the deep structure, and also various intervening levels of representation between deep and surface structure. Although the precise degree of abstractness of deep structures has been, and continues to be, a matter of controversy, the existence of such abstract structures characterizes most versions of transformational-generative grammar. When the existence of such abstract representations is taken into account in discussing the way in which children acquire their first language, a potential problem arises. If the best way of characterizing the structure of a language involves abstract underlying structures, then it is probably justifiable to assume that, in acquiring a language, the child internalizes these abstract structures. This implies, in turn, that he must also internalize rules for passing from these abstract structures to the more concrete levels of analysis. The argument then continues by claiming that there is no way, in terms of our current knowledge of learning abilities, in which the child, presented only with the data of adults using the language around him, could induce these abstract principles from these data. Moreover, it is argued that the rules needed to pass from deep to surface structure are subject to a number of highly specific constraints: again, it is not clear how these constraints, which are highly abstract in nature, could be induced by the child from the raw data presented to him by adult speech. More generally, if the child is viewed simply as a tabula rasa, as having no predisposition to analysing data in terms of one formal system rather than any other one, then it is difficult or impossible to explain how the child does in fact come to acquire his first language within a relatively short period of time.

This learnability problem evaporates if one makes the crucial assumption underlying orthodox transformational work on language universals. The reason why the child acquires his first language so effortlessly is that the crucial abstract principles of transformational-generative grammar are innate: they are available to the child from birth (or, perhaps, are available from a certain period soon after birth as part of the maturational process, but at any rate are preprogrammed at birth), so that the child does not have to learn them, but can use them in figuring out which particular language, of those permitted by the general theory of transformational-generative grammar, is being spoken in his speech community: although the general theory (and, equivalently, the set of innate abstract principles internal to the child) allows an infinite number of possible languages, the types of languages are greatly restricted to those permitted by the constraints imposed by the theory.

Given the simple observation that children learn their first language so readily, one might wonder whether an even stronger claim could not be made, namely that the language as a whole is innate. This would assume that a child born into a given speech community is already preprogrammed with knowledge of the language of the speech community, presumably having inherited it from his parents. However, further observation soon shows that this scenario, though clearly simplifying the learnability problem, cannot be correct. It would imply that a child could only learn, or at least would much more readily learn, the language of his parents, irrespective of the language of the surrounding community. Now, it is known from observation that children acquire, with approximately equal facility, the language of whatever speech community they happen to grow up in, quite irrespective of the language of their parents or their more remote ancestors; this can be seen most clearly in the case of children who are brought up by speakers of a language different from that of their natural parents. Thus it cannot be the case that the language as a whole is innate – note that this was established on the basis of empirical observation, rather than by speculation. At best certain principles common to all human languages would be innate, which would thus facilitate the child's task in acquiring whichever language he happens to be exposed to, with no preference for one language over any other. This now brings in the last link in this argument: since the abstract principles claimed to be innate are the same for all children, irrespective of ethnic background, they must be neutral with respect to differences among languages, i.e. they must be universal. One can thus establish an equation between language universals and innate ideas: language universals would be those innate linguistic principles which facilitate the child's language-learning task.

Once one makes this equation, it is but a short step to justifying the methodology of language universals research adopted by Chomsky. Since the universals in which one is interested are abstract principles, there is no way in which the analysis of surface structures of a wide range of languages would provide any relevant data. Rather, one should investigate relations between abstract and more concrete levels of representation, in order to factor out the abstract principles which constrain language structure (and which are, thus, language universals or, equivalently, innate ideas). In principle, one could argue that this should lead to study of the detailed transformational-generative grammars of a number of languages, but given the limitations on resources devoted to linguistic research, in practice this is not feasible. In terms of the weighting of breadth as against depth of coverage of languages, the position outlined in this section clearly favours concentrating on depth, with preference for the detailed abstract study of a single language rather than casting the net more widely but with less depth. From this come the general methodological tenets outlined at the beginning of the section: the most profitable way to study language universals is to study a single language in depth, in terms of an abstract analysis of that language – the universals themselves are then of an abstract nature (abstract constraints on a system involving abstract levels of representation); since language universals are equated with innate ideas, the latter provide an obvious explanation for the former, and the only way in which one might need to extend the consideration of explanatory principles would be to ask whether there is in turn an explanation for the innate ideas.

In sections 1.1.2–3, we will consider practical reasons why this research strategy for language universals, despite its internal coherence, suffers from a number of serious defects, leading to its rejection in the present book. To conclude this section, however, we will examine some more general weaknesses of the argumentation leading to the research paradigm. These weaknesses stem mainly from the fact that the argumentation is almost entirely aprioristic, with virtually no appeal to actual data supporting the position being argued for: indeed the only direct appeal to facts, namely that children learn any language with comparable facility, served only to establish a non-universal (the specific language as a whole cannot be innate). Of course, in any science it is necessary to establish hypotheses which may, in the initial stages, be largely aprioristic, but it is important then to test out these hypotheses, to see to what extent they do fit with the data range to be explained. The real problem with the kind of aprioristic argumentation summarized in this section is that it is not, given present techniques, subject to any kind of empirical test, i.e. is not potentially disconfirmable. More specifically, the claims about what is inherently easy or difficult to learn are not based on any actual research on ease of learnability, so that again one must simply take on trust that some things are easily learned and others less so, others perhaps being impossible to learn. Finally, as will be shown in more detail in section 1.1.3, any argument based on an abstract analysis is no stronger than is that abstract analysis itself, and given the wide range of competing abstract analyses of, say English syntax, one must again simply take on trust that one analysis, rather than another, is the psychologically real analysis (or, at least, the best that we can, in our present state of knowledge, advance as the psychologically correct analysis). Generalizing these remarks, the research paradigm outlined in this section is characterized by a number of questionable assumptions that are crucial to the argumentation, these assumptions being for the most part untestable, at least at present, so that acceptance of the paradigm becomes simply a matter of faith.

1.1.2 THE DATA BASE

In this section, we will establish some more practical reasons why the study of language universals must operate with data from a wide range of languages, then look at some of the implications of this for the practice of research on language universals. A priori, there seems to be no reason to assume either that language universals research should require a wide range of languages – in section 1.1.1 we outlined a coherent paradigm which did not make this requirement – or that it should not, and one can easily come up with analogies from other investigations for either of these two positions. For instance, if one wanted to study the chemical properties of iron, then presumably one would concentrate on analysing a single sample of iron, rather than on analysing vast numbers of pieces of iron, still less attempting to obtain a representative sample of the world's iron. This simply reflects our knowledge (based, presumably, on experience) that all instances of a given substance are homogeneous with respect to their chemical properties. On the other hand, if one wanted to study human behaviour under stress, then presumably one would not concentrate on analysing the behaviour of just a single individual, since we know from experience that different people behave differently under similar conditions of stress, i.e. if one wanted to make generalizations about over-all tendencies in human behaviour under stress it would be necessary to work with a representative sample of individuals (even if the study were restricted to a single society, let alone a cross-cultural study).

Since one of the things we want to find out in work on language universals is the range of variation found across languages and the limits placed on this variation, it would be a serious methodological error to build into our research programme aprioristic assumptions about the range of variation. Moreover, as we shall see in the following paragraphs, there is evidence from fairly basic research on language universals that, in certain crucial cases that have arisen in work to date, data from a wide range of languages were in fact necessary to have a reasonable chance of validating a given language universal.

First, there are certain language universals that simply cannot be predicated of an individual language. In particular, implicational universals are of this kind. We shall look at implicational universals in more detail in section 1.2.2, for the moment it suffices to note that an implicational universal always involves at least two linguistic properties, which we may symbolize as p and q, related to one another as an implication (condition), i.e. 'if p, then q'. As a simple example, we may take the following actual example: if the basic word order of a language is verb – subject – object (VSO), then it will have prepositions (rather than postpositions). In this example, the property p is 'having VSO basic word order' and q is 'having prepositions'. The combination of these two properties can be seen, for instance, in Welsh, with a sentence like *gwelodd y dyn y cwcw* 'the man saw the cuckoo', literally 'saw the man the cuckoo', and a prepositional phrase like *yn y tŷ* 'in the house'. Note, however, that Welsh does not provide any evidence for stating the universal as an implication: indeed, if we were only investigating Welsh, we might be led to conclude that a language must have VSO word order and must have prepositions. Investigation of other languages, however, soon shows this generalization to be untrue. English, for instance has subject – verb – object (SVO) word order and prepositions, as in *the man saw the woman* and *in the room*. Conversely, Japanese has subject – object – verb (SOV) basic word order and postpositions, as in *Hanako ga Taroo o butta* 'Hanako hit Taroo', literally 'Hanako SUBJECT Taroo DIRECT – OBJECT hit', which illustrates both the basic clause-internal word order and the existence of postpositions (such as *ga* marking the subject and *o* marking the direct object). The fourth logical possibility – a language having basic VSO word order and postpositions – is excluded by the implicational universal.

If we were to base our study on any single language, then we would be led to make a statement stronger than the implicational universal, as we noted above with respect to the Welsh data. Only consideration of data from a range of languages enables us to see that of the four logical combinations – (a) VSO order and prepositions, (b) VSO order and postpositions, (c) word order other than VSO and prepositions, (d) word order other than VSO and postpositions – one, namely (b), is systematically absent. Of course, each individual language must be consistent with an implicational universal, otherwise it would be a counterexample, but no individual language provides the kind of evidence that would be needed to justify positing an implicational universal. (The only exception to this

would be where a given individual language has more than one construction in a given area, in which case it might be possible to establish an
implication on the basis of data from the two constructions within the same
language; this possibility is illustrated in chapter 7, for relative clauses.)

In addition to such examples where data from a range of languages is
absolutely necessary, even aprioristically, in the establishment of language
universals, there are other examples where failure to consider a range of
languages has led to the positing of putative language universals which
then crumble as soon as one is presented with data from other languages.
As illustration, we shall take one example from the most recent variant of
transformational-generative grammar, the extended standard theory.
Here, it is argued that, if we treat $\bar{\bar{X}}$ as a cover symbol for various kinds of
phrase (e.g. noun phrases, verb phrases, adjective phrases), then there is a
general (i.e. language-independent) expansion rule $\bar{\bar{X}} \rightarrow \text{Spec}_{\bar{X}}\ \bar{X}$, i.e. that
a phrase $\bar{\bar{X}}$ (a phrase whose head constituent is X, so that noun phrase
would be symbolized $\bar{\bar{N}}$) consists of the immediate constituents
Specifier-of-$\bar{X}$ and $\bar{X}$. In terms of actual phrase types, if X is noun, then
$\text{Spec}_{\bar{X}}$ would be, for instance, an article (determiner); if X is verb, then
$\text{Spec}_{\bar{X}}$ would be an auxiliary. The language-independent schema given
above for the expansion of $\bar{\bar{X}}$ says nothing about the relative order of $\text{Spec}_{\bar{X}}$
and $\bar{X}$, this being left as a parameter on which individual languages may
vary. However, the schema does make claims about the relative order of
$\text{Spec}_{\bar{X}}$ and $\bar{X}$ across phrase types within a given language. Interpreted as an
absolute, exceptionless universal (see section 1.2.3), it claims that in a
given language, for all phrase types either the Specifier precedes or it
follows, i.e. either determiners precede nouns and auxiliaries precede
verbs, or determiners follow nouns and auxiliaries follow verbs. Interpreted as a tendency, it says that languages would tend to adhere to this
generalization, although it would always be open to an individual language
to violate the universal.

This universal was originally proposed on the basis of English data, and
in English it is indeed the case that determiners precede their noun (as in
the book) and that auxiliaries precede their verb (as in *must go*). There are
clear counterexamples to the principle as an absolute universal: for instance, in Malay determiners follow their noun (e.g. *surat itu* 'that letter',
literally 'letter that'), while auxiliaries precede their verb (e.g. *sedang
membaca* 'is reading', *akan membaca* 'will read'). In fact, in current work
within the extended standard theory, it is usually stated, or at least allowed
as a possibility, that the schema may be a tendency, rather than an absolute
universal. However, even this claim turns out to be invalid as an attempt to
characterize variation across languages. The number of languages in which
determiners follow nouns and auxiliaries follow verbs is small, while there

are many languages – including most languages of the widespread canonical SOV type (see chapter 4) – that have determiners preceding the noun but auxiliaries following the verb, as in Japanese *kono hon* 'this book', *aisite iru* 'loves', literally 'loving is'. In other words, in terms of the actual distribution of word order types along these two parameters (determiner relative to noun, auxiliary relative to main verb), the schema makes incorrect claims, even as a statement of a tendency.

Note that the weakness of the one-language approach to language universals illustrated here is not simply that a given putative universal turns out to be wrong. This is almost inevitably going to be the case whatever data base one adopts for research on language universals, since certain attested language types are simply very rare, and might very well not be included even within a comprehensive sample of the world's languages: for instance, click consonants as regular phonemes are restricted to Khoisan and neighbouring Bantu languages in southern Africa; very few languages, perhaps restricted to the Amazon basin, have object – verb – subject (OVS) as their basic word order. The point is rather that, once the putative universal concerning the order of $Spec_{\bar{X}}$ and $\bar{X}$ was formulated by proponents of the extended standard theory, they made no attempt to establish, say by looking even at a few other languages with different word order possibilities, whether or not their generalization stood some chance of being a valid cross-language generalization. What is even more disturbing is that attempts to bring such data to the attention of practitioners of the one-language approach to universals meet with lack of interest, rather than any attempt to work out the implications of the new data for the over-all theory. Although in principle the one-language approach always leaves it open to other linguists to test universals formulated on the basis of English against other languages, in practice it is all too rare for such feedback to have any impact.

As a final point relative to the use of one language or a wide range of languages as the basis for work on language universals, we might note that within transformational-generative grammar, and even within Chomsky's own work, there is a major difference between work on syntax and work on phonology: while the former has proceeded almost exclusively in terms of work on English, the development of generative phonology has always recognized the importance of data from other languages. As a nice illustration of this, we may note that Chomsky's *Aspects of the theory of syntax*, though a work on syntactic theory rather than specifically the analysis of English, uses almost exclusively examples from English; whereas Chomsky and Halle's *The sound pattern of English*, where the title explicitly refers to English, includes also reference to a hundred other languages, some of which are used crucially in the resolution of general theoretical issues of phonology. This discrepancy seems not to have been discussed by proponents of the one-language approach to language universals.

From the theoretical and practical deficiencies of trying to work on language universals on the basis of a single language, one might think that the ideal would be to base the study of language universals on simultaneous investigation of all languages of the world. However, there are two very obvious reasons why this is impossible. First, we know that many languages have become extinct without ever having been recorded, or without being recorded in sufficient detail to be of value to our enterprise, in addition to which, given language change, many new languages will arise in the future; clearly, these two sets of languages are unavailable to us, and therefore a large number of actual human languages (defined as languages that were, are, or will be spoken) are not amenable to investigation. Secondly, the estimated number of languages spoken in the world today is so large that, if we were to await investigation of each language before embarking on research on universals, we would probably never even initiate our main task. Although estimates of the number of different languages vary considerably, they tend to cluster around the 4,000 mark.

In practical terms, then, the problem with which we are faced is establishing a representative sample of human languages in order to be able to carry out work on language universals that is both manageable in practical terms and likely to be free of bias from concentrating unduly on a single language or group of languages. The population from which we draw our sample is limited to the languages actually spoken today, plus some of the better documented extinct languages (though, given the absence of native speakers, certain questions concerning a dead language will necessarily go unanswered). Behind this statement, there are two assumptions that are necessary to such work on language universals, but which should not go unstated. One is that, at least within a time-span of several thousand years in either direction from the present, there has been no significant sense in which human language has evolved, i.e. no sense in which human language as a whole today is different in essence from that of ten thousand years ago; more specifically, it assumes that all human languages spoken today represent the same level of evolution. The more specific assumption seems reasonable, given that no structural features of language have been found that can unequivocally be correlated with more or less civilized social structure (however the latter is defined). The more general assumption is, however, beyond the possibility of empirical confirmation or disconfirmation, but lies at the basis of all work, of whatever orientation, that treats human language as a homogeneous phenomenon.

The second assumption is that the range of human languages spoken in the world today is sufficiently large and varied to include examples of virtually all the kinds of structure that are possible in human language. This second assumption is much more questionable than the first, especially since we know that in certain respects the languages of the world are decidedly skewed in favour of certain structures and against others: thus, click consonants are restricted to a small part of southern Africa, languages with object-initial word order seem restricted to one part of South America, whereas languages with verb-final word order can be found in every continent. What, then, if this assumption should turn out to be false? In this eventuality, research on language universals will simply be impossible, and in practice researchers working within the same paradigm of language-universals research as is presented in this book simply make the assumption that the range of attested languages is sufficiently wide. In practice, significant results have been achieved by making this assumption. Moreover, although there is skewing on certain parameters, there are other parameters (for instance in the syntax of relative clauses; see chapter 7) where representatives of different types are found scattered across the world, so that in certain areas, at least, we can be reasonably sure that the totality of the world's languages does represent a reasonable population from which to draw our sample – it is not just the case that this is the only population we have.

Assuming that we have a reasonable population, the next problem is to decide on what kind of sample we are going to use from this population, given the impracticality of attempting to work with all the world's languages. Here, there are certain biases that must be avoided in establishing the sample, although not all work on language universals has necessarily done so. First, it is essential that the languages chosen in the sample must be from a range of genetic language families. Since members of a single language family, by definition, have certain traits in common because they have inherited them from their ancestor language, restriction of the sample to a single language family would not enable us to distinguish between common properties that are genuine language universals and those that are chance properties of the given genetic group. Likewise, biasing the sample in favour of one language family would give the impression that accidental structural properties common to that language family are in fact more widespread than they are. With respect to guarding against genetic bias, there is a specific proposal in the literature, devised by Alan Bell, which we shall outline briefly.

Bell argues that, in establishing a sample of languages, one should ensure that each 'group' of languages should be given equal representation, where a group is defined as a genetically related set of languages separated from their common ancestor by a time-depth of 3,500 years. On this criterion, for instance, the Indo-European family would consist of 12 groups. Bell gives the following as the number of groups in the language stocks of the world:

Dravidian	1	Na-Dene	4
Eurasiatic	13	Austric	55 (approximate)
Indo-European	12	Indo-Pacific	100 (estimate)
Nilo-Saharan	18	Australian	27 (approximate)
Niger-Kordofanian	44	Sino-Tibetan	20 (approximate)
Afroasiatic	23	Ibero-Caucasian	4
Khoisan	5	Ket	1
Amerind	150 (estimate)	Burushaski	1

(Many of the stocks are dubious as established genetic units – for instance, Amerind, which groups together virtually all the native languages of the Americas, or Indo-Pacific, which groups together all the non-Austronesian languages of New Guinea – but in terms of the ratio of languages from different stocks, whether or not individual stocks are considered to be established genetic units, this table does provide a reasonable working hypothesis.) The total number of groups is 478, so that in a sample of 478 languages each stock should be represented by one language from each group. In practice, any sample will almost certainly be smaller, to achieve a reasonable practical compromise between depth and breadth of coverage, although the ratios will of course be the same. With a smaller sample, one disadvantage is that stocks with only one or a few groups tend automatically to be excluded. In terms of work to date on language universals, it is clear that the samples used involve many skewings, which, while not unexpected, does seriously call into question whether or not their results are representative of human language as a whole. Thus Indo-European languages are grossly over-represented, for obvious social reasons: speakers of these languages are more readily available, and grammars of these languages are more readily available. At the other extreme, languages of New Guinea, which ought to make up about 20 per cent of a representative sample, are usually completely missing: speakers of the relevant languages are rarely available outside New Guinea, and there are few detailed grammars of any of these languages. Until good descriptions of a wider range of languages are available to linguists working on language universals, this skewing is likely to remain in their samples, even where the existence of the skewing and of its disadvantages are recognized.

In addition to guarding against genetic bias, it is also necessary to guard against areal bias, i.e. against selecting an unrepresentatively large number of languages, even if from different genetic groups, from the same geographical area. This is because, as discussed in more detail in section 10.2, languages spoken in the same geographical area tend over time to influence one another and come, through borrowing or shared innovation, to have features in common that are not necessarily language universals, or even particularly frequent cross-linguistically. A good example would be the diffusion of click consonants from the Khoisan languages into neighbouring Bantu languages. Therefore, in addition to ensuring that the languages in a sample are representative genetically, they must also be representative areally. At present, there are no specific suggestions for a general solution to this problem, comparable to Bell's for genetic bias, but at least one can say that, in establishing a sample free of genetic bias, one should also choose the individual languages so that, as far as possible, no two languages are picked that are known to have been in close areal contact. In general this poses no serious practical problem, although in a very few instances there is the potential for conflict in guarding against both genetic and areal bias: for instance, inclusion of a representatively large number of New Guinea language groups might lead to an areal bias in favour of New Guinea.

In addition to these two obvious biases that should be guarded against, and against which it is relatively easy to guard (at least in theory, i.e. not taking into account practical problems of availability of language material), in an ideal sample one would also want to guard against biases in favour of or to the detriment of classes of languages defined by major typological features. For instance, it would be quite possible to come up with a sample of languages that would be representative genetically and areally, but where all the languages, or at least an overwhelming majority, would have the basic order subject – object – verb, this being the most frequent basic word order in the world's languages. In particular, where it is known, hypothesized, or suspected that a given typological variable may correlate with the phenomenon under investigation, care should be taken to guard against such typological bias.

In sum, then, to carry out detailed work on language universals one needs a representative sample of languages, representativeness being defined in particular as absence of genetic, areal, or typological bias.

1.1.3   DEGREES OF ABSTRACTNESS

In section 1.1.1, we noted that one of the differences between the two main approaches current in research on language universals concerns the degree of abstractness that is involved in stating language universals. Within Chomsky's approach, language universals are primarily constraints on the relation between abstract structures and more concrete structures, i.e. necessarily involve a considerable degree of abstractness. In Greenberg's approach, on the other hand, universals are stated primarily in terms of more concrete levels of analysis. In this section, we shall illustrate these differences in somewhat more detail, concentrating in particular on the following two questions. The first is whether there is any validity to surface structure universals, i.e. to universals that require only a minimum of abstract analysis. The second will be the empirical status of universals that require reference to very abstract analyses. Throughout the discussion, it is important to bear in mind that we are not dealing with a strict dichotomy between abstract statements on the one hand and concrete statements on the other, but rather that there is a continuum between the two. Thus, many of the specific universals that have been proposed by Greenberg and those influenced by him require some degree of abstractness. Greenberg's original contribution on word order typology, by referring to such parameters as the relative order of subject, verb, and object in the clause, assumes that it is possible to identify the subject of an arbitrary clause in an arbitrary language. However, identification of a subject requires a certain amount of abstract analysis (there is no physical property that is common and unique to subjects across all sentences of all languages), and indeed, as we shall see in chapter 5, there is considerable controversy surrounding the identification of subject in many sentence types in many languages, and even concerning the validity of the notion subject at all. But it does still remain true that a statement about the nature of surface-structure subjects is less abstract than one about deep-structure subjects.

The answer to the first question posed above, namely whether or not there are any valid concrete universals, is in a sense given illustratively by the discussion of the body of this book, concerned as it is with a range of recent proposals concerning surface structure universals. Moreover, in discussing not only proposals for actual language universals but also suggested explanations for language universals in these later chapters, it should become clear that concrete universals can not only be established with a degree of rigour that is not possible with more abstract formulation, but that such universals can then be integrated into a much broader perspective on human language than is possible with purely formally stated universals, irrespective of the degree of abstractness required in their formulation.

In the present section, we shall concentrate, therefore, on the second of the two questions posed above, the empirical validity of abstract universals, the crucial point here being that an abstract universal is no stronger than (and may even be weaker than) the analysis on which it is based, i.e. if a given abstract analysis is controversial then so too will be any universal that builds on it. Rather than giving a general discussion of the pros and cons here, we shall examine a specific example that has arisen in recent work in relational grammar, an offshoot of transformational grammar which, while rejecting some of the tenets of transformational grammar, does share with it a predilection for stating universals in terms of abstract structures. A number of the world's languages have a so-called impersonal passive construction, in which, in surface structure, the verb has no overt subject, the agent being expressed, if at all, as an agentive phrase; however, the objects of the verb, including the direct object of a transitive verb, remain just as in the ordinary active sentence. This can be contrasted with the English-type (personal) passive, where there is an overt subject, corresponding to the direct object of the active sentence. We may illustrate the impersonal passive by some examples from Welsh:

Lladdodd y   ddraig y   dyn.   (1)
killed   the dragon the man
'The dragon killed the man.'

Lladdwyd   y   dyn gan y   ddraig.   (2)
killed-PASSIVE the man by the dragon
'The man was killed by the dragon.'

In stating the relationship between the active and passive sentences, a straightforward, superficial statement would be to say that the subject of the active corresponds to the agentive phrase of the passive, with the result that the passive has no overt subject. However, this violates two putative universals of relational grammar. According to the Motivated Chomage Law, it should be impossible for the subject of the active to be demoted to an agentive phrase unless some other noun phrase is advanced to subject position (i.e. the demotion of the subject is contingent upon the advancement of some other noun phrase into that position). The Final 1 Law says that a clause invariably has a final subject, i.e. a subject at the end of the operation of all cyclic rules. Sentence (2) clearly lacks a surface subject, and this is not at issue. In order to maintain the validity of these putative universals, it is necessary to assume, within relational grammar, that some noun phrase (a dummy noun phrase, whose origin is not at issue here) is inserted into subject position in the impersonal passive construction, thereby causing the demotion of the original subject; the dummy subject does not show in surface structure, or at least has no phonological realization.

We must now consider whether or not this putative universal involves any empirical claim. On the basis of the data and discussion given here, there is no empirical claim involved. If this analysis is available for impersonal passive constructions, then it is clearly impossible to construct a set of data that would be a counterexample to the Motivated Chomage Law and/or the Final 1 Law, since proponents of these laws would simply say that at an intermediate level of abstractness the sentence in question does indeed have a subject, only this subject is never realized overtly. Note that we cannot say that the analysis proposed within relational grammar is wrong, in the sense that there are counterexamples to it; rather, this analysis makes no empirical claim, so that it is impossible to construct even a potential counterexample to the hypothesis.

In the present work, it will be maintained that the only language universals that are of empirical interest are those to which potential counterexamples can be constructed. Putative universals which simply test the ability of linguists to come up with abstract analyses that are consistent with any conceivable set of data may tell us something about linguists, but they do not tell us anything about language.

1.2 CLASSIFICATION OF LANGUAGE UNIVERSALS

1.2.1 FORMAL AND SUBSTANTIVE UNIVERSALS

In the transformational-generative literature on language universals, one distinction that has played a major role is that between formal and substantive universals. Although this distinction will play a smaller role in the present book, some discussion of the distinction will be necessary, if only to place the present work in its broader context.

Substantive universals are those categories, taken in a wide sense, that are posited as language universals. In syntax, for instance, they might include such categories as verb, noun, noun phrase, subject, direct object, main verb. In phonology, a clear example would be the distinctive features of Jakobsonian phonology. Although substantive universals delimit the class of possible human languages relative to the class of logically possible languages, they can do so in two ways. On the one hand, a substantive universal may be a category that must be present in each individual human language (in phonology, vowel would be a good candidate). On the other hand, the set of substantive universals in a given area might represent a set from which individual languages select a subset, i.e. they would define the total range available to natural languages, items from outside this range being defined as impossibilities. This second possibility is again well represented by the Jakobsonian theory of distinctive features, which claims that the phonological system of any arbitrary language will make use of no distinctive feature not contained in the list, although it is not necessary that any individual language should make use of the whole set (thus English does not make distinctive use of the feature Checked). Another way of characterizing the difference between the two types would be as follows:

the first distinguishes what is necessary in a language from what is unnecessary, the latter distinguishes what is possible from what is impossible.
In combination, they distinguish necessary characteristics of human
languages, possible characteristics, and impossible characteristics.

Formal universals are rather statements on the form of rules of grammar. Again, it would be necessary here to distinguish among necessary,
possible, and impossible properties of rules of grammar in human
language. As an example, we may take the claim that no language can have
a formal rule that operates by giving a left–right inversion of a string of
arbitrary length. In slightly more concrete terms, this says, for instance,
that no language could form questions by simply inverting the word order,
so that the question corresponding to *this is the house that Jack built* would
be *built Jack that house the is this?* This particular formal universal seems
to stand the test of verification in a wide range of languages; it is a special
case of a more general formal universal proposed within transformational-
generative grammar, namely that transformations are structure-dependent
operations, to which we return in section 1.2.3.

Throughout most of the development of transformational-generative
grammar, it has been held that the constraints delimiting the class of
possible rules are formal universals, and indeed most of the work on universals within this approach to syntax has been concerned with just such
formal constraints. However, there have also been suggestions that at least
part of the problem of delimiting the set of rules might be in terms of
substantive universals, such that there would be a certain set of rules,
subject to variation in detail in individual languages, from which the individual language would select, at least in order to build up its core syntactic
processes. One candidate for such a rule would be passive (personal
passive), characterized as a process whereby the original subject is deleted
or demoted to an agentive phrase while the original object is advanced to
subject position; beyond this core, individual languages would vary, for
instance, as to whether or how they mark the voice change on the verb or
the noun phrases. Thus English uses the auxiliary *be* with the past participle to mark the voice change on the verb, and the preposition *by* to mark
the agentive phrase in the passive, as in *the man was hit by the woman*,
whereas Latin would use a different ending on the main verb, in addition
to changes in the case of the noun phrases, e.g. active *mulier* (NOMINATIVE)
hominem (ACCUSATIVE) *videt* 'the woman sees the man', passive *homo*
(NOMINATIVE) *ā muliere* (preposition + ABLATIVE) *vidētur* 'the man is seen
by the woman'. In the present work, the existence of such substantive
universals plays a significant role, as can be seen from the treatment of
such topics as the cross-language comparison of relative clause constructions (chapter 7).

1.2.2   IMPLICATIONAL AND NON-IMPLICATIONAL UNIVERSALS

For certain properties of language, it seems that we can state whether or not they are found in natural language without reference to any other properties of the given language. For instance, the statement that all languages have oral vowels makes absolutely no reference to any other items that must or must not be present. Such universals are non-implicational. Many other statements about language universals, however, relate the presence of one property to the presence of some other property, i.e. state that a given property must, or can only, be present if some other property is also present. In section 1.1.2, an example of an implicational universal was introduced: if a language has VSO basic word order, then it has prepositions. As illustrative material, we shall discuss this example from word order typology more thoroughly. Two properties are involved: the presence or absence of VSO as the basic word order, and the presence or absence of prepositions. Let us symbolize presence of VSO word order as p (whence absence of VSO word order is not-p), and presence of prepositions as q (whence absence of prepositions is not-q). The universal can now be symbolized: if p, then q. Logically, there are four possibilities for combining these various parameters:

(a) p and q

(b) p and not-q

(c) not-p and q

(d) not-p and not-q

The implicational statement is to be interpreted (by definition) rigidly in terms of the interpretation of material implication in standard propositional calculus, which means that if the implicational statement 'if p, then q' is true, then the possibilities (a), (c), and (d) above are allowed, whereas logical possibility (b) is disallowed. In section 1.1.2, we demonstrated that this is indeed the case with our particular example: there are languages like Welsh with both VSO and prepositions (type (a)); there are languages like English with no VSO but with prepositions (type (c)); there are languages like Japanese with no VSO and no prepositions (type (d)); but type (b) – VSO but no prepositions – is not attested. In formulating implicational universals, it is important that the rigid interpretation of material implication be followed, and in particular to note that a given implicational universal always allows three of the logical possibilities while disallowing one; only attestation of the disallowed fourth logical possibility counts as a counterexample to an implicational universal.

Although it is important always to keep in mind the logical definition of implication, in order to avoid making pointless language universal statements there is one other factor that should be borne in mind, namely that in order for an implicational universal to be a reasonable claim to make, each of the three permitted possibilities should in fact be represented. As an example of a universal that falls foul of this requirement, we may note the following: if a language has nasalized vowels, then it also has oral vowels. In a sense, the universal is true, and certainly there are no counterexamples, i.e. no languages which have nasalized vowels (p) but lack oral vowels (not-q). However, of the three permitted possibilities, only two are in fact attested: languages with both nasalized and oral vowels (p and q), and languages with oral vowels but no nasalized vowels (not-p and q); there are no languages with no vowels at all (not-p and not-q). In a situation like this, where one of the classes has no representatives, one can in fact make a stronger claim, in this case the non-implicational universal: all languages have oral vowels. This, together with the statement that nasalized vowels are possible, renders the original implicational universal superfluous.

In addition, the most significant kind of implicational universals are those where there is a reasonably large number of languages within each of the three permitted classes. An obvious example of an implicational universal that fails to meet this criterion of significance would be the following: if a language is English, then the word for the canine quadruped is *dog*. Case (a) is represented by one and only one language, namely English; case (b), the excluded logical possibility, is indeed not represented, i.e. there are no counterexamples; case (c), i.e. a language which is not English but has the word *dog* in this meaning, has at least one member, the Australian language Mbabaram; case (d), i.e. languages which are not English and which have a different word for the canine quadruped, comprise probably all the other languages of the world. As illustration, an obviously stupid example was chosen here simply to illustrate the general point – presumably no-one would seriously have proposed this as a significant language universal; but it is important to guard against introducing the same deficiency in more covert form. For instance, if a given property or set of properties is only found in a single language in the sample, then any implicational statement that includes this property or set of properties as p may in fact merely be stating a property that is peculiar to that one language. In the present state of our knowledge of object-initial languages, for instance, with only one such language described in detail (the Carib language Hixkaryana), it would be premature to attempt to correlate its object-initial word order as p with any other properties as q.

1.2.3 ABSOLUTE UNIVERSALS AND TENDENCIES

Another parameter along which universals can be classified is that distinguishing absolute universals, i.e. those that are exceptionless, and those that exist as tendencies, but do still have exceptions. This distinction is independent of that between implicational and non-implicational universals, giving over all a fourfold classification. There are absolute non-implicational universals, such as: all languages have vowels. There are absolute implicational universals, such as: if a language has VSO as its basic word order, then it has prepositions. There are non-implicational tendencies, such as: nearly all languages have nasal consonants (although some Salishan languages have no nasal consonants). Finally, there are implicational tendencies, such as: if a language has SOV basic word order, it will probably have postpositions (but Persian, for instance, is SOV with prepositions).

One question that immediately arises here is whether it is justifiable to talk about something being a language universal but nonetheless having exceptions. In most other sciences, one is not permitted to have arbitrary exceptions to supposedly general laws. However, in descriptive linguistics, it is clear that we very often have to make general rules to which there are then individual exceptions: in English, for instance, one can state a very general rule for the formation of the past tense of verbs or the plural of nouns – and the validity of these rules can be seen from the way in which they extend to new lexical items – yet there are still exceptions to these rules. Clearly, a universal which has no exceptions is stronger, preferable to one that does have exceptions, so that a priori there are arguments both in favour and against having statements of universal tendencies.

We can come closer to the validity of universal tendencies by adopting a slightly different approach. In a representative sample of languages, if no universal were involved, i.e. if the distribution of types along some parameter were purely random, then we would expect each type to have roughly an equal number of representatives. To the extent that the actual distribution departs from this random distribution, the linguist is obliged to state and, if possible, account for the discrepancy. One way of looking at a universal tendency, perhaps the best way of looking at one, is as a statistically significant deviation from random patterning. An absolute universal, in this sense, is just the extreme case of deviation from random distribution: certain logical possibilities fail to occur at all, rather than just being rare. An interesting universal to examine from this viewpoint is the claim, now known to be a universal tendency: in basic word order, the subject precedes the object. A number of languages are now known to violate this universal, for instance Malagasy with VOS word order and Hixkaryana with OVS basic word order. However, the disparity between the number of languages violating the universal (probably less than 1 per cent of the world's languages) and those that conform to it is massive. To say that the universal has no validity because there are counterexamples to it, and to leave the discussion at that, would be to abrogate one's responsibility as a linguist to deal with significant patterns in language. Of course, this says nothing about the reasons for the discrepancy, although non-linguistic reasons that have been suggested for the discrepancy hold little water: for instance, object-initial word order can hardly be considered a relict phenomenon found only in languages that have been pushed into backwaters by the major civilizations, with other word orders, when one realizes that the development of OVS word order in Hixkaryana, on the basis of comparison with other Carib languages, seems to be a relatively recent innovation. Explanations for the predominance of word orders where the subject precedes the object seem more likely to have a psychological basis, in terms of the salience of the agent in the agent–action–patient situation, and the high correlation between semantic agent and syntactic subject: we return to some aspects of this problem in section 1.3.2 and chapters 6 and 9.

Until recently, the acceptance of universal tendencies as valid statements could have been held as a further criterion distinguishing Greenberg's approach to language universals (which allowed such tendencies) as opposed to Chomsky's (which did not) – indeed, one criticism that was made by transformationalists against Greenberg's surface structure universals was that so many of the latter are tendencies. More recently, however, even within the mainstream transformationalist school – especially in the development of the extended standard theory – tendencies, in addition to absolute universals, have come to be accepted, paralleling the acceptance of markedness into generative phonological theory. In the current version, a given constraint on the form of grammars is not to be seen (or at least, is not necessarily to be seen) as an absolute constraint excluding all possibility of violation, but rather as a characterization of the unmarked case, the case to which languages correspond unless their grammar contains a specific instruction to the effect that the constraint does not apply to a certain set of constructions. (Thus, the grammar of Japanese would have to contain a statement to the effect that its word order, with determiners before nouns but auxiliaries after main verbs, violates the universal ordering implied by the $\bar{\bar{X}} \rightarrow Spec_{\bar{X}}\ \bar{X}$ convention, as discussed in section 1.1.2.) On this particular point there is, then, no longer any difference in principle between Chomsky's and Greenberg's positions. The coherence of Chomsky's methodological position does, however, seem seriously threatened by this innovation: if one examines only a single language, then there would be no indication a priori, other than by looking at a number of other languages, whether a given property of this language represented the marked or the unmarked state of affairs.

Since the word order claim implied by the $\bar{\text{X}}$ schema is questionable even as a tendency, we shall illustrate the possibility of tendencies using examples that have been used within transformational-generative grammar, in terms of another claim, namely that syntactic processes in natural languages are structure-dependent. This means that, in order to know whether a transformation is applicable and, if so, in order to apply the transformation, it is necessary to identify certain features of the syntactic structure of the sentence at the appropriate stage of derivation. In the statement of passive in English transformational grammar, for instance, it is necessary to identify a string with the structure noun phrase – auxiliary – verb – noun phrase; in relational grammar, essentially equivalently for present purposes, a structure involving both a subject and a direct object within the same clause would be required. Keeping, for ease of exposition, to the traditional transformational format, the structural change would then instruct us to alter that syntactic structure by placing the first noun phrase, preceded by the preposition *by*, at the end of the string, placing the second noun phrase at the beginning of the string, and adding *be* plus the past participle ending at the end of the auxiliary. The important thing about this rule is that it refers only to syntactic structure. It does not, for instance, contain operations of the kind: take the first word (whatever its syntactic role in the structure) and shift it to the end, or: invert the order of words in the string (without paying any attention to the syntactic structure). It would be easy to invent an artificial language that used exclusively syntactic processes of this kind, but any attempt to do so would lead to an artificial language quite unlike actual human languages.

However, there are some areas in some human languages that seem to make use of structure-independent processes of just this kind. For instance, a number of languages have a rule whereby clitics – constituents that have no independent stress of their own, but are pronounced as part of the adjacent word – must appear in sentence-second position. One such language is Serbo-Croatian. We may illustrate this by starting with a sentence that has no clitics, e.g. *Petar čita knjigu danas* 'Peter reads (the) book today'. If we want to include a clitic in the sentence, for instance the unstressed first person singular dative pronoun *mi* 'to me', then this must come after the first word: *Petar mi čita knjigu danas*. Serbo-Croatian word order is relatively free, so that in the sentence given first any of the 24 possible permutations of the four words is grammatical, with the same cognitive meaning. However, if the clitic *mi* is inserted, it will always appear after the first word, whatever the syntactic function of that word, e.g. *danas mi Petar čita knjigu, knjigu mi čita danas Petar*. In this simple example, each major constituent of the sentence is a single word, so the question naturally arises what happens if the first constituent consists of two words, as when we replace *Petar* by *taj pesnik* 'that poet' to get *taj pesnik čita knjigu danas*. In such a sentence, it is possible to place the clitic quite literally after the first word of the sentence, to give *taj mi pesnik čita knjigu danas*, despite the virtual incomprehensibility of a literal translation into English: 'that to me poet reads the book today'. However, it is also possible to place the clitic after the first major constituent, i.e. in this case after the whole noun phrase *taj pesnik*, to give *taj pesnik mi čita knjigu danas*.

Clearly, given the behaviour of clitic placement in Serbo-Croatian, it is not possible to maintain that syntactic processes are invariably structure-dependent, since the Serbo-Croatian rule requires one solely to identify the first word of a sentence, irrespective of syntactic structure. However, it still remains true that most syntactic processes in natural languages, including Serbo-Croatian, are structure-dependent, and even with Serbo-Croatian clitic placement the fact that the second position rule can be violated to avoid breaking up a major constituent shows that there is still some pressure towards structure-dependence here. We can thus conclude that in human language there is a tendency towards structure-dependence, though individual exceptions do occur. (It remains dubious, however, whether this is a specifically linguistic property, since in general structure-independent operations are difficult for people to perform on temporally sequenced strings; for instance, it is difficult to give a fluent reading of the alphabet, or a well-known telephone number, backwards without practice.)

In much recent work on language universals, in place of the term tendency it has been more usual to say statistical universal, referring to the fact that the universal in question has only a certain statistical, rather than absolute, validity. In the present book, the more transparent term tendency has been preferred, especially since the term statistical universal might be useful in speaking of universal statistical properties of languages (such as the claim that redundancy in language is always around 50 per cent).

1.3 EXPLANATIONS FOR LANGUAGE UNIVERSALS

Within the transformational-generative approach to language universals, given the scenario outlined in section 1.1.1, it is clear that the question of explaining language universals has an obvious solution: they are there because they are innate. However, this explanation is never argued for on independent grounds, and so the only reason for accepting innateness seems to be the absence of any plausible, comprehensive alternative. In outline in this section, and in somewhat more detail at appropriate places in the body of the book, we shall examine some other alternative explanations. There will be no attempt, however, to reduce all universals to a single explanation: in many instances, there seems to be no verifiable explanation for even well-established universals; in other instances, different universals seem to require different kinds of explanation, surely no surprise in examining a phenomenon like language which interacts so closely with so many other facets of human cognition and behaviour. Particular attention will be paid to cognitive, functional, and pragmatic explanations, as these seem particularly fruitful sources of explanation of formal properties of language. In section 1.3.1, however, we examine, for completeness, a non-viable explanation.

1.3.1 MONOGENESIS

Monogenesis, or a common genetic origin for all the world's languages, might seem an obvious explanation for language universals: the universals in question would simply have been accidental properties of the putative ancestor language (Proto-World), and the only reason why they would be found in all of the world's languages today would be that all of these languages have retained these traits of the ancestor language without change (whereas the parameters on which languages vary would represent those areas where individual languages have undergone change, without there being necessarily any other common property binding together the language universals). One disadvantage of monogenesis as a putative explanation of language universals is that it is completely speculative and untestable: if all the world's languages descended from a single ancestor – and this question must remain open – then the time-depth between this ancestor and our earliest attestations of language is so great that we would have no hope of establishing this monogenetic origin, or of tracing the changes that separate Proto-World from attested languages.

However, there are more compelling disadvantages which exclude monogenesis from consideration as even a possible explanation for a wide range of language universals, and therefore force us to look elsewhere for possible explanations. For the monogenesis explanation to work, it would be necessary for the universal in question to have been a property of the ancestor language, and to have been passed down through individual intermediate stages to each descendant language. However, in section 1.1.2, we saw that there are certain language universals, in particular implicational universals, that cannot be predicated of individual languages. For instance, in order to approach the universal that VSO word order implies prepositions, it is not enough to know that there is a language with VSO word order and prepositions, one must also know that there are languages with other word orders and either prepositions or postpositions, but no languages with VSO word order and postpositions. There is no way in which information of this kind could be encoded in the structure of a single language, and therefore no way in which the information could be transmitted from ancestor language to descendant languages.

1.3.2   INNATENESS AND OTHER PSYCHOLOGICAL EXPLANATIONS

In previous sections, we have already mentioned innateness as a possible explanation for language universals, in particular with reference to Chomsky's paradigm for research on language universals (see especially section 1.1.1). Here, we shall merely reiterate that as an explanation for language universals, especially when viewed without a priori commitment to Chomsky's paradigm, innateness remains empty because it is not subject to any independent verification – rather, it is just a name given to the set of language universals, and using this name should not blind us to the fact that a name is not an explanation. It is important also to emphasize that the onus is not on those who reject innateness to come up with alternative explanations, as is sometimes implied in the literature from the innatist viewpoint. Advocates of innateness are simply arguing that in the absence of any alternative coherent explanation for language universals, innateness is the only possibility they can think of. Instead of serving to deepen our understanding of language universals, the absence of any possibility of testing innateness as an explanation serves rather to divert researchers from considering alternatives that may be testable. We should note that this is not to be taken as a rejection of innateness: it may well be the case that at least some language universals are to be explained ultimately in terms of human genetic predispositions, but at the present stage of investigation hardly any such claims are amenable to independent verification.

It is, however, possible that certain language universals can be correlated with other aspects of human cognitive psychology that are amenable to independent testing. In chapter 9, for instance, we shall see that a certain hierarchy of noun phrases, which has significant relevance to cross-language generalizations, also correlates highly with an independently verifiable hierarchy of salience of entities in perception. In a sense, one could argue that this only pushes the need for explanation one stage further back, since one must in turn account for the hierarchy of salience, which may be determined by innate principles. There are two things to note in reply to this. First, any explanation necessarily pushes the problem back one stage further, since the explanation itself then becomes an object requiring explanation (one could equally ask for an explanation of how a particular proposed set of innate ideas comes to be innate). Second, in explanation the most important criterion in evaluating progress is that seemingly disparate phenomena be shown to have a common explanation, and in the example chosen this was achieved by showing how both linguistic properties and propensities in rating the importance of entities in describing situations can be related to the same notion of perceptual salience.

1.3.3 FUNCTIONAL AND PRAGMATIC EXPLANATIONS

Another approach to explanation of language universals would be to argue that certain universals serve to make language more functional, either as a communication system in general, or more particularly relative to the communicative needs of humans. Many linguists are sceptical of functional explanations, pointing out, quite correctly, that there are numerous instances in which language seems to be dysfunctional. For instance, the existence of synonyms might seem to be a needless luxury, and even more clearly the existence of homonyms would seem to create needless complication by having potential confusion through identical names for different concepts. Nonetheless, there are clearly some bounds which must be placed on such dysfunctional features of language – for instance, one could not imagine a functioning language in which all lexical items were homophonous – so that strategies to reduce dysfunctional elements may play a certain role in explaining language universals.

The essence of functional explanations in syntax is that the given language universal facilitates recovery of the semantic content from the syntactic structure, whereas violation of the universal would make such recovery more difficult. The example discussed here relates to the more detailed discussion of relative clauses in chapter 7. In chapter 7, one of the main claims is that certain positions in a sentence are harder to relativize, cross-linguistically, than are other positions. Thus, genitives are harder to relativize (e.g. *the man whose son ran away*) than are subjects (*the man who ran away*), for instance in that some languages readily form the latter kind of construction but not the former; constituents of embedded sentences are likewise harder to relativize than those of main clauses (e.g. *the man who ran away* is a construction type more common cross-linguistically than *the man that I think ran away*). Some languages distinguish two constructions for forming relative clauses: the one having a pronoun left behind in the position relativized – as if one were to say in English *the man that I saw him* rather than just *the man that I saw*; the other having no such pronoun. The distribution of these two constructions is constrained by the following universal: retention of the pronoun is found with positions that are more difficult to relativize, while the pronoun is not retained in positions that are easier to relativize. Even in English, though perhaps this usage is non-standard, pronouns are retained in certain subordinate clause positions that cannot be relativized directly, e.g. *the road that I know where it leads* (cf. the ungrammatical **the road that I know where leads*). The construction that preserves the pronoun provides more direct access to the semantic information contained in the sentence: in processing *the man that I saw him*, it is clear that *him* refers to the object of the relative clause, since this is precisely the configuration (*I saw him*) that one finds in simplex sentences. Where there is no pronoun, however, more processing is required in order to work out that in *the man that I saw* it is necessary to interpret *the man* as object of *saw*. The generalization is thus functional: in positions where, for independent reasons (ease of forming relative clauses), semantic processing would be more difficult, that syntactic structure is used which would be most explicit in providing direct access to the semantic content.

This kind of functional explanation could, of course, be carried over to any kind of communication system, and is not necessarily restricted to one used by humans. When one looks at pragmatic explanations, however, there are certain instances where there seems to be a clearer correlation between properties of language structure and properties of language use in human communities. One such universal is the presence in human languages of a deictic system for referring to the speaker and hearer, i.e. the existence of first and second person pronouns (as opposed to third person noun phrases, including third person pronouns where these exist). One could easily construct an artificial language which did not have such a deictic system, and where people would be forced to refer to themselves and their interlocutors by proper names or other paraphrases. However, it is clear that such a language would be very different from any known human language, and it is therefore hardly accidental that the presence of a deictic system of person reference correlates so highly with the basic use of human language in face-to-face interaction.

1.4 SUMMARY

In this chapter, we have contrasted, with exemplification, two radically different views of language universals and language universal research. The one, advocated by Chomsky, argues that the best way of studying language universals is by the detailed, abstract study of an individual language, the main explanation for language universals being that they are innate properties of the human. The other, advocated by Greenberg, and also in this book, says that research on language universals requires a wide range of languages as its data base, believes that a number of language universals can be stated in terms of concrete levels of analysis, and has an open mind on possible explanations for language universals, considering in particular psychological and functional (including pragmatic) factors. In presenting this contrast, we have tended to concentrate on the differences, and in fairness these should not be taken to indicate an absolute, unbridgeable chasm between the two approaches. For instance, Chomsky has never maintained that one cannot come up with language universals by studying a range of languages, or that no universals can have a functional explanation. Conversely, the present work acknowledges that there do seem to be some formal universals, and does not exclude innateness as a possible, eventual explanation for some language universals. However, the difference of emphasis is clear, since the two camps do make very different claims about the most reasonable way, given limited resources, of making most progress in research on language universals. In this chapter, and in more detail in the body of the book, it should become clear that, in addition to work on the detailed study of individual languages, research on language universals also crucially requires work based on data from a wide range of languages if vitally important generalizations are not to be missed.

NOTES AND REFERENCES

There are few general books, as opposed to collections of articles, dealing specifically with language universals, especially from the viewpoint of the Greenbergian approach. Conversely, many works on general linguistics or on the structure of specific linguistic theories inevitably contain some of the author's ideas on language universals. Greenberg (1966a) is, as implied by the subtitle, concerned with specific problems of markedness rather than being a general account of language universals research.

Among collections of articles, pride of place must clearly go to Greenberg (1966c): the Introduction and Memorandum, Hockett (1966), and especially the seminal essay by Greenberg (1966b) himself, can be regarded as initiating the current interest in research on language universals on the basis of a wide range of languages. The Stanford Language Universals Research Project published, for its duration, a journal *Working Papers on Language Universals* (1969–76), and a further result of this project is the four-volume set Greenberg *et al.* (1978). The universals project at the University of Cologne also produces working papers: *Akup* (*Arbeiten des Kölner Universalien-Projekts*).

For Chomsky's views on language universals, reference may be made to Chomsky (1965), chapter 1; there is also a somewhat negative reference to Greenberg's 'statistical universals' on page 118. A particularly clear statement of many of the key issues emerges in Chomsky & Hampshire (1968).

In section 1.1.2, the analogy with iron is taken from Sampson (1975, 114–16), although Sampson does not consider that other analogies would work equally well in the opposite direction. The universal that VSO languages have prepositions is number 3 in the list given by Greenberg (1966b, 110). I have selected this particular example in this chapter because it is very straightforward, although more substantial examples of absolute implicational universals are cited in later chapters. This particular example is not beyond controversy, since Smith (1980, 155) gives Papago as a VSO language with postpositions; however, reference to the grammatical sketch in Saxton & Saxton (1969) suggests that there are both prepositions and postpositions, e.g. *wui g Chuk-shon* or *Chuk-shon wui* 'to Tucson' (pages 130–1) – in the former, *g* is an unstressed pronoun frequently used with third person noun phrases, as in *bei at g Pancho g wisilo* 'Pancho got the calf' (page 118). The critique of the $\bar{X}$ convention universal of determiner and auxiliary order is discussed by McCawley (1978, 214). For a slightly different approach to justifying the need for language universals research to use a wide data base, see Comrie (1978d). My discussion of the data base in generative phonology refers to Chomsky & Halle (1968). For an attempt to bridge the gap between the need for solid descriptions of individual languages and the need for data from a wide range of languages, see the language description framework proposed by Comrie & Smith (1977); the *Lingua Descriptive Studies* series, consisting of individual language descriptions in accordance with this framework, started publication with Derbyshire (1979).

Bell's discussion of sampling is in Bell (1978). For a general survey of genetic classification of the world's languages, see Voegelin & Voegelin (1977).

In section 1.1.3, the discussion of the impersonal passive reviews some of the points made in Comrie (1977a). Perlmutter (1978) argues that, in conjunction with certain other principles of relational grammar, the Motivated Chomage Law and the Final 1 Law do make empirical predictions concerning the impersonal passive, but Wachtel (1979) shows that none of the predictions depends crucially on these two laws.

In section 1.2, the distinction of formal and substantive universals follows Chomsky (1965, 27–30); for Jakobsonian distinctive features, consult Jakobson *et al.* (1963). The suggestion that there may be a set of transformations as substantive universals is made by Bach (1965); in application to the passive, the idea is further developed, within the framework of relational grammar, by Johnson (1974). The distinction of implicational and non-implicational, absolute and tendency, follows (apart from some terminology) the Memorandum in Greenberg (1966c, xix–xxi). My information on Mbabaram *dog* 'dog' is from R. M. W. Dixon (Australian

National University, Canberra), who notes that this form is a regular development from *gudaga* (found as such in some other Australian languages), not a loan from English. The detailed description of Hixkary-ana referred to is Derbyshire (1979). The information that some Salishan languages lack nasal consonants is from Hockett (1955, 119). For word order in Malagasy, see in particular Keenan (1976a), which also shows the inadequacy of arguments that the putative subject in Malagasy is anything other than a subject. For the claim that OVS order in Hixkaryana may be an innovation, see Derbyshire & Pullum (1981) and references cited there. The Serbo-Croatian examples are based on data in Browne (1974). The claim that redundancy in natural language is around 50 per cent is made, specifically for phonology, by Hockett (1966, 24).

In section 1.3, reference should be made to Timberlake (1977, 160–5) for some discussion of the relationship between salience and linguistic parameters. The functional explanation for pronoun retention in relative clauses is given by Keenan (1975, 406–10). The discussion of relative clause formation in Irish in McCloskey (1978) provides an excellent illu-stration of how typological research (in particular, universals in pronoun retention in relative clauses) and language-specific description can inter-act. For a discussion of what a language without first and second person pronouns might look like, see Lyons (1977, 640–6); Japanese does come close to such a language, in that in natural discourse first and second person deixis are left to be inferred from markers of deference or politeness rather than expressed overtly, although it is still the case that Japanese has noun phrases with, synchronically, specifically first and second person reference.

2

LANGUAGE TYPOLOGY

2.1 TYPOLOGY AND UNIVERSALS

At first sight, the study of language universals and the study of language typology might seem to be opposites, even in conflict with one another: language universals research is concerned with finding those properties that are common to all human languages, whereas in order to typologize languages, i.e. to assign them to different types, it is necessary that there should be differences among languages. The contrast can thus be summed up as one between the study of similarities across languages and the study of differences among languages. Yet, in practice, the two studies proceed in parallel: typically, linguists who are interested in language universals from the viewpoint of work on a wide range of languages are also interested in language typology, and it is very often difficult to classify a given piece of work in this area as being specifically on language universals as opposed to language typology or vice versa: book and article titles including *typology* or *universals* often seem arbitrary, though the arbitrariness is sometimes removed, as in the title of the present book, by including both.

The discussion of the preceding chapter should, however, point the way towards recognizing that there is in fact no such conflict between universals research and typological research, rather these are just different facets of a single research endeavour. In the present section, we shall demonstrate this more thoroughly. In chapter 1, we argued that a theory of language universals must make a three-way division among logically possible properties of a human language. It must specify which properties are necessary to a human language; which properties are impossible for a human language; and, residually, which properties are contingently possible, but not necessary, for a human language. (The rigid division into three classes would, of course, have to be weakened slightly to take into account tendencies as well as absolute universals.) We can thus say that, over all, the study of language universals aims to establish limits on variation within human language. Typology is concerned directly with the study of this variation, and this makes it clearer why the two studies run so close together, since both are concerned with variation across languages, the only difference being that language universals research is concerned primarily with limits on this variation, whereas typological research is concerned more directly with possible variation. However, neither conceptually nor methodologically is it possible to isolate the one study from the other.

In terms of methodology, this shows perhaps most clearly in the interaction between language typology and implicational universals, whether absolute or tendencies. In carrying out a typology of languages on some parameter, one establishes a certain number of logically possible types, and then assigns each language of the sample to one or other of these types. If all the logical possibilities have actual representatives, and there is no marked skewing of membership among the various types, then this result, though perhaps of typological interest, is not particularly interesting from the viewpoint of universals: it demonstrates that there are no restrictions on language variation with respect to the chosen parameter. Where, however, some of the logical possibilities are not represented, or are represented by a statistically significant low or high number of representatives, then the typological result does become of importance for the statement of language universals. We may illustrate this by returning to one of the examples discussed in chapter 1, namely Greenberg's universal that languages with VSO basic word order have prepositions. As discussed in section 1.2.2, there are four logical possibilities: VSO and prepositions; VSO without prepositions; non-VSO with prepositions; non-VSO without prepositions. When we assign languages to these four logically possible types, we find a large number of languages falling into the first, third, and fourth categories, but none falling into the second. Thus what originally started out as a typological endeavour, namely the cross-classification of languages in terms of basic word order (VSO versus non-VSO) and the presence versus absence of prepositions, turns out to lead to the establishment of a language universal.

Implicational universals are a particularly clear case of the interaction between universals and typology, given the interpretation of the universal as a set of four logical possibilities only three of which are actually represented. However, in principle any typological parameter may be of significance for language universals research if it turns out that some of the logical possibilities are unrepresented or have a statistically significant low level of representation. This can again be illustrated with one of Greenberg's universals, this time a word order tendency mentioned in section 1.2.3, namely that in basic word order the subject tends to precede the object. If we work, like Greenberg, in terms of the three clause constituents S, O, and V, then there are six logical possibilities for arranging these linearly: (a) SOV, (b) SVO, (c) VSO, (d) VOS, (e) OVS, (f) OSV. Types (a)–(c) are all consistent with the universal just stated, and indeed the vast majority of the world's languages belong to one or other of these three types (at least to the extent that they have a basic word order – see further chapter 4). Type (d) has only a very small number of representatives, type (e) even fewer and more geographically restricted, while we are still awaiting a detailed description of any language with OSV basic word order, although preliminary indications suggest that some languages of the Amazon region do have OSV as their basic word order. Thus typologizing languages in terms of the six logically possible permutations of S, O, and V leads to the recognition of a universal tendency for subjects to precede objects in unmarked word order.

An even more straightforward example of typology leading to the establishment of a universal would be the universal mentioned in section 1.2.2 that all languages have vowels. If one were to typologize languages into those that have vowels and those that do not, then all languages would fall into the first class. Typologically, the result is, perhaps, trivial (all languages belong to one type), but in terms of universals it is a valid empirical generalization, once again illustrating the complementarity, rather than antagonism, between typology and universals.

There is another sense in which universals and typology go hand in hand. In order to do language typology, it is necessary to establish certain parameters along which one is going to typologize the languages of the world. Now, the selection of any parameter as a valid parameter for cross-language typological comparison assumes that this parameter is indeed valid in the analysis of any language. Thus carrying out any piece of language typology involves making certain assumptions about language universals. We can illustrate this once again by considering Greenberg's seminal work on word order universals, in particular basic order of S, V, and O within the clause. In order to typologize languages according to their basic word orders, the following presuppositions are made: (a) all languages have a basic word order; (b) in the syntactic structure of a clause in any language, the categories subject, object, and verb are relevant. Neither of these assumptions is logically necessary, and, as we will see in more detail in chapter 4, there is good reason for assuming that neither of them is in fact an absolute language universal. Thus, there seem to be some languages that do not have a basic word order, or at least not a basic word order defined in terms of S, O, and V (so-called free word order languages). There seem to be some languages where either there is no category subject, or where the various properties of subject are distributed across more than one noun phrase (see chapter 5), so that in either case it is not possible to point to a given noun phrase as being unequivocally the subject of a clause, and therefore not possible to determine the linear order of the subject relative to other constituents.

It is important to realize that the caveats expressed in the previous paragraph do not invalidate the kinds of word order universals that Greenberg talks about, although they do restrict somewhat their scope. All that is required is that we should establish further language types, say by making an initial typological dichotomy between languages that have a basic word order statable in terms of S, O, and V, and languages that do not; the first of these types will then divide into six logically possible subtypes, and we can proceed as before, except that our six types will now cover only a subset of the world's languages, i.e. the universal is of more restricted application. In fact, this kind of procedure is widespread in the study of typology or universals. If, for instance, one wants to study typological properties of tone languages, and perhaps come up with universals of tone, then the fact that many languages are non-tonal simply means that those languages are irrelevant to the project at hand, and this is not taken to invalidate the internal study and typologization of tone languages. Likewise, in studying the typology of case systems, or passive constructions, languages that lack case systems, or have no passive construction, are irrelevant to the endeavour at hand, rather than being counterexamples to it.

Implicit in the above discussion is another way in which typology and universals research interrelate, namely that the possibility of arriving at significant universals is very closely bound up with the typological parameters that one uses, implicitly or explicitly, in describing variation among the languages of the sample. A particularly clear example is provided here by the history of research into colour systems across the languages of the world. In very general terms, colour perception involves three parameters: hue (correlating with wave-length), brightness, and saturation, of which the first two are most important for present purposes. Traditional study of colour terms in different languages has emphasized the different physical ranges that are covered by individual colour terms in different languages, i.e. on the fact that different languages have a different number of colour terms and have different boundaries between adjacent colour terms. Thus in Hanunoo, a Philippine language, there are four basic colour terms: *(ma)lagtiʔ* covers English *white*, but also all other light tints, irrespective of the colour to which they would be assigned in English; likewise, *(ma)biru* covers *black*, but also dark tints of other colours; *(ma)raraʔ* covers approximately the range of English *red*, *orange*, and *maroon*; while *(ma)latuy* covers approximately the range of English *yellow*, and lighter tints of *green* and *brown*. As long as one looks at boundaries between adjacent colour terms on the colour chart, it seems that all one can say is that English and Hanunoo are radically different: Hanunoo has nothing corresponding to the boundary between English *yellow* and *green*, while conversely English has no clear boundary where Hanunoo discriminates between *(ma)biru* and *(ma)raraʔ*.

With hindsight, we can perhaps recognize that this was an undesirable way to classify colour systems, given that even within a single language, say English, native speakers often disagree among one another, or with themselves on different occasions, as to the precise boundary lines between adjacent colours, although they are much more likely to agree on assigning colour names to colours that are more central to the range of a given colour term. Criticism of the traditional, cultural-relativistic view of colour terms came not, however, so much from aprioristic qualms of this kind, but rather from the typological research of Berlin and Kay on colour systems of a wide range of languages (over a hundred in the initial publication). Instead of asking about boundaries between different colour terms in a language, Berlin and Kay ask rather about the focus of a colour term, i.e. the colour that native speakers consider the most typical referent of that colour term. In the answers to this question, Berlin and Kay noticed a clear pattern emerging. First, even where colour term boundaries are very different across languages, there is agreement as to foci: thus the focus of Hanunoo *(ma)lagtiʔ* is the same as that for English *white*; the foci are the same for *(ma)biru* and *black*; the same for *(ma)raraʔ* and *red*; the same for *(ma)latuy* and *green*. Moreover, if one looks at the number and location of foci across a range of languages, a hierarchy, or series of implicational universals, emerges: all languages have foci for 'black' and 'white'; if a language has three basic colour terms, then the third has the focus of 'red'; if a language has five basic colour terms, then the foci of 'green' and 'yellow' are those added to this list (but if there are four terms, the fourth may be either 'green' or 'yellow', with no hierarchical preference among these two); six-term colour systems add 'blue'; seven-term systems add 'brown'. This is diagrammed below:

```
white                 green
          >  red  >                >  blue  >  brown
black                 yellow
```

The above statement as a hierarchy is readily turned into a series of implicational universals, of the following form: if a language has a colour term with focus 'blue', then necessarily it has colour terms with foci 'white', 'black', 'red', 'green', 'yellow'. More generally: if a language has a colour term with focus x, then it also has a colour term for each focus to the left of x in the diagram.

The main illustrative point in the above example is that, by slightly changing the questions asked, i.e. by changing the basis of typological comparison, it was possible to come up with a universal where previously it had been assumed that all one could do was typologize among all the logically possible types. In fact, Berlin and Kay's work also has more far-reaching implications for work on language universals and typology and even for descriptive linguistics, some of which will emerge in the discussion of later chapters. For instance, there is evidence that the hierarchy of foci given above can be correlated with colour perception, thus providing one example of a psychological explanation of a linguistic universal (cf. section 1.3.2). Secondly, it indicates that some, at least, of human categorization is not in terms of sharp boundaries between adjacent concepts, as assumed in much work on semantic structure, but rather in terms of well-defined foci with hazy (fuzzy) boundaries, i.e. in terms of prototypes rather than in terms of necessary and sufficient conditions.

2.2 TYPOLOGICAL PARAMETERS

In principle, one could choose any linguistically relevant parameter along which to typologize languages. If one makes the distinction between language universals and language typology, then the range of relevant parameters is restricted somewhat, namely to those parameters along which languages do in fact vary. Thus, once it is established that all languages have vowels, the parameter presence versus absence of vowels is no longer of interest for the study of variation across languages, and this generalization passes exclusively into the domain of language universals.

However, it is clear that some typological parameters turn out to be more significant, more interesting than others. In section 2.1 we illustrated this with reference to colour terms: of the two typological parameters appealed to in that discussion, it turned out that classification of colour terms according to their boundaries provided little significant insight into cross-language variation, since the range of logical possibilities and the range of attested systems are more or less the same; whereas classifying colour systems according to the foci of colour terms turned out to be of immense importance in typologizing colour systems and in coming up with language universals, since given the universal implied by the hierarchy of foci, the task of typologizing can be simplified by and large to specifying the cut-off point on the hierarchy for each language in question. Another lesson of this particular example is that there is no a priori way of knowing which particular parameter or set of parameters will turn out to be significant for research into typology and universals, rather the selection of parameters advances hand in hand with typological study as a whole. As a result of typological studies to date, we do have some idea of what parameters are most likely to be significant, and several of these are illustrated and discussed in subsequent chapters. However, there are undoubtedly many significant parameters whose significance has not yet been recognized, so that the illustrations given in the present book can be no more than illustrations.

Perhaps the best way to illustrate what is meant by the difference between significant and insignificant typological parameters is by means of
illustrations of some non-significant parameters, some particularly clear
examples being provided by phonological systems. Thus, in principle one
could typologize the languages of the world into two classes: those with a
palatal nasal phoneme and those without; the first group would include
such languages as French, Spanish, Hungarian, Malay, while the second
would include such languages as English, German, Turkish, and Hawaiian. Likewise, in principle one could typologize languages into those
that have front rounded vowel phonemes, such as French, Hungarian,
German, and Turkish in the above list, versus those that do not, i.e.
Spanish, Malay, English, and Hawaiian from this list. (Reference is to the
standard language in each case.) However, having once carried out these
classifications, there is then little further one can do with these typologies
in terms of the over-all typological structure of the languages in question.
If one attempted to correlate these two phonological features with one
another then, with the given eight-language sample as illustrative material,
we would find no correlations: there are four logically possible classes, and
each is represented within the sample: French and Hungarian have both a
palatal nasal and front rounded vowels; Spanish and Malay have a palatal
nasal, but no front rounded vowels; German and Turkish have no palatal
nasal, but do have front rounded vowels; while English and Hawaiian have
neither a palatal nasal nor front rounded vowels. Not only do these two
phonological parameters not correlate with one another, but equally they
do not correlate with any non-phonological parameters, i.e. our choice of
typological parameters turned out to be arbitrary, of no significance
beyond the fact that we can divide languages up into classes on the basis of
these parameters.

With these non-significant parameters we might contrast many of the
word order parameters used by Greenberg in his study of word order
universals, for instance the order of S, O, and V in the clause, the order of
relative clauses with respect to their head noun, the order of adpositions
relative to their noun (i.e. whether the language has prepositions before the
noun or postpositions after it), etc. Although these parameters are all
logically independent of one another, it turns out that there is a high
degree of correlation among them, leading in some instances to the statement of absolute implicational univerals, as is discussed in greater detail in
chapter 4. Thus, the fact that using these parameters enables us to come up
with implicational statements of the type 'if VSO, then prepositional', or
'if SOV, then usually postpositional', implies that we have not just selected arbitrary parameters, but rather that our choice of parameters tells us
something significant about the structure of the languages concerned, and

about cross-language typology in general. This also illustrates another way in which typology and universals research are intimately related: if we have a set of significant parameters whose values none the less show a high degree of correlation, then the network of relations among these parameter values can equally be expressed in the form of a network of implicational universals (absolute or tendencies).

Clearly, the more widespread the net of logically independent parameters that can be linked in this way, the more significant is the typological base being used. At the opposite extreme from non-significant, individual typological parameters like the presence versus absence of a palatal nasal phoneme, one might imagine a holistic typology, i.e. some set of typological parameters that are logically independent but in practice correlate so highly with one another that they enable us to typologize the whole, or at least a large part, of the structure of an arbitrary language. This is, for instance, what is done in biological classification, where typologizing an animal as a mammal subsumes a significant correlation among a number of logically independent criteria (e.g. viviparous, being covered with fur, having external ears, suckling its young). Over the history of linguistic typology, a number of attempts have been made to provide such holistic typologies of languages. One of these, morphological typology, with its classification of languages into isolating, agglutinating, fusional, sometimes with the addition of polysynthetic, will be discussed in section 2.3. More recently, on the basis of generalizations of Greenberg's work on word order typology, some linguists have suggested that word order types (such as VO versus OV) likewise define holistic types, a question to which we return in chapter 4.

The discussion in the relevant parts of the present book is rather critical of claims about holistic typologies, arguing that the empirical bases for the claims about holistic types are usually weak or lacking, so that while it is not logically impossible that there may be holistic types corresponding to mammal in biological classification, experience to date is rather against this possibility: while we can state often wide-ranging correlations among logically independent parameters, these correlations are not sufficiently strong or sufficiently wide-ranging to give holistic types rather than cross-classification of languages on different parameters.

However, it does sometimes remain the case that a given language makes much greater use of some property than does the average natural language, so that we can argue that use of this property, though not defining the holistic type of the language in question, does nonetheless permeate a significant part of its structure. Obvious examples would be the classification of a language as being a case language, or as being tonal. Tonal languages differ very much from one another on other parameters: some,

like Vietnamese, are isolating, each word consisting of just a single morpheme, while others, such as most Bantu languages, have complex mor-
phologies, mainly of an agglutinating type; some tonal languages are verb-
final, like Burmese, whereas others are SVO, like Vietnamese. But the fact
that lexical and/or morphological distinctions can be carried by tone does
represent an important general characteristic common to all such
languages, and there are many properties common to the phonological
processes that are found across tone languages but which have no immediate counterpart in non-tonal languages.

As a different example of the same kind of phenomenon, we might refer
to the role of animacy in Yidiny. Many languages have structural reflections of degrees of animacy (e.g. the distinction between living and
non-living entities, within the former between human and animals, and
within animals between higher and lower animals), as will be discussed in
more detail in chapter 9, but Yidiny happens to have a particularly large
number of logically independent reflections of animacy in its structure. In
Yidiny, animacy is basically a question of degree, rather than of absolute
cut-off points, so that where a given structural feature correlates with
animate rather than inanimate, this usually means that it is more likely to
be used with a noun phrase whose referent is higher on the animacy hierarchy, rather than that it will necessarily be used with noun phrases with
referents above a certain point on the hierarchy, and never used with those
below that cut-off point, although in certain instances there are cut-off
points. One reflection of animacy is in the choice of demonstrative pronouns, where for instance 'that' is more likely to appear as *ŋunʸdʸu-* with
noun phrases higher in animacy, and is obligatory in this form with human
noun phrases, but as *ŋuŋgu-* with noun phrases lower in animacy. Of two
possessive constructions, one placing the possessor in the genitive (e.g.
ŋadʸin dungu 'my head') and the other simply placing the possessor in
apposition to (in the same case as) the head noun phrase (e.g. *ŋayu dungu*
'my head', literally 'I head'), either can in principle be used with any kind
of possessor noun phrase, but in fact the genitive is more likely the higher
in animacy the possessor is. The case of the patient in a derived intransitive
construction called the antipassive (see section 5.3) can be in either the
dative or the locative: here, as with the demonstratives, there is, in part, a
cut-off point, in that noun phrases with human reference must stand in the
dative case, but otherwise either the dative or locative is possible, preference for the dative correlating with degree of animacy, as in *bunʸa
wagudʸanda* (DATIVE) *wawa:dʸinʸu* 'the woman saw the man' (literally
'woman man saw'); *ŋayu balmbi:nʸdʸa* (LOCATIVE)/*balmbi:nda* (DATIVE)
wawa:dʸinʸu 'I saw the locust'; *ŋayu walba:* (LOCATIVE) (less commonly,
walba:nda (DATIVE)) *wawa:dʸinʸu* 'I saw the stone'. The constructions

where animacy is relevant are very different from one another: form of the demonstrative, case marking of a patient which is not a direct object, choice of possessive construction; therefore the fact that animacy is relevant to each of these constructions provides our basis for saying that animacy in Yidiny is more significant in the typological characterization of this language than in the characterization of most languages. We can thus say that high relevance of animacy is a language-specific typological feature of Yidiny. It does not serve as a significant parameter in more general typology, in particular in that the set of languages where animacy is not particularly relevant does not form a natural class. Nor is it the basis for a holistic typologization of Yidiny, since in most of Yidiny structure animacy is not relevant. Other examples of language, language-group, or language-area specific typological parameters will occur at various points in subsequent chapters.

2.3 MORPHOLOGICAL TYPOLOGY

Although a number of bases for holistic typologies have been suggested over the history of typological studies, there are two which are particularly important, at least from a historical point of view. The first of these, morphological typology, was predominant in the nineteenth and early twentieth centuries, although it also retains an established place in textbooks of general linguistics; this is the subject of the present section. The second, word order typology, is discussed in chapter 4. Although the view expressed in the present book is that neither of these does in fact provide the basis for a holistic typology, each of them can serve to provide typologization of a significant part of language structure.

Although morphological typology has a long history, going back at least to the beginning of the nineteenth century, there has been a tendency for some of the tenets of this typology to become ossified, and in the present section we aim not only to give an account of the traditional lore concerning morphological typology, but also to look at some improvements that can and must be made if the fullest advantage possible is to be drawn from this way of typologizing languages. But first, we will examine the traditional classification.

Morphological typology usually recognizes three canonical types of language: isolating, agglutinating, and fusional, to which is sometimes added a fourth: polysynthetic (or incorporating). An isolating language is one which has no morphology, i.e. at least ideally, a language where there is one-to-one correspondence between words and morphemes. An example of a language which comes close to the isolating type is Vietnamese, as can be illustrated by the following sentence:

Khi tôi đến nhà bạn tôi, chúng tôi bắt đầu làm bài.
when I come house friend I PLURAL I begin do lesson
'When I came to my friend's house, we began to do lessons.'

Each of the words in this sentence is invariable, there being no morpho-logical variation for, for instance, tense (cf. English *come/came, begin/began*) or case (note that Vietnamese has *tôi* for both 'I' and 'my'); perhaps even more strikingly, plurality is indicated, in the case of pro-nouns, by the addition of a separate word rather than by morphological means, so that the plural of *tôi* 'I' is *chúng tôi* 'we'. Moreover, it is in general true that each word consists of just a single morpheme, with the possible exception of *bắt đầu* 'begin', which is arguably a word on some criteria, e.g. unity of meaning, although it can be segmented, at least etymologically, into two morphemes: *bắt* 'seize' and *đầu* 'head'; we shall return below to some problems in establishing whether or not one has in fact one-to-one correspondence between words and morphemes.

In some discussions of morphological typology, one comes across the term monosyllabic language, in addition to or in place of isolating language. Although there is a certain correlation between isolating and monosyllabic languages, the two parameters are in principle distinct, and for purposes of morphological typology it is isolating structure that is relevant. Thus one could imagine a language where there is no morphology but where each word (=morpheme) may consist of any number of syll-ables. Conversely, one could imagine a language with some morphology but where the morphology was restricted to changes in consonants and tone, without affecting the monosyllabic nature of the word. We therefore retain the term isolating here.

In an agglutinating language, a word may consist of more than one morpheme, but the boundaries between morphemes in the word are always clear-cut; moreover, a given morpheme has at least a reasonably invariant shape, so that the identification of morphemes in terms of their phonetic shape is also straightforward. As an example, Turkish will serve, the illus-tration being from the declension of nouns. In Turkish, nouns vary for both number and case (and also other parameters not treated here, e.g. possessor), with a system of two numbers (singular, plural) and six cases (nominative, accusative, genitive, dative, locative, ablative). However, for a given noun form it is always possible to segment clearly into lexical stem, number affix (zero in the singular, *-lar* in the plural), and case affix (zero in the nominative, *-ı* in the accusative, *-ın* in the genitive, *-a* in the dative, *-da* in the locative, *-dan* in the ablative), as in the following paradigm of the word *adam* 'man':

	Singular	Plural
Nominative	*adam*	*adam-lar*
Accusative	*adam-ı*	*adam-lar-ı*
Genitive	*adam-ın*	*adam-lar-ın*
Dative	*adam-a*	*adam-lar-a*
Locative	*adam-da*	*adam-lar-da*
Ablative	*adam-dan*	*adam-lar-dan*

(Note that the plural affix always precedes the case affix.) As is suggested by the term agglutinating (cf. Latin *gluten* 'glue'), it is as if the various affixes were just glued on one after the other (or one before the other, with prefixes).

In a fusional language, however, there is no such clear-cut boundary between morphemes, the characteristic of a fusional language being that the expression of different categories within the same word is fused together to give a single, unsegmentable morph. This can be illustrated by Russian declension: Russian has a two-way number distinction (singular, plural), and a six-way case distinction (nominative, accusative, genitive, dative, instrumental, prepositional). In Russian, moreover, even the fused affixes do not have invariant shape, since in different declension classes different affixes are used. This is illustrated below with declensional forms of the noun *stol* 'table' (declension Ia) and *lipa* 'lime-tree' (declension II):

	Ia		II	
	Singular	Plural	Singular	Plural
Nominative	*stol*	*stol-y*	*lip-a*	*lip-y*
Accusative	*stol*	*stol-y*	*lip-u*	*lip-y*
Genitive	*stol-a*	*stol-ov*	*lip-y*	*lip*
Dative	*stol-u*	*stol-am*	*lip-e*	*lip-am*
Instrumental	*stol-om*	*stol-ami*	*lip-oj*	*lip-ami*
Prepositional	*stol-e*	*stol-ax*	*lip-e*	*lip-ax*

Clearly, there is no way in which a form like genitive plural *stol-ov* 'of tables' can be segmented into an affix for number and an affix for case, rather the whole affix *-ov* is a single affix combining expression of both case and number (a portmanteau morph). And even knowing that *-ov* is the genitive plural affix in declension Ia, we have no way of predicting the genitive plural affix in declension II, which happens to be zero.

In place of the term fusional, one sometimes finds the term flectional, or even inflectional, used in the same sense. This is not done in the present work to avoid a potential terminological confusion: both agglutinating and fusion-al languages, as opposed to isolating languages, have inflections, and it is therefore misleading to use a term based on *(in)flection* to refer to one only of these two types. The availability of the alternative term fusional neatly solves the terminological dilemma.

The fourth morphological type, which is sometimes, though by no means always, included, is polysynthetic or incorporating. Although these two terms are sometimes used interchangeably, it is possible and advisable to make a distinction between them. Incorporation refers to the possibility of taking a number of lexical morphemes and combining them together into a single word. In a limited way, this is possible in English with various processes of compounding, as when the lexical morphemes *swim* and *suit* are com-pounded together to give *swimsuit*. In some languages, however, this process is extremely productive, giving rise to extremely long words with a large number of incorporated lexical morphemes, often translating whole sen-tences of English, as in Chukchi *tə-meyŋə-levtə-pəɣt-ərkən* 'I have a fierce head-ache', which contains three lexical morphemes: *meyŋ-* 'great, big', *levt-* 'head', and *pəɣt-* 'ache', in addition to grammatical morphemes *t-* (first person singular subject) and *-rkən* (imperfect aspect).

Polysynthesis, however, refers simply to the fact that, in a language of this type, it is possible to combine a large number of morphemes, be they lexical or grammatical, into a single word, often corresponding to a whole sentence of English, as in Eskimo (Siberian Yupik) *angya-ghlla-ng-yug-tuq* 'he wants to acquire a big boat', literally 'boat-AUGMENTATIVE-ACQUIRE-DESIDERATIVE-3SINGULAR'. In Eskimo, in contrast to Chukchi, a given word contains only one lexical morpheme, all the others being grammatical, i.e. Eskimo is poly-synthetic, but not incorporating. We thus see that incorporation is a special case of polysynthesis, namely where lexical morphemes can be combined together into a single polysynthetic complex, and we shall therefore use polysynthetic as a cover-term for this type as a whole.

One of the reasons for the omission of polysynthetic from many lists of morphological types is that its inclusion destroys the homogeneity of the over-all morphological typology. Although we classified the Chukchi and Eskimo examples given above as instances of polysynthesis, they are also clearly instances of agglutination: in the Chukchi example, we can segment off the individual lexical and grammatical morphemes, and these are more-over largely invariable (the major exception being the, largely predictable, occurrence of the vowel *ə* to break up consonant clusters, especially at morp-heme boundaries); likewise, in the Eskimo example, we can readily segment off the individual grammatical suffixes, and these are again constant in form. (In a more thorough study of both Chukchi and Eskimo, it would become apparent that both languages also have a certain amount of fusion, although this does not interact with polysynthesis.) Thus agglutination and poly-synthesis represent different parameters, which can operate independently, rather than different values of the same parameter.

However, to exclude polysynthesis from morphological typology for this reason is not necessarily justified, in particular because polysynthetic languages do, in a very real sense, provide the counterpoint to isolating languages in terms of the number of morphemes per word: in isolating languages, each word consists of just one morpheme, whereas in a poly-synthetic language, or rather in an ideal polysynthetic language, each sen-tence consists of just one word, this word in turn consisting of as many morphemes as are necessary to express the intended meaning. Over all, this suggests abandoning morphological typology in terms of a single parameter that is designed to cover all morphological types, and rather to operate with two parameters. One of these parameters will be the number of morphemes per word, and its two extremes will be isolating and polysynthetic. The other parameter will be the extent to which morphemes within the word are readily segmentable, its two extremes being agglutination (where segmentation is straightforward) and fusion (where there is no segmentability). We may refer to these two parameters as the index of synthesis and the index of fusion. Note that the index of fusion is, by definition, irrelevant in dealing with isolating languages. Otherwise, what are traditionally called polysynthetic languages become languages with a high index of synthesis (in addition, they may or may not also have a high index of fusion; for reasons discussed below it is inevitable that a language with a very high index of synthesis will also have a low index of fusion, even though the two parameters are logically independent). The traditional class of agglutinating languages corresponds to those with a low index of fusion (and, in terms of the tradi-tional fourfold classification, an intermediate index of synthesis, i.e. neither isolating nor polysynthetic). Finally, the traditional class of fusional languages corresponds to those with a high index of fusion (bearing in mind that isolating languages have neither a high nor a low index of fusion: this index simply does not apply to them).

The preceding discussion has surreptitiously introduced another aspect of morphological typology. At the outset of our discussion we assumed, very simplistically, that the typology would consist of three or four ideal types, among which we could distribute the languages of the world. In fact, how-ever, although we can establish these ideal types, the majority (perhaps all) of the world's languages do not correspond exactly to one or other of these types, but rather fall between the two extremes on each of the indices of synthesis and fusion. Thus instead of providing a discrete typology, morpho-logical typology provides us with a continuous typology, i.e. for a given language we can assign that language a place along the continua defined by the index of synthesis and the index of fusion. We shall illustrate this, and some of the other attendant problems, in the following paragraphs, starting with the index of synthesis.

In terms of the synthetic–analytic dimension, there are clearly some languages that at least approach the analytic end of the spectrum, i.e. where there is almost one-to-one correspondence between words and morphemes; Vietnamese, cited above, is a good example. However, there is probably no language that even approaches the opposite end of the spectrum, i.e. there is no language where it is obligatory to combine as many morphemes as possible into a single word, i.e. where there would be absolute identity between the word and the sentence. Although in Eskimo, for instance, it is easy to find sentences consisting of just a single word that consists in turn of a large number of morphemes, it is just as easy to find sentences consisting of more than one word, and there are many instances where it is not possible to combine morphemes together into a single word: as noted above, Eskimo has no way of combining lexical morphemes together, so that if a given lexical morpheme has no semantically equivalent grammatical morpheme, then there is no way in which that lexical morpheme can be combined together with any other lexical morpheme into a single word. Even in Chukçhi, which does have the possibility of combining lexical morphemes together, there are severe constraints limiting the possibilities of doing so: for instance, there is no way of incorporating a transitive subject or most intransitive subjects into the verb, so that while a sentence of three words like *tumɣe kupren nantəvatən* ' the friends set the net ' (literally ' friends net set ') can be reduced to two by incorporating the direct object, giving *tumɣət koprantə-vatɣʔat*, there is no way in which the subject ' friends ' can in turn be incorporated to give a one-word sentence containing the three lexical morphemes. The index of synthesis is thus best viewed as an index of the degree of deviation from the ideal analytic type in the direction of synthesis.

But even in trying to apply the index of synthesis in practical terms, for instance by dividing the number of morphemes by the number of words, certain practical problems arise which indicate that still further attention must be paid to the theoretical bases of morphological typology. Perhaps the most obvious, and the most widely discussed in the literature, is the question of establishing word boundaries, and thence the number of words in a sentence: even in Vietnamese, we noticed this problem with the expression (one word or two?) *bắt đầu* ' begin '. While the canonical definition of the word as a ' minimal free form ' gives a lot of mileage, and is particularly useful in dealing with languages rich in polysynthesis, where the individual morphemes are frequently clearly not minimal free forms, problems can arise in much more mundane cases, e.g. with the English definite article in *the man*, or the French unstressed pronouns in *je le vois* ' I see him ' (literally ' I him see '), where, despite the orthographic conventions, there is little reason for assuming that *the*, *je*, or *le* is a free form, i.e. pronounceable in isolation (other than by linguists). But whether *je le vois* is counted as one word or three can make a significant difference to the index of synthesis for French.

Another problem for the index of synthesis arises when one tries to count morphemes, in languages with either zero morphs or portmanteau morphs. In English, the plural *cat-s* is clearly two morphemes, but less clear is the number of morphemes in the singular *cat*: just one morpheme, or a lexical morpheme *cat* plus a grammatical zero morpheme? In terms of cross-language comparison, a decision one way or the other can again be of extreme importance for the statistics involved, since if English *cat* consists of just one morpheme, then English will be reduced in degree of synthesis relative to Russian, where the singular *košk-a* has an affix just as much as does the plural *košk-i*. In analysing a Spanish verb form like *cantas* 'you sing', should this be analysed as two morphemes (stem *cant-* or *canta-* and affix *-s* or *-as*), or should one rather factor out all the categories which are fused together in that ending (second person, singular, present tense, indicative mood, first conjugation), giving, together with the lexical morpheme, as many as six morphemes? While a consistent decision can be made, at least arbitrarily, the precise decision made will radically alter the comparison between a language like Spanish, with widespread occurrence of portmanteau morphs (especially in the verb system), and an agglutinating language like Turkish, where there is little or no controversy surrounding the number of morphemes in a word (except, perhaps, for the counting of zero morphs).

Turning now to the index of fusion, we should recall the two components of agglutination that were mentioned above: segmentability of morphemes, and invariance of morphemes, of which the former is perhaps more important in previous treatments of agglutination, although the second should also not be left out of account, especially in comparing agglutination with fusion – which is, after all, what the index of fusion does. Here, we can take agglutination as the norm: clearly segmentable and invariant morphemes, and define the index of fusion as deviation from this norm. The extreme deviation from this norm would thus be suppletion, where there is absolutely no segmentability and no invariance, as with English *went* as the past tense of *go*. Thus a language which represented the ideal fusional type would have all of its morphology in terms of suppletion; if it also had an ideally high index of synthesis, then each sentence would simply be totally and unsegmentably distinct from every other sentence of the language. Given that a language consists of an infinite number of sentences, this is clearly a practical impossibility, which means in practice that as the index of synthesis gets higher, the ratio of agglutination to fusion must also increase; more radically stated, there can be no such thing as an ideal fusional polysynthetic language. This demonstrates the advantage of taking isolating structure and agglutinating structure as the bases from which deviations are calculated by the two indexes.

We may now look at problems internal to the index of fusion, starting with segmentability and then turning to invariance. The problem with segmentability is that it is not itself an all-or-none categorization, but rather involves degree of segmentability. In the Turkish declension given above, segmentation was clear-cut in every instance. If we look at declension in Hungarian, however, the situation is not quite so straightforward, as can be seen in the following forms, singular and plural, nominative and accusative, of *ház* 'house', *asztal* 'table', and *folyó* 'river'.

Nominative singular	*ház*	*asztal*	*folyó*
Accusative singular	*házat*	*asztalt*	*folyót*
Nominative plural	*házak*	*asztalok*	*folyók*
Accusative plural	*házakat*	*asztalokat*	*folyókat*

It is clear that there are lexical morphemes consisting of at least *ház*, *asztal*, and *folyó*, that there is an accusative suffix consisting of at least *-t*, and a plural suffix consisting of at least *-k*. It is thus equally clear that the accusative plural forms consist of three morphemes. What is not clear, however, is where exactly the morpheme boundary should be drawn in those instances where the accusative or plural consonant is preceded by a vowel that is not there in the corresponding nominative or singular form, e.g. is *házat* to be segmented *ház-at* or *háza-t*, is *asztalokat* to be segmented *asztal-ok-at* or *asztalo-ka-t*, or conceivably *asztalo-k-at*? Reasons can be advanced for both logical possibilities, i.e. both for including the vowel as part of the stem and for not doing so, and at present the segmentation problem seems irresolvable. This case thus differs from the Turkish case, where segmentation was straightforward. However, it differs at least as much from the Russian case illustrated above, since in Hungarian it is clear that each of the morphemes involved does have some segmental content (e.g. accusative *-t*, plural *-k*), whereas in Russian there is no way in which any of the segments in the suffixes can be identified as exclusively indicating either case or number. Somehow, we want to indicate a degree intermediate between ready segmentability and impossibility of segmentation.

If invariance is included as a further characteristic of agglutinative morphology, then the problem of intermediate cases is even worse. First, we should illustrate that segmentability and invariance are indeed distinct from one another. In Turkish, in general morphemes are both readily segmentable and invariant, but there are some exceptions: in particular, the first person plural suffix on verbs is readily segmentable, but has two radically different forms, *-ız* and *-k*, which occur in different tense-aspect-mood forms, cf. aorist *yap-ar-ız* 'we make', conditional *yap-sa-k* 'if we make'. Although there is clear lack of invariance, there is no problem of segmentability, i.e. the situation just illustrated is more agglutinative than Russian declension (where there is neither segmentability nor invariance), but less agglutinative than Turkish noun inflection (where there is both segmentability and invariance).

In some instances, variability of morpheme shape is completely predictable in terms of general phonological rules of the language in question. In Turkish, for instance, rules of vowel harmony account for the different shapes of the plural morpheme in *adam-lar* 'men' versus *ev-ler* 'houses' (*-lar* after back vowels, *-ler* after front vowels, since vowel harmony precludes the presence of both front and back vowels in the same word). Such instances, presumably, should not be considered violations of invariance, since the variability of the morpheme is an inevitable consequence of other rules of the language. Elsewhere, however, variability in the shape of a morpheme represents a continuum reaching its extreme with suppletion, but going through a range of intermediate values in terms of the degree of variation and the degree of its predictability: thus the alternations of the stressed vowels in English *divine–divinity* and *strong–strength* are comparable in terms of the phonetic distance between alternants, but whereas the former alternation is essentially predictable in morphological terms, the latter is idiosyncratic.

A good illustration of the problems that arise in practice when one tries to calculate the index of fusion can be seen by comparing noun declension in Finnish and Estonian, two genetically very closely related languages. First, consider the Finnish forms, for *jalka* 'leg' and *lippu* 'flag':

Nominative singular	*jalka*	*lippu*
Genitive singular	*jala-n*	*lipu-n*
Partitive singular	*jalka-a*	*lippu-a*
Partitive plural	*jalko-j-a*	*lippu-j-a*

With the limited data given here, segmentability is no problem: the plural suffix is *-j*, the genitive suffix *-n*, and the partitive suffix *-a*; likewise, there is little variability in morpheme shape: the consonant alternations *k – ⌀* and *pp – p* are largely (though not quite) accountable for in terms of syllable structure (the second member of each pair occurs in a closed syllable), and the appearance of *o* in *jalkoja* is accountable for morphologically (though not phonetically). The situation is very different in Estonian, however:

Nominative singular	*jalg*	*lipp*
Genitive singular	*jala*	*lipu*
Partitive singular	*jalga*	*lippu*
Partitive plural	*jalgu*	*lippe*

Although these forms can all be derived diachronically from proto-forms close to the actual Finnish forms given above, there is no longer any ready segmentability or invariance. Etymologically, all the forms are different allomorphs of the stem, i.e. each is non-segmentable and the alternation among the four forms of each word is completely unpredictable in phonetic terms. If one adopts the alternative analysis of segmenting off the final vowels as case or case–number suffixes, then the degree of variation in the stem is reduced, but variation is introduced into the suffixes, e.g. 'partitive singular' is *-a* after *jalg*, but *-u* after *lipp-*. This example serves to illustrate not only the problems involved in assigning an index of fusion to a morphological system like that of Estonian, where there are weak traces rather than clear indications of segmentation, but also the more general point that a relatively short time-span can serve to alter a language's morphological typology from a fairly clear-cut agglutinating structure to one that is much more strongly characterized by fusion.

We may summarize this rather detailed discussion of morphological typology by saying that there are two major indices, independent of one another, that are needed in morphological typology: the index of synthesis, measuring the number of morphemes per word (low in isolating languages, high in polysynthetic languages), and the index of fusion (measuring the difference between agglutination and fusion). There are numerous problems in practice in quantifying these indices; in particular, the index of fusion actually refers in turn to two logically independent parameters, segmentability and invariance of morphemes. Despite the long history of morphological typology studies, it is clear that many quite basic problems of definition have still not really been faced, which is why such immense practical problems arise as soon as one actually tries to do, rather than just talk about, morphological typology.

Although morphological typology does serve the useful purpose of presenting an overview of the morphological structure type of a language, it remains unclear whether it can be considered a significant typological parameter (or set of parameters) in the sense of correlating with other parameters outside morphology. Of course, there are some few parameters with which morphological types correlate by definition. In chapter 8, for instance, one of the types of causative construction with which we will be concerned is the morphological causative, whereby a causative is related to its non-causative equivalent morphologically, each being a single word, e.g. Turkish *öl-dür* 'cause to die, kill', in relation to *öl* 'die'. Clearly, such a causative construction can only exist in a language that is not isolating, but this follows logically from the definition of the isolating type as having no morphology, and does not represent a correlation among logically independent parameters. Our over-all conclusion is, thus, that morphological typology has a secure, but restricted, place in language typology, and it is to be hoped that general linguistics textbooks will not continue indefinitely to give the impression that this is the only, or most insightful, way of classifying languages typologically.

NOTES AND REFERENCES

For a general survey of approaches to language typology, including references to more detailed historical studies of language typology, see Greenberg (1974). My own thinking on the relation between universals and typology has been influenced and clarified by Keenan (1978).

The universal that subject usually precedes object in basic word order is number 1 in Greenberg (1966b, 110). The preliminary material referred to on object-final languages is to be found in Derbyshire & Pullum (1981).

The information on Hanunoo colour terms is from Conklin (1955). The initial publication on universals of colour foci is Berlin & Kay (1969). This work has been subject to considerable refinement and criticism, though its results seem to stand up at least as universal tendencies. The explanation in terms of perception is to be found in Kay & McDaniel (1978), which also includes more recent references on colour terminology and on perceptual and linguistic theories utilizing prototypes and fuzzy sets.

Universals of tone rules, though with an explicit areal bias to West Africa, are discussed by Hyman & Schuh (1974). Dixon (1977, 110–12) discusses the widespread relevance of animacy in Yidiny.

The major classical work on morphological typology, building on earlier work by the Schlegel brothers, is Humboldt (1836); it was Humboldt who established the fourfold typology by including polysynthetic. The Chukchi example is from Skorik (1961, 102), and the Siberian Yupik Eskimo example from Jacobson (1977, 2–3).

The approach to morphological typology adopted here owes much to Sapir (1921), chapter 6; in particular, Sapir introduces the parameters of synthesis and technique (the latter approximating to index of fusion). The quantification of indices of synthesis and fusion is introduced by Greenberg (1960). Various possibilities for measuring the indices of synthesis and fusion are discussed by Altmann & Lehfeldt (1973, 108–12); despite

the title ('general language-typology'), this book is concerned almost exclusively with quantitative typology. A more detailed account of agglutination versus fusion in Finnish and Estonian may be found in Comrie
(forthcoming, b).

There are several works that give an overview of the typological structure of one or more languages – indeed, one can argue that this material
should be readily retrievable from any good grammar. Meillet & Cohen
(1952) provide overviews of most language families discussed (a third,
substantially revised, edition is in preparation). Sketches of several
languages (Easter Island, Japanese, and Mandarin Chinese) are included
in Lehmann (1978b). Briefer, more introductory sketches of a larger
number of languages are included in Shopen (1979a, b). See also the references to work by Sandra A. Thompson and John A. Hawkins in the
notes and references for chapter 3.

Detailed typological overviews of a range of syntactic topics are included
in Shopen (forthcoming): these volumes could well serve as a set of further
readings in conjunction with the present book.

3

THEORETICAL
PREREQUISITES

This chapter is not so much a study of language universals and typology as such, but rather an outline presentation of some of the notions that will be relevant in the discussion of particular aspects of universals and typology in subsequent chapters. However, section 3.5 does present a synthesis of the material in the rest of the chapter that is relevant directly to language typology, in the form of some contrasts between basic clause structure in English and Russian.

Much of the detailed discussion of the body of the book is concerned, in one way or another, with the valency of predicates, i.e. with the number and kind of noun phrase arguments that a particular predicate (usually, a verb) can take. An obvious example, from traditional grammar, would be the statement that the verb *give* takes three arguments: subject, direct object, and indirect object. Another way of describing the valency of the verb *give* would be to say that it takes an agent (the giver), a patient (the gift), and a recipient. There are thus several terminologies within which we can describe the valency of a verb, and in the present chapter we shall be looking at three such terminologies in particular: semantic roles, pragmatic roles, and grammatical (syntactic) relations. In addition, there will also be a brief discussion (section 3.4) of morphological cases, especially in relation to grammatical relations. The aim of this chapter is clearly not to provide an exhaustive account of the various kinds of relation a predicate can contract with its arguments, but rather to clarify certain more specific issues that will be of relevance for the subsequent discussion.

3.1 SEMANTIC ROLES

Recent interest in semantic roles within descriptive linguistics stems largely from the work, originally using English material, within the framework of case grammar. This model made explicit an important point that had received virtually no treatment within previous models of transformational-generative grammar, namely that the various grammatical relations of English bear only a very loose correlation with semantic roles, and that therefore some other vocabulary, in addition to grammatical relations, is required to give a complete account of the syntax and semantics of valency in English. Thus, if one takes the sentences *John opened the door with the key*, *the key opened the door*, *the door opened*, then simply to say that the subjects of these sentences are, respectively, *John*, *the key*, and *the door* fails to recognize that the semantic role of the subject is different in each example, a difference that can be described by assigning the semantic roles, respectively, of agent, instrument, and patient. Conversely, simply to describe the grammatical relations of these sentences fails to note that although *the door* is sometimes direct object and sometimes subject, yet still its semantic role remains constant (as patient); although *the key* is sometimes a non-direct object and sometimes a subject, again it always fulfils the same semantic role, of instrument.

In relation to straightforward examples like the English examples just discussed, the problem seems to have a ready solution, but this is not so when one turns to a wider range of data. In particular, one major problem that arises is the justification of the set of semantic roles, and the justification of particular assignments of semantic roles. The former problem can be seen in the tendency for the list of semantic roles to grow with each new contribution to the literature. Thus if one distinguishes between agent, defined say as the conscious initiator of an action, and instrument as the means used by the agent to carry out the action, then one needs a third semantic role for *the wind* in *the wind opened the door*, say natural force, since the wind is neither a conscious initiator nor a tool used by some conscious initiator. The second problem can be illustrated by considering a sentence like *John rolled down the hill*: here, it would be misleading to consider John simply as a patient, as he would be in the sentence *Mary rolled John down the hill*, since at least one possible interpretation of the former sentence is that John consciously initiated his roll down the hill; on the other hand, it is equally misleading to classify John simply as an agent, since he is also undergoing the rolling action.

Given our interests in the present book, we shall not attempt to provide a general solution to the problem of enumerating and assigning semantic roles, but rather limit ourselves to the following two more restricted objectives – elsewhere, in the course of the exposition, we will often make informal use of terms from case grammar. First, our discussion will be limited to a relatively narrow area within the totality of semantic roles, namely the area concerned with such roles as agent, force, instrument, experiencer, and patient, the last-named being treated essentially as unmarked, i.e. the others are described primarily in terms of their deviation from patient. Secondly, we will assume that in order for a distinction of semantic role to figure in a universal inventory of semantic roles, it must be the case that at least one possible language has some grammatical correlate of this semantic distinction. In practice, this means that justification of a semantic role requires such evidence from an actual language. This avoids the problem of multiplying the number of semantic roles to encompass all possible conceptual distinctions.

The most important point that we want to make concerning the relations among agent, force, instrument, and patient is that this is not so much a set of discrete semantic relations, but rather a continuum, the labels representing different points along this continuum. The continuum as a whole can be regarded as a continuum of control, and we shall use this term rather than the set of discrete labels, except informally. Our task is therefore to ascertain whether distinctions in terms of control find formal linguistic reflection in one or more languages, correlating with the conceptual distinction that can be drawn among conscious initiator (*John* of *John opened the door*), mindless initiator (*the wind* of *the wind opened the door*), mindless tool (*the key* of *John opened the door with the key*), and entity affected by the action (*the door* in each of these examples).

If we take an English sentence like *we fell to the ground*, then there is no grammatical indication of the degree of control that we exercised: it may have been the case that we deliberately fell down (full control), it may have been the case that we fell owing to our carelessness (potential control not exercised), or it may have been the case that we inadvertently succumbed to a hostile universe or were pushed (no control). In some languages, however, it is possible to express this kind of distinction in certain constructions. For instance, in Bats there are two ways of translating this English sentence, of which (1) has the intransitive subject in the absolute case, and (2) – the less usual construction – has the intransitive subject in the ergative, usually reserved for transitive subjects:

Txo (ABSOLUTIVE) *naizdrax kxitra.*   (1)

Atxo (ERGATIVE) *naizdrax kxitra.*   (2)

The difference is entirely one of control: version (2) implies that we had more control over the event described, perhaps in that we deliberately fell, or more likely in that we should have exercised control but failed to do so; (2) cannot, however, be used to describe a situation where we fell through no fault of our own. Essentially the same distinction is found in Chickasaw, except that here the distinction is shown by different sets of person-and-number affixes on the verb:

Sa-ttola. (3)

Ittola-li. (4)

Both can be translated into English as 'I fell down', but (4), the more marked form, indicates that I fell down on purpose. Although such distinctions, correlating with different degrees of control, are found sporadically across the languages of the world, we are not aware of any language where the case marking or verb agreement system is completely general in this respect, i.e. where this part of the morphology would be determined purely in terms of semantic roles. In Bats, this opposition is restricted to a small (and apparently dwindling) set of intransitive verbs, and also occurs only with first and second person pronouns. In Chickasaw, there are numerous verbs which seem simply to require one or other set of affixes, irrespective of degree of control, e.g. *ĩla-li* 'I am different', with no indication that I am deliberately being different.

Another area where differences in degree of control show up quite frequently across languages is in causative constructions, as discussed in more detail in chapter 8. For the present, we will restrict ourselves to giving some examples where the degree of control retained by the causee is different depending on the case used to encode this semantic role. In Japanese, for instance, there are two ways of translating 'Taroo made Ziroo go', in the first of which *Ziroo* is in the accusative (postposition *o*), in the second with the postposition *ni* (which is used for a variety of semantic roles, e.g. recipient, location, instrument):

Taroo ga Ziroo o ikaseta. (5)

Taroo ga Ziroo ni ikaseta. (6)

The difference is that (5) assigns minimal control to Ziroo, while (6) allows that Ziroo may have retained greater control: for instance, (5) often corresponds to 'Taroo forced Ziroo to go', while (6) corresponds to 'Taroo got Ziroo to go, persuaded him to go, got him to go by asking nicely'. A similar distinction with the causative of a transitive verb is found in the following Kannada examples:

Avanu nanage (DATIVE) *bisketannu tinnisidanu.* (7)
'He caused me to eat (fed me) a biscuit.'

Avanu nanninda (INSTRUMENTAL) *bisketannu tinnisidanu.* (8)
'He got me to eat a biscuit.'

Sentence (7) implies little or no control retained by the causee (person caused to do the action), and might be appropriate, for instance, for someone feeding a baby or force-feeding someone on hunger strike, while (8) suggests rather that the causer worked indirectly on the causee to get him to eat the biscuit, for instance by persuading him without the use of force.

On the parameter of control, it might seem that there is no distinction between experiencer and patient, since in general one does not have control over one's own sensory experiences: one can choose whether or not to look at something, but one cannot choose (except metaphorically) whether or not to see something. However, there is a crucial difference, in that for an entity to be an experiencer presupposes that it must be sentient, capable of receiving sensory experiences, and this is crucial in distinguishing experiencer from patient, and also in distinguishing experiencer from non-patient on the continuum of control: an experiencer has no (necessary) control over the reception of sensory impressions. Although many languages treat experiencers just like initiators of actions, as in English *I hit the man* and *I saw the man*, there are also many languages that distinguish them. In Lak, for instance, the dative case is used for the subject of a verb of perception, whereas the ergative is the usual case for the subject of a transitive verb:

> *Buttan* (DATIVE) *ussu xxal x̄unni.*   (9)
> 'Father saw brother.'

> *Buttal* (ERGATIVE) *bavxxunnu ur ču.*   (10)
> 'Father sold the horse.'

Causative constructions again sometimes evince a distinction between experiencer and non-experiencer causee. In French, for instance, the causee in the causative of a transitive verb can usually be expressed either by a noun phrase in the dative (preposition *à*) or by the use of the preposition *par* 'by':

> *J'ai fait manger les gâteaux à/par Paul.*   (11)
> 'I made Paul eat the cakes.'

Where the verb expressing the result is one of perception, however, the experiencer-causee can only stand in the dative:

> *J'ai fait voir les gâteaux à/*par Paul.*   (12)
> 'I made Paul see the cakes.'

From the preceding discussion, it might seem that the continuum of control and the distinction of experiencer from patient are concerned with animacy, but in fact it is crucial to keep these two parameters apart. Notions like control and experiencer refer to a relation between the predicate and one of its arguments. The scale of animacy, however, to which we return in more detail in chapter 9, is concerned with an inherent property of noun phrases, irrespective of their role within a particular construction. Thus the noun phrase *the man* is always high in animacy, although it may vary in degree of control, having high control in *the man deliberately hit me*, minimal control in *I hit the man*, and either high or low control in *the man rolled down the hill*, depending on the particular interpretation assigned. The distinction between the relations and inherent properties is particularly clear in an opposition like that between Bats sentences (1) and (2): the noun phrase 'we' is very high in animacy in both examples, but the degree of control is different. More generally: a high degree of animacy is necessary for a noun phrase to be interpreted as having a high degree of control or as an experiencer, but is not a sufficient condition.

3.2   PRAGMATIC ROLES

By pragmatic or discourse roles, we refer to the different ways in which essentially the same information, or the same semantic content, can be structured differently to reflect the flow of given and new information. A simple way of illustrating differences of pragmatic role of noun phrases is by taking question and answer sequences:

—*Who saw Bill?*—*John saw Bill/him.*   (13)

—*Who did Bill see?* —*Bill/he saw John.*   (14)

In such interchanges, as indeed in any natural discourse, it is normally the case that the speaker and hearer share certain information in common, but that there is also some information that they do not share. Thus in (13), the questioner assumes that both he and his interlocutor know that someone saw Bill, and the questioner wants a piece of new information; this new information is given by the answerer as the noun phrase *John*. Likewise, in (14), the questioner assumes as common knowledge that Bill saw someone, and requests a piece of new information, provided by the answerer as *John*. In talking about pragmatic roles, as opposed to semantic roles, we are not restricted solely to noun phrases, since the new information may be the verb phrase, as in (15), or even the whole sentence, as in (16), but for the present purposes we will in fact restrict ourselves to the pragmatic functions of noun phrases:

—*What did Bill do?* —*Bill/he went straight home.*   (15)

—*What happened?* —*Bill went straight home.*   (16)

The terminology for describing pragmatic functions is even less standard than that for describing semantic roles, the differences being conceptual as well as purely terminological, but for present purposes we will need to make only two distinctions; we will therefore introduce the terminology used here for these distinctions, and stick to this terminology throughout the rest of the book. The essential piece of new information that is carried by a sentence will be referred to as its focus. Thus the focus of (13) is *John*, that of (14) is *John*, that of (15) is *went straight home*, and that of (16) is *Bill went straight home*. The use of question and answer sequences is particularly useful in illustrating focus distinctions, since the nature of the question forces the answerer (assuming he is being cooperative) to select a particular part of his reply as focus. However, the distinction between focus and non-focus can be applied to any sentence.

In English, in general, there is no grammaticalized indication of focus, although focus is usually shown intonationally in the spoken language by being assigned sentence stress (intonation nucleus). In some languages, however, there is such grammaticalization. In Hungarian, for instance, the focus must immediately precede the finite verb (as must the question word in a special question). Thus the question 'who saw Zoli?' could be phrased as either (17) or (18) in Hungarian, and likewise the reply 'Vili saw Zoli' could be either (19) or (20), but no other word orders are possible, because they would involve separating the focus from before the verb:

Ki látta Zoli-t?	(17)
Zoli-t ki látta?	(18)
Vili látta Zoli-t.	(19)
Zoli-t Vili látta.	(20)

(In these examples -*t* is the accusative (direct object) suffix; *látta* 'he saw' is used when the direct object is definite, otherwise *látott*.) In Hungarian, incidentally, this rule operates independently of grammatical relations, so that if the focus is direct object then it also must immediately precede the verb:

Ki-t látott Zoli? or *Zoli ki-t látott?*	(21)
'Who(m) did Zoli see?'	
Zoli Vili-t látta or *Vili-t látta Zoli.*	(22)
'Zoli saw Vili.'	

Even in English, there is one instance where focus is the determining factor in word order, namely with special questions, where the *wh-* word expressing the focus must be sentence-initial (or part of the sentence-initial noun or prepositional phrase), so that although direct objects normally follow the main verb in English, we still have *who(m) did Bill see?* It is by no means necessary for a language to exhibit this relevance of focus, since in Mandarin Chinese, for instance, one has the word order *Zhāngsān kàn shéi?*, literally 'Zhangsan see who?' for English 'who does Zhangsan see?'

The second distinction that we need to introduce is that between topic and comment. Again, the easiest way to appreciate this distinction is to look at mini-dialogues where the choice of topic is forced. In English, for instance, if one person asks a question like *and what about Bill?*, then his interlocutor is forced, assuming he is being cooperative, to select *Bill* as topic of his reply. Thus if a dialogue starts out by A saying *Bill sold the car*, and B then asks *and what about John?*, then A must continue by saying something about John, for instance *John sold the bike*, *John didn't sell his car*. Conversely, if B had said *and what about the bike?*, then A would have had to give a reply with *the bike* as topic, e.g. *Bill didn't sell the bike*, or *John sold the bike*. From the fact that *John sold the bike* is felicitous as an answer to either question, we observe that in general English does not have any grammaticalization of topic versus non-topic (comment) status. Some languages, however, do, for instance Japanese, with a special topic marker *wa* to indicate the topic of the sentence.

Although in general English does not have grammaticalization of topic or focus, there are some more restricted kinds of topic and focus that can be grammaticalized. These are contrastive topic and focus, i.e. where one wishes to select one topic or focus from a delimited set of topics or focuses. With topics, this is indicated in English, especially spoken English, by preposing the topic noun phrase, as in *John, I know*; the implication is that, of the various entities that constitute the potential range of topics, there is one, namely John, that I do know, whereas I am not indicating whether or not I know the others. With focus, the construction is with sentence-initial *it's X that*, where *X* represents the focused noun phrase. Thus if someone offers me a range of books and asks which particular book I want to take, I can reply by saying *it's that one over there that I want*. In English, however, these are not general topic or focus constructions, so that it would be inappropriate, for instance, to introduce a chapter by saying *in this chapter it's relative clauses that we're going to talk about*, even though *relative clauses* is the intended focus.

With pragmatic roles, as with semantic roles, we must emphasize that we are concerned with relations between noun phrase arguments and their predicate, and not with inherent properties of noun phrases. This is essential in order to distinguish adequately between, on the one hand, topic and focus, and, on the other, definiteness and indefiniteness. In answer to the question *what did you see?*, the focus may be either definite or indefinite, i.e. *I saw the dog* or *I saw a dog*. The former will be used if the answerer assumes that his interlocutor can identify the dog being referred to in the context or situation, for instance if this dog had already been mentioned in the earlier discourse; the latter, with the indefinite article, will be used if the answerer assumes that this identification cannot be made. In the first instance, *the dog* is in a sense old information, in that it is already available to speaker and hearer as referring to some known entity, but what is important is not the pragmatic nature of this noun phrase on its own, but rather its pragmatic relation to the rest of the sentence: although the presence of the dog in the store of speaker–hearer shared knowledge is presupposed, what is new is the precise relation of this entity to the action of my seeing. In the reply *a dog*, the dog in question is both presented per se for the first time, and related to my seeing for the first time. The terms given versus new information are potentially confusing because of this distinction between inherent and relational pragmatic properties of noun phrases, and to avoid this potential confusion we use definite/indefinite as inherent terms and topic and focus as relational terms.

3.3 GRAMMATICAL RELATIONS

Most descriptions of English syntax, and of the syntax of many other languages, have assumed that, perhaps in addition to semantic and pragmatic roles of the kind discussed in the earlier part of this chapter, there are also purely syntactic relations contracted between a noun phrase and its predicate, which, however closely they may correlate with semantic or pragmatic relations, cannot be identified with them. These might be called syntactic relations, though recent tradition has in fact determined that the usual name is grammatical relations, and this is the term that will be used in the present book: it should, however, be borne in mind that the term grammatical here does have the narrow sense of syntactic. Grammatical relations that are commonly proposed in traditional and recent literature are subject, direct object, and indirect object.

While the function of semantic roles and pragmatic roles can readily be understood in terms of the need for language to express semantic relations and package them in some way in terms of information flow, it is much less obvious why human language should require grammatical relations, or more generally why human language should require syntax (in the linguists' sense of syntax) at all. Although attempts have been made to do away with syntax by trying to argue that everything can be accounted for in terms of either semantics or pragmatics, no such attempt strikes us as even nearly approaching success, and it therefore seems to remain a truth about human languages that they do have syntaxes, and that many of them do have grammatical relations that cannot be reduced to semantic or pragmatic primitives. In this book, we accept that such grammatical relations do exist, but unlike much recent work on grammatical relations (in particular, relational grammar), we argue that much of syntax can be understood only in relation to semantics and pragmatics, or more specifically that grammatical relations cannot be understood in their entirety unless they are related to semantic and pragmatic roles. This point will be illustrated in somewhat more detail in chapter 5, when we look more specifically at one grammatical relation, subject. For the moment, suffice it to say that at least many aspects of the nature of grammatical relations can be understood in terms of the interaction of semantic and pragmatic roles: for instance, many facets of subjecthood can be understood by regarding the prototype of subject as the intersection of agent and topic.

In much work on grammatical relations, it is taken for granted that certain grammatical relations exist as given by the general theory – in particular: subject, direct object, indirect object, versus other (oblique) noun phrases that bear some other relation to the predicate – and that the linguist looking at an individual language has to work out which noun phrases in this particular language evince these particular relations. In the present work, a different approach is assumed, namely that in order to say that a given grammatical relation exists in a given language this claim must be justified both language-internally and cross-linguistically. Language-internally, this means that a number of logically independent criteria must be established that serve to identify the grammatical relation in question as being syntactically significant in the language in question. Cross-linguistically, the problem is more difficult, and the following is more in the nature of a suggestion: in assigning the same name to grammatical relations established independently in different languages, it must be the case that the relations in the two languages have a reasonable degree of overlap, for instance in terms of occurrence in translation equivalents. Although there remain many unclear instances, this clearly excludes any analysis of a language where the only claimed occurrences of subjects were in translations of English prepositional phrases with the preposition *notwithstanding*.

One way of illustrating this is to take an example which is often treated as a grammatical relation, and show how under this approach it would probably, on available evidence, not be a grammatical relation, namely indirect object in English. In much traditional grammar this term is used very loosely, as when, for instance, we are told that the indirect object may either precede the direct object without a preposition (as in *I gave John the book*), or follow the direct object with the preposition *to* (as in *I gave the book to John*). Since these are, rather, different syntactic encodings of the same semantic role, this use of the term indirect object seems to be referring to a semantic role (in more current terminology, recipient) rather than to a grammatical relation; the noun/prepositional phrases *John* and *to John* seem to have little, other than semantic similarity, in common, as can be seen by contrasting their different abilities to become subject of the passive: *John was given the book*, but not **John was given the book to*.

Orthodox relational grammar deliberately avoids this pitfall, and would claim that in the version *I gave John the book* the noun phrase *John*, despite its semantic role, is a direct object, while restricting the term indirect object to the equivalent argument in the version *I gave the book to John*. The question which is not addressed by this assignment, however, is what evidence there is internal to English for the establishment of a separate grammatical relation of indirect object. There might seem to be a good test, in that indirect objects do permit the alternation between the two construction types shown above with *give*, i.e. corresponding to a construction with an indirect object there will be an alternative construction where that noun phrase appears as a direct object. However, this criterion – apart from being just a single criterion, and therefore not really satisfying the need for a set of logically independent criteria – fails on two major counts. First, the alternation in question is in large measure lexically conditioned, so that in many constructions where one might expect intuitively to find an indirect object the alternative without the preposition *to* is impossible, as in *I attribute our failure to his malevolence*, versus **I attribute his malevolence our failure*; presumably this objection could be answered (though at the risk of circularity) by saying that the *to* argument of *attribute* is not an indirect object. Secondly, this alternation applies not only to putative indirect objects, but also to benefactives, as in the alternation between *I bought this book for John* and *I bought John this book*. While one might again, circularly, avoid the problem by saying that in English benefactives are a subclass of indirect objects, this runs into further problems, since for many speakers the behaviour of such alternative benefactive constructions under passive is different from that of recipient constructions, since many speakers allow *John was given the book* but not **John was bought the book*. In English, then, there seems to be no evidence for, and circumstantial evidence against, the existence of a distinct grammatical relation of indirect object. Similar caveats can be applied to putative indirect objects in many other languages, and this particular grammatical relation seems to be the one that requires most re-thinking cross-linguistically.

After this negative demonstration, we shall outline a positive demonstration, using Huichol as the illustrative language. In Huichol, there are several logically independent tests that enable us to set up two grammatical relations of subject and (direct) object (we parenthetize *direct*, since there is no grammatical relation of indirect object with which it contrasts). Subjects are characterized

(a) by having distinct suffixes for a limited number of noun phrase types, whereas all non-subjects have a distinct set of suffixes for such noun phrase types; in (23), the subject suffix is *-tɨ*:

> *Tɨɨri   yɨnauka-tɨ me   -wa*
> children four   3PLURAL 3PLURAL
> *-zeiya uukaraawicizɨ yɨhuuta-me.*   (23)
>   see   women   two
> 'Four children see two women.'

(b) by triggering a separate set of verb agreement prefixes; in (24), the prefix *pe-* is unequivocally a subject prefix:

> *Eekɨ pe   -nua.*   (24)
> you 2SINGULAR arrive
> 'You arrived.'

(c) in that only subjects can trigger the possessive reflexive prefix *yu-*, so that in (25) the stick is unequivocally in the possession of the one doing the beating and not of the person being beaten or some third party:

> *Mɨɨkɨ yu-kɨye -kɨ   me*
> they   stick INSTRUMENTAL 3PLURAL
> *-pe-i   -kuuwaazɨ*   (25)
>   3SINGULAR beat
> 'They beat him with their/*his stick.'

(d) in that, where the subject of certain time clauses is coreferential with the subject of the main clause, a special suffix must be added to the verb of the time clause, e.g. *-ka* in (26); in all other instances (i.e. unlike subjects, even if other noun phrases are coreferential), a different set of suffixes is used, e.g. *-ku* in (27):

> *Nee ne   -nua -ka, paapaa ne*
> I   ISINGULAR come   tortilla ISINGULAR   (26)

-p-ii   *-Päti.*
  3SINGULAR give
'When I arrived, I gave him a tortilla.'

Uuka nua   -ku, nee ne   -petia.   (27)
girl   arrive   I   ISINGULAR leave
'When the girl arrived, I left.'

These four tests are clearly logically independent of one another, yet all serve to identify a single set of noun phrases, thus establishing a grammatical relation language-internally. Moreover, the degree of overlap between these noun phrases and subjects in translation equivalents in other languages is so close that we have no hesitation in referring to this grammatical relation as subject.

For direct objects in Huichol there are two criteria:

(a) verb agreement, since in addition to the prefixes for subject agreement, Huichol has a distinct set of prefixes for direct object agreement:

Taame eeki te   -meci   -zeiya.   (28)
we   you IPLURAL   2SINGULAR see
'We see you.'

(b) possibility of appearing as subject of a passive, since in Huichol only direct objects have this property:

Tiiri   me   -puutiweiya.   (29)
children 3PLURAL   beat-PASSIVE
'The children were beaten.'

The conjunction of these two logically independent properties serves to identify the grammatical relation of direct object language-internally. In comparison with other languages, the noun phrases thus identified correlate highly with direct objects, which justifies the use of this term to refer to this grammatical relation (though a more neutral term like prime object might be preferable, since Huichol has no separate grammatical relation of indirect object). The overlap is not, however, complete here, since in a Huichol sentence with both a patient and a recipient it is the recipient, rather than, as in many languages, the patient that is direct object:

Nee waakanaari ne   -meci   -tikiiti eeki.   (30)
I   chickens   ISINGULAR 2SINGULAR give you
'I gave the chickens to you.'

Eeki̱ tumiini pe   *-puuzeiyast̄iari*   (31)
you money 2SINGULAR show-PASSIVE
'You were shown the money.'

But notwithstanding the discrepancy in certain instances, the degree of over-lap elsewhere is large enough to justify the identification. Thus our use of the same terms subject and direct object as in discussing other languages is justified by the overlap cross-linguistically in their use: while the assignment of individual noun phrases to these grammatical relations in Huichol is determined by language-specific criteria associated with each grammatical relation.

In the particular example chosen, that of Huichol, all of the criteria for each grammatical relation converge on a single noun phrase in each con-struction (at least, in the present state of our knowledge of Huichol syntax). It is, however, conceivable that different sets of criteria might make for different groupings of arguments into different grammatical relations. Examples of this, and their implications for universals and typology of grammatical re-lations, will be discussed further in chapter 5, with particular regard to sub-jects. For the present, we may note that one particularly widespread instance of this kind of split is found between intransitive and transitive constructions in many languages, so that in translations of (32) and (33) it is sometimes the case that some criteria group *John* and *Bill* together as a single grammatical relation, while others group *John* and *Harry* together:

John arrived.   (32)

Bill hit Harry.   (33)

Since we shall need to refer, relatively informally, to some such examples before they are introduced more thoroughly in chapter 5, we will introduce the following terminology to refer to the various arguments: the intransitive subject (e.g. *John* of (32)) will by symbolized S; that argument of the transitive construction that correlates most closely with agent will be symbolized A (e.g. *Bill* of (33)), and that one that correlates most highly with patient will be symbolized P (e.g. *Harry* of (33)). Grouping of S and A together will be referred to as the nominative–accusative system; grouping of S and P to-gether as the ergative–absolutive system.

3.4 MORPHOLOGICAL CASES

In terms of a traditional grammatical discussion of clause structure, it might seem strange that so far we have not spoken of morphological cases, such as nominative, accusative, ergative, absolutive, since in the traditional grammars, especially of highly inflected languages like Latin, the discussion of grammatical relations, also semantic roles, is closely linked to that of case, with equation or near-equation being drawn between subject and nominative, or direct object and accusative, for instance. In the present section, largely as a counter-influence to this traditional view, we will emphasize the extent to which there can be discrepancy between grammatical relations and morphological cases, in particular noting some examples where the distribution of morphological cases is completely irrelevant to the operation of syntactic processes. Towards the end of this section, we will also note some examples where, despite a discrepancy between grammatical relations and morphological case, the latter does still play some role in the conditioning of certain syntactic processes.

We shall start with a relatively straightforward example of such discrepancy, concerning the cases used to express the direct object in Russian. In positive sentences, the direct object normally stands in the accusative; in negated sentences, the direct object may stand in either the accusative or the genitive, but our present interest is naturally focused on instances where the direct object under negation is in the genitive:

Maša kupila šapku. (34)
'Masha bought a cap.'

Maša ne kupila šapki. (35)
'Masha didn't buy a cap.'

One syntactic process of Russian that is sensitive to grammatical relations is passive, since only the direct object of an active verb can appear as the subject of the corresponding passive. Both (34) and (35), despite the different case markings of the noun *šapk-*, have corresponding passives where this noun phrase appears as subject, in the nominative form *šapka*:

Šapka byla kuplena Mašej. (36)
'The cap was bought by Masha.'

Šapka ne byla kuplena Mašej. (37)
'The cap wasn't bought by Masha.'

This is, then, a clear instance of discrepancy between grammatical relations and morphology, moreover one where the grammatical relations clearly win out.

To avoid misunderstanding, it should be emphasized that what we are claiming is that there is here a discrepancy between syntax and morphology, i.e. that the morphology is arbitrary relative to the syntax (or, equivalently except for emphasis, the syntax is arbitrary relative to the morphology). We are not claiming that the morphology is arbitrary in any absolute sense – although there probably are many instances where morphology is simply arbitrary. For instance, the use of the genitive for a negated direct object can be given a natural interpretation as a special case of the use of the genitive in quantified expressions in Russian, compare the genitive singular in *ni šapki* 'not a (single) cap' and the genitive plural in *mnogo šapok* 'many caps'.

A particularly far-reaching discrepancy between morphology and syntax is to be found in Kalaw Lagaw Ya (the Western Torres Strait language), the discussion here being restricted to the Saibai dialect. Different classes of noun phrase have completely different morphological systems when they appear as S, A, or P of a clause. Thus, singular pronouns have different forms for each of these three (e.g. S *ngay*, A *ngath*, P *ngoena* 'I'); singular proper names have a nominative–accusative case marking system (e.g. S/A *Kala*, P *Kala-n*); non-plural common nouns have an ergative–absolutive case marking system (e.g. S/P *burum* 'pig', A *burum-an*); non-singular personal pronouns and plural common nouns have only one form for all three functions (e.g. S/A/P *ngoey* 'we', *burum-al* 'pigs'). However, there seems to be no other process in the language that is sensitive to these distinctions. For instance, verb agreement operates consistently on an ergative–absolutive basis: verbs agree in number with their S if intransitive, and with their P if transitive, totally independent of the case marking:

Ngay/ngi/garkaz/burum/Kala/Gibuma pathiz (SINGULAR).   (38)
'I/you/the man/the pig/Kala/Gibuma left.'

Ngoey/ngitha/garkoez-il/burum-al pathemin (PLURAL).   (39)
'We/you/the men/the pigs left.'

Ngath/garkoez-in/Kala/ngoey/garkoez-il ngin/burum/Gibuma-n
   mathaman (SINGULAR).   (40)
'I/the man/Kala/we/the men hit you/the pig/Gibuma.'

Ngath/garkoez-in/Kala/ngoey/garkoez-il ngitha/burum-al   (41)
   mathamoeyn (PLURAL).
'I/the man/Kala/we/the men hit you/the pigs.'

Although much recent work on syntax, especially syntactic typology, has emphasized the frequent irrelevance, for syntactic purposes, of morphological distinctions of this kind, some recent work has shown that at least in some restricted instances some morphological differences are important for the operation of syntactic processes. The example used here is of coordination in Yidiny. First, we should note that, in English, when transitive and intransitive sentences are coordinated as in (42) below, it is possible to omit the subject of the intransitive clause only if it is coreferential with the subject (A) of the preceding transitive clause:

The man/I hit the woman/you and ran away.   (42)

Thus the interpretation of (42) is that the man/I ran away, not that the woman/you ran away: in English this is rigidly determined syntactically, and only this interpretation is possible even in situations where the alternative interpretation would be as plausible or more so. In Yidiny, however, the interpretation, or at least the preferred interpretation, is determined by the case of the noun phrases in the transitive clause. In Yidiny, pronouns have a nominative–accusative case marking system, while other noun phrases have an ergative–absolutive case marking system, as in the first clause of each of the following examples:

Biṃbi:ŋ   *gudʸugudʸu*
father-ERGATIVE rainbow-ABSOLUTIVE
   wawa:l, biṛi   *gundʸi:nʸ*.   (43)
   saw   PARTICLE returned
'Father saw the rainbow, and it returned.'

ŋayu   *nʸuninʸ*   *bandʸa:ṛ, wanda:nʸ*.   (44)
I-NOMINATIVE you-ACCUSATIVE followed fell-down
'I followed you, and I fell down.'

ŋayu   *bama*   *bandʸa:ṛ, wanda:nʸ*.   (45)
I-NOMINATIVE person-ABSOLUTIVE followed fell-down
'I followed the person and I/he fell down.'

The rule determining the interpretation in Yidiny is the following: the controller of the interpretation (i.e. the noun phrase in the first clause interpreted as coreferential with the omitted noun phrase of the second clause) must be in either the absolutive or the nominative case: thus, in (43) the controller is the absolutive noun phrase, in (44) the nominative pronoun, and in (45) it can be either the absolutive noun phrase or the nominative pronoun.

   This morphologically conditioned pattern, however, exists only for the interpretation of coordinate constructions. Elsewhere, these morphological differences are irrelevant to syntactic processes, which work for the most part on an ergative–absolutive basis (cf. the discussion of Dyirbal syntax in section 5.3). It thus remains true that in general morphology can deviate quite widely from the syntactically relevant parameters, though there are also instances where morphology overrides the otherwise valid syntactic parameters.

3.5 ILLUSTRATION: ENGLISH AND RUSSIAN CLAUSE STRUCTURE

In this section, we will illustrate the interaction of the various parameters discussed in the preceding sections – semantic roles, pragmatic roles, grammatical relations, and morphological cases – by contrasting some of the properties of clause structure in two languages, English and Russian. Although these two languages are genetically related within the Indo-European family, they differ considerably from one another in terms of this interaction, and therefore the contrast between them does serve to illustrate two radically different solutions to the problem of integrating all of these parameters, i.e. we are contrasting two radically different types along this parameter.

In English, there is a very high correlation between grammatical relations and word order, indeed word order is the basic carrier of grammatical relations, especially of subject and direct object, as can be seen by comparing the following two sentences:

John hit Mary.   (46)

Mary hit John.   (47)

The position immediately before the verb is reserved for the subject, while the position immediately after the verb is reserved for the direct object. Even in the corresponding questions, with subject–auxiliary inversion, it is still the case that the subject precedes the main verb, as in *did John hit Mary?*, *did Mary hit John?* Changing the word order, as in changing (46) to (47), therefore changes the grammatical relations, and ultimately the meaning of the sentence.

From the pair of examples just given, one might imagine that an alternative statement could be given, namely that the word order is determined by semantic roles, with the agent preceding the verb and the patient following. However, further data serve to show that this alternative is incorrect, and that in English it is precisely grammatical relations and word order that correlate. This can be seen in examples where the subject is an experiencer or an instrument rather than an agent:

John saw Mary.   (48)

The stone hit John.   (49)

Perhaps most clearly, it can be seen in passive sentences, where the subject is usually a patient, and the agent follows the verb:

John was hit by Mary. (50)

Mary was hit by John. (51)

The correlation between word order and grammatical relations in English is so strong that native speakers have no difficulty in interpreting pairs of sentences like (46) and (47), where the interpretations of John hitting Mary and Mary hitting John are equally plausible in terms of real-world likelihood; and sentences like (52) below are interpreted as nonsense (at least, in terms of real-world interpretations), rather than a plausible interpretation being assigned that violates this syntactic determination of word order:

The stone saw Mary. (52)

We have already illustrated in passing another property of English clause structure, namely that a given grammatical relation can be associated with a wide range of semantic roles: the subjects in the above sentences included agents, patients, instruments, and experiencers. English has a number of syntactic processes which serve to put the same semantic role in different grammatical relations, and to have the same grammatical relation serving a number of semantic roles. Thus the passive construction places a patient in subject position, even though the agent is the more basic semantic role correlating with subjecthood for two-place predicates. The rule of subject-to-object raising, which relates sentences like (53) and (54), means that a role that is expressed as subject of a subordinate clause can also be expressed as direct object of a main clause:

I believe that Mary hit John. (53)

I believe Mary to have hit John. (54)

The embedded subject may itself encode a variety of semantic roles, as can be seen in the following examples:

I believe that the stone hit Mary. (55)

I believe the stone to have hit Mary. (56)

I believe that John saw Mary. (57)

I believe John to have seen Mary. (58)

I believe that John was hit by Mary. (59)

I believe John to have been hit by Mary. (60)

As a last illustration, we may take the rule of object-to-subject raising, which relates sentences like (61) and (62), enabling the object of an embedded construction to appear also as subject of the main clause:

It is easy to solve this problem. (61)

This problem is easy to solve. (62)

Many such constructions are frequently used in natural discourse, so that even though some constructions, like many instances of subject-to-object raising and passives with an expressed agent, are very rare in the spoken language, this variety of the language does still provide sufficient illustration of the operation of syntactic processes that destroy any close correlation between semantic roles and grammatical relations.

A similar situation can be observed in English with lexical, as opposed to syntactic, relations among the valencies of verbs. Thus English has many verbs that can be used either transitively or intransitively. When used transitively, the subject will be an agent; when used intransitively, the verb will have a patient as subject:

John opened the door. (63)

The door opened. (64)

In English, morphological marking of noun phrases plays a marginal role. To be sure, most pronouns have a nominative versus accusative distinction, as in:

I saw him. (65)

He saw me. (66)

However, the existence of this case distinction does not provide for any greater freedom of word order: **him saw I* and **me saw he* are simply ungrammatical in the modern language. Moreover, except in very straightforward examples like the above, the correlation between case and grammatical relation is rather weak: for instance, many speakers of English have the pattern illustrated below:

John and I saw Mary. (67)

Me and John saw Mary. (68)

Here, the difference between *I* and *me* is conditioned by word order, in turn conditioned by register ((68) is more colloquial than (67)), although there is no difference in grammatical relations. Finally, probably few native speakers of English consistently differentiate, in production and comprehension, between such putative minimal pairs in prescriptive grammar as *John knows more people than I* (sc. *than I do*) and *John knows more people than me* (i.e. he doesn't just know me).

In English, pragmatic roles play a very small role in the syntactic structure of sentences. Thus a sentence like *John hit Mary*, with that word order, could be used to answer any of the questions *who hit Mary?*, *who did John hit?*, *what did John do to Mary?*, *what did John do?*, *what happened to Mary?*, *what happened?* Differences among at least some of these will, of course, be carried by differences in intonation: the nucleus of the intonation pattern (the sentence stress) will fall on the focus. But in general, in English it is not possible to carry differences of pragmatic structure by simply varying the word order: *John hit Mary* and *Mary hit John* represent different distributions of semantic role, and cannot be used to encode differences of pragmatic structure. There is, however, a weaker correlation involving pragmatic structure, because in English the choice between alternative syntactic means of encoding the same semantic structure is often determined by pragmatic considerations, one of the principles being a preference to make the topic subject wherever possible, thus leading to a correlation between subject and topic. For instance, in answer to the question *what do you think of these problems?*, it is more natural to reply *these problems/they are easy to solve* than *it's easy to solve these problems/them*, i.e. there is preference for making *these problems/they* subject of the reply.

Russian clause structure is determined by a very different weighting of these principles, as can be seen by starting with variations on Russian sentence (69):

Tanja ubila Mašu. (69)
'Tanya killed Masha.'

In Russian the basic marker of grammatical relations is not the word order, but rather the morphology. In the example given above, the form of the noun ending in -*a* is nominative (the case used for subjects) and that in -*u* is accusative (the case used for direct objects); the citation forms of the two names, as indicated in the English translation, are *Tanja* and *Maša*. Changing the word order does not affect the distribution of grammatical relations or of semantic roles. In fact, any of the six logically possible permutations of the three words *Tanja*, *ubila*, *Mašu* is a grammatical Russian sentence meaning 'Tanya killed Masha'.

Although all six permutations have the same semantic roles and the same grammatical relations, they are by no means equivalent, in particular they differ in terms of the pragmatic roles expressed. The basic principle in Russian (especially in non-affective use) is that the topic comes at the beginning of the sentence, and the focus at the end. Thus the following question-and-answer pairs reflect the normal word order to be used in answer to that particular question:

—Kto ubil Mašu? —Mašu ubila Tanja.   (70)
'—Who killed Masha? —Tanya killed Masha.'

—Kogo Tanja ubila? —Tanja ubila Mašu.   (71)
'—Who did Tanya kill? —Tanya killed Masha.'

—Valja ubila Natašu. —A Tanja? —Tanja ubila Mašu.   (72)
'—Valya killed Natasha. —What about Tanya?
 —Tanya killed Masha.'

—Valja ubila Natašu. —A Mašu? —Mašu ubila Tanja.   (73)
'—Valya killed Natasha. —What about Masha?
 —Tanya killed Masha.'

Note that in examples (72) and (73), the distinction between the nominative (*Tanja*) and the accusative (*Mašu*) is crucial to understanding whether the question is about the killer or the victim: this is not brought out in the English translations, which would, to carry the same amount of information, have to be more explicit, e.g. (72) *and who did Tanya kill?*, (73) *and who killed Masha?* Our initial observation is thus that English and Russian differ in that in English word order is determined by grammatical relations and independent of pragmatic roles; in Russian, morphology is determined by and carries grammatical relations, while word order is determined by pragmatic roles.

In addition, there is a difference between English and Russian in terms of the interaction of semantic roles with grammatical relations. In the discussion of English above, we noted that a given grammatical relation, in particular subject, can carry a variety of semantic roles. Although to some extent this is also true of Russian, the range of the syntactic–semantic discrepancy is much smaller, in that in many instances where English would use a non-agentive subject Russian either requires or prefers a non-subject. A particularly clear instance of this can be seen in the description of actions where there is no agent or where the agent is not mentioned. Here English can quite freely use non-agentive subjects, as in:

The lightning killed Tanya. (74)

The bullet killed Tanya. (75)

Although literal translations are possible in Russian, the preference is rather for an impersonal construction: the verb remains in the active, but has no subject, standing instead in the third person singular neuter; the natural force or instrument stands in the instrumental, thus giving as translations of the English sentences above:

Tanju ubilo molniej. (76)

Tanju ubilo pulej. (77)

The noun phrase *Tanju* is in the accusative; the noun phrases *molniej* and *pulej* are the instrumentals of *molnija* 'lightning' and *pulja* 'bullet', respectively.

In somewhat similar manner, many experiencers which are expressed by subjects in English are expressed by noun phrases in the dative case in Russian, so that, for instance, the translation of 'Tanya is (feels) cold' must be *Tane* (DATIVE) *xolodno*: here, *xolodno* is an impersonal, subjectless, form of the adjective *xolodnyj* 'cold'. The closest nominative-subject equivalent, *Tanja xolodna(ja)*, the adjective being in the feminine form agreeing with *Tanja*, would have a quite different meaning, for instance that Tanya is dead and her body is cold, or that she is frigid, but certainly not with Tanya as experiencer.

The closer relation that obtains in Russian between grammatical relations and semantic roles can also be seen in the fact that some syntactic processes are subject to semantic role constraints, in addition to syntactic constraints, where their closest analogues in English are subject only to syntactic constraints. Thus the constructions referred to in English transformational-generative syntax as equi-NP-deletion require that the subject of the subordinate clause be coreferential with the appropriate noun phrase of the main clause, irrespective of semantic role:

I persuaded the doctor to examine Tanya. (78)

I persuaded Tanya to be examined by the doctor. (79)

In (78), the omitted noun phrase is subject and agent of the subordinate clause; in (79), the omitted noun phrase is subject and patient of the subordinate clause. In Russian, there is a literal translation of (78), but not of (79), the version offered below being at best decidedly weird to native speakers of Russian, even though it does not violate any syntactic constraint:

> *Ja ugovoril vrača osmotret' Tanju.*   (80)

> **Ja ugovoril Tanju byt' osmotrennoj vračom*   (81)

Although further work is needed to establish the precise nature of the constraint, it seems at the very least that in a clause that contains both an agent (expressed or implied) and a patient, equi-NP-deletion cannot delete the patient. Note that in the interpretation of the English example (79), it is necessary to assign some degree of control over the situation of being examined to Tanya, and in order to translate this example into natural Russian this degree of control must be expressed, as in:

> *Ja ugovoril Tanju podvergnut' sebja osmotru.*   (82)
> 'I persuaded Tanya to submit herself to an examination.'

In looking at lexical relations, it emerges that Russian does have a similar range of possibilities to English for expressing similar or identical semantic roles by different syntactic constructions, but in nearly all such instances Russian, unlike English, must provide overt marking on the verb of the different semantic role of the grammatical relations. Thus, corresponding to a transitive construction with an agentive subject like (83), the intransitive construction with a patient subject requires the suffix -*s'* on the verb:

> *Tanja zakryla dubovuju dver'.*   (83)
> 'Tanya closed the oak door.'

> *Dubovaja dver' zakryla-s'.*   (84)
> 'The oak door closed.'

(The noun *dver'* 'door' happens to have the same form for nominative and accusative, but the fact that the noun phrase containing *dver'* is direct object in (83) but subject in (84) is shown by the distinction between the nominative adjective *dubovaja* and accusative *dubovuju*.) A further example of this difference between English and Russian is illustrated by the following pair, where Russian must distinguish between *po-sejal* and *za-sejal*, while English uses *sowed* in both:

> *Kolxoznik po-sejal pšenicu v pole.*   (85)
> 'The collective-farmer sowed wheat in the field.'

> *Kolxoznik za-sejal pole pšenicej.*   (86)
> 'The collective-farmer sowed the field with wheat.'

Turning to syntactically different means of encoding the same set of semantic roles, we find that Russian lacks many of the constructions that are found in English. For instance, Russian has no syntactic equivalent of object-to-subject raising, so that in an example like (87) there is no way of making *problemu* 'problem' (accusative case) into subject (as *problema*) in the nominative:

> *Legko razrešit' ètu problemu.* (87)
> 'It is easy to solve this problem.'

Given the free word order of Russian, it is, however, possible simply to move the noun phrase *ètu problemu* to the beginning of the sentence, to give (88):

> *Ètu problemu legko razrešit'.* (88)

Since sentence-initial position correlates strongly with topic in Russian, and rather weakly with topic in English, sentence (88) is in a sense a functional equivalent of English *this problem is easy to solve*, so that the same pragmatic function is served, but by very different syntactic means. Russian does have a passive construction, but its use is much less frequent than is the English passive (even than the English passive in the spoken language). The usual functional equivalent of English *Masha was killed by Tanya* in Russian would be the active with the word order direct object-verb-subject, rather than the passive construction of (90):

> *Mašu ubila Tanja.* (89)

> *Maša byla ubita Tanej.* (90)
> 'Masha was killed by Tanya.'

The usual equivalent of the English agentless passive is a subjectless construction, with the verb in the third person plural, i.e. as if one were to say in English *they've killed Masha* in the meaning *Masha has been killed*:

> *Mašu ubili.* (91)

Since Russian has free word order, it is actually possible to carry out pragmatic role variations on the passive sentence (90) in much the same way as with an active sentence, and even possible to give a passive sentence with the same word order and pragmatic role distribution as the active:

> *Tanej byla ubita Maša.* (92)

Indeed, the basic function of the Russian passive seems to be not so much pragmatic as stylistic: it is characteristic of certain written styles, in particular scientific writing.

One particularly enlightening way of generalizing the above differences between Russian and English would be to say that in English the grammatical relations play a much greater role than in Russian. First, the grammatical relations in English are more independent than in Russian, with a low correlation in English between grammatical relations and either semantic roles or pragmatic roles (or morphology, which is virtually nonexistent). Secondly, there is a wider range of syntactic processes in English than in Russian where grammatical relations and changes in grammatical relations are relevant. In Russian, semantic and pragmatic roles (and even morphology) play a greater role than in English.

However, it is important to realize, in conjunction with the discussion of chapter 2, that what we have here is a difference of degree between English and Russian: it is not the case that English syntax operates solely in terms of grammatical relations while Russian syntax avoids grammatical relations. Relevance of pragmatic roles in English can be seen, for instance, in the formation of special questions and relative clauses, where the constituent questioned or relativized must appear in clause-initial position, irrespective of its grammatical relation:

Who saw you?   (93)

Who(m) did you see?   (94)

The man who saw me ran away.   (95)

The man who(m) I saw ran away.   (96)

Even in varieties of English that lack the *who/whom* distinction, the interpretation of sentences like (93)–(96) is unambiguous because of the general word order principle that the position before the main verb is reserved for the subject. In spoken English, especially, further constructions of this kind are possible, for instance the movement of contrastive topics to sentence-initial position, irrespective of grammatical relation:

That book over there, I wouldn't read in a million years.   (97)

Conversely, in Russian there are some instances where grammatical relations are crucial. For instance, there is a rule of verb agreement whereby verbs agree with their subject, and, as the following examples show, there is no way in which this can be reformulated as agreement with agent or topic:

Tanja ubila (FEMININE) *Kolju.*   (98)
'Tanya killed Kolya.'

Kolja byl ubit (MASCULINE) *Tanej.*   (99)
'Kolya was killed by Tanya.'

Kolju ubila (FEMININE) *Tanja.*   (100)
'Kolya, Tanya killed.'

(Tanya is a girl's name, Kolya a boy's.) The relevance of the grammatical
relation of direct object in Russian is shown by the fact that only direct
objects can become subject of the passive construction. There are also a few
instances where Russian allows the same verbal form to be used even with
rearrangement of the syntactic encoding of semantic roles, although such
examples are few indeed, for instance:

Tanja povernula mašinu nalevo.   (101)
'Tanya turned the car to the left.'

Mašina povernula nalevo.   (102)
'The car turned to the left.'

Rabočie gruzili drova na baržu.   (103)
'The workmen were loading wood onto the barge.'

Rabočie gruzili baržu drovami.   (104)
'The workmen were loading the barge with wood.'

(In the perfective aspect, however, the verb forms in (103) and (104) would
have to be distinguished as *na-gruzili* and *za-gruzili*, respectively.) And
finally, as we noted above, there are many instances in Russian of discrepancy between semantic role and grammatical relation, for example experiencer subjects as in (105), quite apart from discrepancies occasioned by
the, admittedly marginal, existence of the passive:

Tanja videla Kolju.   (105)
'Tanya saw Kolya.'

Even the role of morphology is not an absolute distinction between
English and Russian. In English, some pronouns do have a nominative–
accusative distinction, although as we indicated above its functional load is
minimal. Conversely, in Russian some noun phrases do not make the
nominative–accusative distinction, and in the few instances where the morphology is ambivalent and both interpretations make sense, preference is given

to a subject-verb-direct object interpretation, i.e. (106) below, with *mat'* 'mother' and *doč'* 'daughter', is preferred with the interpretation 'the mother loves the daughter' rather than 'the daughter loves the mother', although for many speakers this does seem to be a preference rather than an absolute:

Mat' ljubit doč. (106)

Although the interaction of semantic, pragmatic, syntactic, and morphological relations does not provide a holistic typology of either English or Russian (for instance, it has nothing to say about the phonology of either), it does characterize a large part of the syntactic differences between the two languages; indeed, we would argue that it provides a much wider-ranging characterization than does word order typology, especially since in terms of basic word order the two languages are remarkably similar. The discussion of this section can therefore be taken as illustration of a significant typological parameter.

NOTES AND REFERENCES

The bases of case grammar may be found in Fillmore (1968). The Bats examples are from Dešeriev (1953, 226). The Chickasaw examples are from Munro & Gordon (1982); Munro & Gordon argue conclusively against the claim that verb agreement in Chickasaw is determined purely by semantic roles. The Japanese, Kannada, and French examples are discussed further in chapter 8. The Lak examples are from Žirkov (1955, 41, 138).

The classic studies of pragmatic roles (informational structure, topic-comment structure, functional sentence perspective) are by such Prague School linguists as Vilém Mathesius and Jan Firbas, but an excellent introduction is provided by Chafe (1976). Most of the contributions in Li (1976) relate more or less directly to the general discussion of section 3.2. For discussion of focus in Hungarian, see Kiefer (1967). Of the vast amount of literature on Japanese *wa*, a good starting point, given the general and English–Japanese contrastive viewpoints, is Kuno (1972).

At the time of writing, the only authoritative published account of (orthodox) relational grammar is the formal description in Johnson & Postal 1980, though a series of more data-oriented essays (Perlmutter, forthcoming) is promised. Reference may also be made to the overview by Johnson (1977b); the other essays in Cole & Sadock (1977) provide a variety of approaches, all linked by acceptance of the importance of grammatical relations, though not all uncritical of relational grammar. A much fuller discussion of the Huichol material is given in Comrie (1982).

In section 3.4, the Kalaw Lagaw Ya examples are from Comrie (1981b). The Yidiny examples and discussion are based on Dixon (1977, 388–92); as noted in my review of the work (Comrie, 1978e, 285), Dixon's discussion of examples where the first clause has an ergative noun phrase and an accusative pronoun is inconclusive; Dixon informs me that a surviving speaker of the Tablelands dialect of Yidiny rejects as ungrammatical the sentence *bama:l ṇanʸanʸ bundʸa:nʸ, wanda:nʸ (person-ERGATIVE I-ACCUSATIVE hit, fell), where there is no potential nominative or absolutive controller. Further arguments in favour of relevance of some morphology in syntax can be found in Shibatani (1977) (Japanese data), and Babby (1980) (Russian data).

The presentation of section 3.5 owes much to discussions with John A. Hawkins (University of Southern California, Los Angeles), who is currently working on similar problems in English–German contrastive syntax. For further discussion of the typology of English, see Thompson (1978). For further discussion of Russian, see Comrie (1979d).

4

WORD ORDER

As has already been indicated in passing, word order typology has played a major role in the recent development of language typology. In large measure, this is because the current interest in language typology using data from a wide range of languages has taken its impetus from Greenberg's seminal article on word order typology: this article not only talked about doing this kind of language universals and typology research, but actually set about doing it. Although Greenberg himself is very cautious about the reliability of his results ('the tentative nature of the conclusions set forth here should be evident to the reader' is how his article starts), this caution has not been shared by all of those who have further developed his ideas, with the result that, as we shall see, generalizations have been claimed that go far beyond anything warranted by the data to hand, and attempts have been made to make word order the basic parameter in a holistic typology. In the present chapter, we will examine Greenberg's original work, then the attempts to generalize beyond his results, and finally some of the more recent critiques of such generalization. Although on occasion critical remarks will be directed at Greenberg's original contribution, it should be borne in mind that these are criticisms that can be made with hindsight, and in no way detract from the pioneering insights provided by Greenberg.

Although we retain the term word order typology, which has become established for referring to this area of typology, it should be noted that, strictly speaking, we are concerned not so much with the order of words as with the order of constituents, i.e. it would be more correct to speak of constituent order typology (cf. Greenberg's term 'the order of meaningful elements'). On the one hand, in saying, for instance, that a given language has subject – verb – object basic word order, it is irrelevant whether the constituents referred to consist of one or more words, so that this characterization applies equally to *John hit Mary* and to *the rogue elephant with the missing*

tusk attacked the hunter who had just noticed that his rifle was unloaded.
Secondly, in addition to being concerned with the order of constituents that
contain one or more words, we are also, in principle, interested in the order of
morphemes less than a word, for instance in the relative order of affixes
(prefixes, suffixes, infixes) and stems.

4.1 WORD ORDER PARAMETERS

This section examines the various major word order parameters that have
been used in recent typological literature, in particular the order of the major
constituents of the clause (subject, object, verb) and of the noun phrase,
although other constructions are introduced where relevant. In typologizing
a language on each of these parameters, we are concerned with the basic
word order of the language in question. Although, in many instances, the
assignment of a given basic word order to a language is unproblematical,
there are also numerous instances where the assignment is more complex or
even, perhaps, impossible. We will discuss examples of this as they arise.

The order of constituents of the clause is one of the most important word
order typological parameters, indeed, as we will see in section 4.2, some
linguists have made it into the major typological parameter. In its original
form, this parameter characterizes the relative order of subject, verb, and
object, giving rise to six logically possible types, namely SOV, SVO, VSO,
VOS, OVS, OSV. As has already been noted in passing, in chapter 1, the
distribution of these types across the languages of the world is heavily skewed
in favour of the first three, more especially the first two, but we can now cite
solidly attested examples of each of the first five basic word orders, and it is
probably only a matter of time before reliable attestations of OSV languages
become available:

Hasan öküz-ü aldı.	(Turkish: SOV)	(1)
Hasan ox ACCUSATIVE bought		
'Hasan bought the ox.'		

The farmer killed the duckling.	(English: SVO)	(2)

Lladdodd y ddraig y dyn.	(Welsh: VSO)	(3)
killed the dragon the man		
'The dragon killed the man.'		

Nahita ny mpianatra ny vehivavy.	(Malagasy: VOS)	(4)
saw the student the woman		
'The woman saw the student.'		

Toto yahos̷ye   *kamara.*   (Hixkaryana: OVS)   (5)
man it-grabbed-him jaguar
'The jaguar grabbed the man.'

Although, in the languages illustrated above, there is general agreement as to the basic word order, there are many languages where the situation is less clear-cut, and perhaps even languages where we are forced to say that, in terms of subject, object, and verb, there is no basic word order: such languages would then be irrelevant to word order typology on this parameter, reducing its range, but not its over-all validity. First, the parameter is only applicable to languages in which the grammatical relations of subject and object(s) exist, and, as we will see in more detail in chapter 5, there are many languages where the criteria identifying subjects seem to split across two noun phrases, thus making it difficult or impossible to specify the linear order of subject with respect to other constituents. Secondly, the parameter is only applicable to languages in which there is a basic word order determined, at least in part, by grammatical relations relative to the verb, and there are some languages where this seems not to be the case. For instance, in Dyirbal and Walbiri, all permutations of major constituents give rise to grammatical sentences, and if there is any preference for one word order over another, it is so slight as to be almost imperceptible. It should be noted that the problem with these languages is inability to determine a basic word order for the language as a whole. It is not just the case that certain limited constructions have a word order differing from that found elsewhere. If this were all that was involved, then we could agree to disregard such limited constructions in favour of the major sentence type in the language. Thus, when we classify English as being basically SVO, we abstract away from the fact that in special questions the word order of the *wh-* element is determined not by its grammatical relation, but rather by a general rule that places such elements sentence-initially, thus giving rise to such OSV orders as *who(m) did John see?* Even in many languages that are often described as having free word order, there is some good indication that one of the orders is more basic than the others. In Russian, for instance, any permutation of S, O, and V will give a grammatical sentence, but the order SVO is much more frequent than all of the other orders put together, and is moreover the preferred interpretation for sentences with the sequence NP – V – NP when the morphology, exceptionally, does not indicate which noun phrase is subject and which one is direct object (as in sentence (106) of chapter 3).

A further problem in assigning basic word order is where the language has a split, i.e. different basic word orders in different constructions. In some instances, this does not lead to undue difficulty in assigning basic word order, where one of the word orders is clearly much more restricted than the other. Thus, the presence of special questions in English where the object precedes the subject does not seriously jeopardize the claim that English is a SVO language, and one can establish a general principle that word order of statements is more basic than that of questions (the more marked sentence type). In many languages, the order of pronouns is different from that of other noun phrases, so that in French, for instance, clitic object pronouns precede the verb, whereas other objects follow:

> *Le garçon a vu la jeune fille.* (6)
> 'The boy has seen the girl.'

> *Le garçon l'a vue.* (7)
> 'The boy has seen her.'

However, it is known that unstressed constituents, such as clitic pronouns, are often, cross-linguistically, subject to special positioning rules only loosely, if at all, relating to their grammatical relation, so sentences with pronouns can be discounted in favour of those with full noun phrases.

There are, however, examples of splits where no such ready solution is forthcoming. A classic example is from German, which has the word order SVO in main clauses but SOV in subordinate clauses:

> *Der Mann* (NOMINATIVE) *sah den Jungen* (ACCUSATIVE). (8)
> 'The man saw the boy.'

> *Ich weiß, daß der Mann den Jungen sah.* (9)
> 'I know that the man saw the boy.'

Controversy continues to rage over which, if any, of these word orders should be considered basic, with a certain tendency for analysts to split on ideological grounds: surface structure typologists tend to opt for main clause order as less marked, while transformational-generative grammarians tend to opt for subordinate clause word order as more basic. Moreover, the parameter does not specify what kind of object is most relevant, so a similar problem arises in languages like Kpelle, where the direct object precedes the verb but other objects follow:

> *È sɛŋ-kâu tèe kâloŋ-pɔ́.* (10)
> he money sent chief to
> 'He sent the money to the chief.'

Turning now to word order within the noun phrase, we may start with the relative order of adjective (A) and noun (N). Here, as with most of the following parameters, there are only two possibilities for basic order (if there is a basic order), namely AN and NA. The former is illustrated, for instance, by English *the green table* or Turkish *büyük şehir* 'large city'; NA order is illustrated by French *le tapis vert* 'the green carpet' or Welsh *llyfr bach* 'a little book'. The examples given here illustrate the basic, by far the most usual, order of adjective and noun in these languages, although in both French and Welsh it is possible for at least some adjectives to precede their noun, and in both languages there is a set of adjectives that usually precede, as in French *le petit prince* 'the little prince', Welsh *yr hen wlad* 'the old country'. It seems to be generally true that languages with the basic word order NA are more tolerant of exceptions of this kind than are languages with the basic word order AN (Greenberg's universal number 19): English examples like *court martial, envoy plenipotentiary*, are marginal, and often not felt synchronically to be sequences of noun and adjective.

Related to adjective–noun order, at least conceptually, is the order of head noun (N) and relative clause (Rel) in the relative clause construction. Again, there are two possible orders, either the head precedes the relative clause as in English, or the relative clause precedes the head as in Turkish:

adam-ın	*kadın -a*	*ver -diğ-i*	*patates*	(11)
man GENITIVE	woman DATIVE	give	his potato	

'the potato that the man gave to the woman'

For further discussion of relative clauses, including this Turkish example, reference should be made to chapter 7, where we will see that there is a further, third, possible order relation between head and relative clause, with the head internal to the relative clause. Although adjectives and relative clauses are similar conceptually, and indeed hard to separate from one another in some languages (e.g. Malay), in many languages they differ in word order: English is AN but NRel, for instance. In English, moreover, many heavy adjectival phrases have the same order as relative clauses, as in *people fluent in three languages*. This suggests that in characterizing languages as AN or NA, preference should be given to the order of simple adjectives rather than to that of more complex adjectival phrases.

Completing our list of constituents of the noun phrase is the relative order of possessive (genitive) (G) and head noun (N), again giving two possible orders, GN and NG. The former is illustrated by Turkish *kadın-ın çavuğ-u* 'the woman's chicken', literally 'woman-GENITIVE chicken-her'; the latter is illustrated by French *la plume de ma tante* 'the pen of my aunt' or Welsh *het y dyn* 'the man's hat', literally 'hat the man'. Although we have not always illustrated problems caused by conflicting word orders within the noun phrase, we may do so here in discussing the characterization of English, which has two possessive constructions, the prenominal Saxon genitive, e.g. *the man's hat*, and the postnominal Norman genitive, e.g. *the roof of the house*. Although the Norman genitive is, textually, the more frequent of the two, and has become more frequent over the historical development of English, it is far from clear, for the modern language, whether one can specify that one of these two constructions is the basic order of head noun and possessive in English.

The last among the major word order parameters to be examined here is whether a language has prepositions (Pr), such as English *in the house* or Welsh *yn y tŷ* (same meaning), or postpositions (Po), such as Turkish *adam için* 'for the man'. The terminology of traditional grammar, though providing the two terms preposition and postposition, does not provide a single term to cover both of these, irrespective of order, and recent typological work has filled this gap by coining the term adposition. If we abbreviate this to Ap, then we can say that English has the order ApN (=PrN), while Turkish has the order NAp (=NPo). Most languages clearly have either prepositions or postpositions, though there may be occasional exceptions (thus Persian is basically prepositional, but has one postposition -*rā* for direct objects); however, there are also languages which are more mixed, such as Estonian, for which it is difficult to say, other than on the basis of slight statistical preponderance, whether the language is prepositional or postpositional. Most Australian languages have neither prepositions nor postpositions. Languages like Estonian and the Australian languages can thus be judged irrelevant, rather than counterexamples, to generalizations about prepositional versus postpositional languages.

Other parameters discussed, though less centrally, by Greenberg and figuring in some of his universals are the following. First, whether auxiliary verbs typically precede the main verb (as in English *will go*) or follow (as in Japanese *aisite iru* 'loves'). Secondly, whether in comparative constructions, the standard of comparison precedes the comparative (as in Turkish *Ankara'dan daha büyük* 'bigger than Ankara', literally 'Ankara-from more big'), or follows it (as in English *bigger than Ankara*); Finnish has both constructions here, the standard following when introduced by the conjunction *kuin* 'than' (e.g. *vanhempi kuin Helsinki* 'older than Helsinki'), but preceding when the standard is in the partitive case (e.g. *Helsinki-ä vanhempi*). Finally, we may distinguish between languages which are overwhelmingly suffixing as opposed to those which are overwhelmingly prefixing; while there are few good examples of the latter type, and few where a large number of prefixes can be added to a given stem, there are some languages with long sequences of suffixes but virtually no prefixes, such as Turkish *bil-mi-yor-um* 'I do not know', literally 'know-NEGATIVE-PROGRESSIVE-1SINGULAR'.

4.2 CORRELATIONS AMONG WORD ORDER PARAMETERS

Most of the parameters listed in section 4.1 are logically independent of one another, for instance in that there is no a priori expectation that the presence of SOV basic word order in a language should correlate more or less well with the presence of AN rather than NA word order. Even in those instances where one might expect, a priori, there to be some correlations, as between AN order and RelN order (these are different kinds of attributive constructions), there are sufficient languages that do not have this correlation – such as English, with AN but NRel – to demonstrate that the correlation is far from necessary. Despite this, it turns out to be the case that there are many statistically significant correlations that can be drawn among these various parameters, and it is one of Greenberg's more specific merits, in addition to initiating general interest in this approach to language typology, to have established so many of these correlations. In section 4.2.1, we shall discuss some of Greenberg's correlations in more detail.

4.2.1 GREENBERG'S CORRELATIONS

Since Greenberg's proposed universals are gathered as an appendix to the work cited in the notes and references to this chapter, we will not simply repeat this list here, but rather state and comment upon some of the more salient of his results. The universals listed by Greenberg contain both absolute universals and tendencies, both non-implicational and implicational universals (though there are in fact more implicational than non-implicational universals – whence our characterization of them as correlations). Throughout, Greenberg's statements are very careful and cautious, based meticulously on his sample of languages and other languages from which he had relevant data. For instance, in the first universal, 'in declarative sentences with nominal subject and object, the dominant order is almost always one in which the subject precedes the object', the statement is as a (strong) tendency, rather than as an absolute, because Greenberg was aware of claims that certain languages have word orders violating this – although the data actually available to Greenberg were not always reliable on this score, we have cited examples above of reliably attested languages with VOS and OVS basic word order.

Another instance of Greenberg's care, especially in contrast to much later work, can be seen in the fact that he consistently avoids generalizing unilateral implications to bilateral implications, where the material does not justify doing so. Thus despite universal 27: 'if a language is exclusively suffixing, it is postpositional; if it is exclusively prefixing, it is prepositional', there is no corresponding universal that would say 'if a language is postpositional, then it is suffixing; if a language is prepositional, it is prefixing' – and this is clearly justifiable, since there are many languages like Huichol that have postpositions but also widespread prefixing, and like Persian that have prepositions but also widespread suffixing.

Thirdly, Greenberg does not take any one single parameter as being the basic determiner of word order typology, and again this caution is amply justified by the nature of the data. Thus word order in the clause is a good predictor of adposition order, at least for VSO languages (exclusively prepositional, by universal 3) and for SOV languages (overwhelmingly postpositional, by universal 4). However, it turns out that it is the order of adposition and noun that provides the best predictor for that of genitives, as per universal 2: 'in languages with prepositions, the genitive almost always follows the governing noun, while in languages with postpositions it almost always precedes'. One, and only one, of the three major basic clause order types gives a good prediction for adjective order: by universal 17, 'with overwhelmingly more than chance frequency, languages with dominant order VSO have the adjective after the noun'.

Fourthly, many of the correlations are stated, where required by the data, not as holistic correlations across all parameters or as simple correlations involving only two of the parameters, but as complex correlations involving conditions among several parameters, as in universal 5, which correlates certain instances of clause order, genitive order, and adjective order: 'if a language has dominant SOV order and the genitive follows the governing noun, then the adjective likewise follows the noun'. Perhaps the most extreme example of such a complex condition is universal 24: 'if the relative expression precedes the noun either as the only construction or as an alternative construction, either the language is postpositional or the adjective precedes the noun or both'.

In keeping with the general principles of the Dobbs Ferry Conference on Language Universals, at which Greenberg's paper was first presented, the emphasis at this stage of research was on establishing a wide range of language universals on a reliable cross-linguistic basis, with little or no attempt to find explanations, or farther-reaching generalizations, underlying these universals. Some of the individual universals proposed by Greenberg do have plausible, reasonably clear, explanations, although it was not the task of the original paper to explore this avenue. In section 1.3.3 we suggested that the tendency for subjects to precede objects (universal 1) may be explainable in terms of the correlation between subject and agent, the correlation between object and patient, and the tendency for agents to be more salient perceptually than patients. Likewise, an explanation can readily be found for universal 15: 'in expressions of volition and purpose, a subordinate verbal form always follows the main verb except in those languages in which the nominal object always precedes the verb'. There are many instances where language has a tendency to mirror temporal order of events by linear order (e.g. in coordinate constructions like *John arrived and sat down*); a wish necessarily precedes its realization, a statement of purpose necessarily precedes its realization, therefore one would expect, other things being equal, that the main clause verb, expressing the wish or intention, would precede the subordinate verb, expressing the (potential) result thereof. The rider 'other things being equal' is necessary to account for the exception noted by Greenberg: if a language otherwise has a strict requirement of sentence-final main clause verb, then this can override the universal correlation of linguistic and temporal order.

Perhaps one of the reasons why many linguists following on from Greenberg's results have been less careful in their statements about correlations is that a large number of Greenberg's universals, however valid they may be as statements of limitations on cross-language variation, do not seem to lend themselves to any ready explanation or generalization. If one looks at universal 2, discussed above, for instance, then it is quite unclear why precisely the order of adpositions should play such a significant role in determining the order of a genitive relative to its head noun: there is no obvious conceptual link between adpositions and genitives, and one would hardly suspect a priori that adpositions would be the central parameter in a holistic typology of word order. Even a generalization of the kind 'adpositions and genitives tend to be placed on opposite sides of the noun' is little more than a formal restatement, with no indication of why this formal generalization should hold. Universal 24 above, in which prehead relative clause position predicts either postpositions or prenominal adjectives (or both) is perhaps the clearest example of a universal which is, in this sense, unintuitive.

Some of Greenberg's empirically ascertained universals do have plausible explanations, and these are the greatest factual merits of his list of universals: progress has been made both empirically and explanatorily. With the less intuitively plausible universals, however, one senses a certain tension between, on the one hand, empirical validity without a coherent conceptual system, and, on the other, plausible coherent conceptual systems which, however, lack empirical validity. This tension will play a major role in the following two sections.

4.2.2 GENERALIZATIONS OF GREENBERG'S RESULTS

In the appendix to his article on word order typology, Greenberg lists 24 logically possible types of language, based on the combinations of the four parameters VSO/SVO/SOV, Pr/Po, NG/GN, NA/AN; of these 24, 15 are actually attested in his sample or in other languages used by him in this piece of work. However, it is noticeable that the distribution of languages among these fifteen attested types is far from even. In fact, four types each contain far more languages than does any of the other eleven, as follows:

(a) VSO/Pr/NG/NA

(b) SVO/Pr/NG/NA

(c) SOV/Po/GN/AN

(d) SOV/Po/GN/NA

$$(12)$$

On the basis of this observation, one might think that in order to establish universal tendencies, rather than absolute universals, of word order typology, it would be possible to work with just these types, neglecting the relatively few languages that fall into the other eleven attested types. If one makes this assumption, then a number of other generalizations seem to emerge from the four types listed above. First, except for the position of the subject in clause order, types (a) and (b) are identical. If one were to omit the subject from consideration, then types (a) and (b) could be combined into a single VO type; types (c) and (d) would then both be characterized as OV. Secondly, on most parameters, types (a) and (b) are precisely the inverse of types (c) and (d): the former are VO, Pr, NG, and NA; the latter are OV, Po, GN, and either AN or NA, the only embarrassment to this generalization being the widespread occurrence of NA basic order in OV languages. However, since we are working with tendencies, we might be prepared to overlook this complication, and work with only two major types in terms of word order, (e) and (f):

(e) VO, Pr, NG, NA

(f) OV, Po, GN, AN

$$(12)$$

Some further support for this view might seem to come from the fact that VOS languages, not included in the original list, tend strongly to adhere to type (e). Data on OVS languages, and even more so OSV languages, which should behave like type (f), are less readily available – indeed, detailed information is really available only for the one language Hixkaryana, which does more or less adhere to type (f), except that, to the extent that Hixkaryana can be said to have adjectives (and relative clauses), these follow the head noun.

Moreover, some of the other parameters discussed tend to correlate with this distinction into two types: type (f) tends also to have prenominal relative clauses, a strong tendency towards suffixing, auxiliary verbs after the main verb, and the standard of comparison before the comparative; while type (e) tends to have postnominal relative clauses, some tendency towards prefixing, auxiliary verbs before the main verb, and the standard of comparison after the comparative.

The kinds of generalization of Greenberg's results noted above are associated with two linguists in particular, Lehmann and Vennemann, and we will examine their contributions in turn. Lehmann argues, first, that the order of subject is irrelevant from a general typological viewpoint, so that we may indeed work with two major types of language, OV and VO. Two comments are in order here. First, as we shall see in more detail in section 4.2.3, while the collapsing of VSO and VOS into a single word order type seems reasonably justified – on other parameters, these two kinds of languages generally behave alike – the inclusion of SVO languages within this same type is questionable. In particular, while the existence of verb-initial word order or of SOV word order seems to correlate highly with various other typological parameters of word order, the existence of SVO word order does not seem to correlate particularly well with any other parameter. Knowing that a language is VSO or VOS, we can predict its values for other word order parameters; knowing that a language is SOV, we can with considerable reliability predict its other word order parameter values; knowing that a language is SVO, we can predict virtually nothing else. Secondly, there is potential terminological confusion in the use of the terms OV language and VO language, and it is essential to be aware of the particular use that each author makes. On the one hand, one could use these terms strictly to refer to the relative basic order of verb and object. On the other hand – and this is Lehmann's usage – one could use VO language to mean a language that has all or most of the word order properties of type (e) above, and OV language to mean a language that has all or most of the word properties of type (f). An actual example will make this clear. In Persian, the basic word order in the clause is SOV, so by the first use of the term OV language it would be an OV language. However, Persian has prepositions, postnominal genitives, postnominal adjectives, and postnominal relative clauses, so that under the second usage it would be a VO language, even though it does not actually have VO basic word order. To avoid the confusion, it is preferable, following Vennemann (see below) to refer to type (e) as operand–operator (or head–adjunct), and type (f) as operator–operand (or adjunct–head).

Lehmann also proposes a formal explanation, or rather generalization, of the observed correlations. He argues that V and O are primary concomitants of each other, and that modifiers are placed on the opposite side of a constituent from its primary concomitant. Thus, in a VO language, the primary concomitant of V is the postverbal O, so modifiers of V (in particular, auxiliary verbs) go to the left of V (AuxV); likewise, V is the primary concomitant of O, so modifiers of O (in particular, adjectives, relative clauses, and possessives) go to the opposite side from V, namely to the right. Conversely, in an OV language: the primary concomitant of V is the O to the left, so other modifiers follow the V (e.g. VAux); the primary concomitant of O is V, to the right, so other modifiers of O go to the left, i.e. adjectives, relative clauses, and possessors precede the object noun.

Apart from problems stemming from generalizing Greenberg's universals, to which we return in section 4.2.3, there are two other specific problems in this explanation. First, the explanation for order within the noun phrase applies strictly only to object noun phrases, and does not generalize directly to subjects or noun phrases in adverbials. One could presumably argue that the order is generalized from objects to other noun phrases, but if this were so one might expect to find languages where the order of constituents within the noun phrase was different for objects and other noun phrases, and such instances are either non-existent or rare. Secondly, the explanation, as is clear from Lehmann's exemplification, makes no distinction between modifiers which are expressed as separate words and those which are expressed as affixes. With regard to modifiers of verbs, this creates few problems, as there is a high correlation between having the auxiliary after the verb and having suffixes, and between having the auxiliary before the verb and having prefixes. With noun modifiers, however, to the extent that there is any correlation it is the reverse: certainly, across a wide range of operator-operand languages, e.g. Turkic languages, most Uralic languages, Quechua, Armenian, possessors precede their head noun, but possessive affixes are suffixed (see further section 10.3.2).

The explanation proposed by Vennemann for the correlations represented diagrammatically by types (e) and (f) above does not suffer from these disadvantages (in part in that it does not consider relations below the word level), although it, too, remains a formal explanation, without any further consideration of the question why this particular explanation should hold. Vennemann argues that in each of the construction types under consideration, i.e. the relation between verb and object (but not subject), between noun and adjective, etc., one of the constituents is an operator (corresponding to the traditional structuralist term adjunct or modifier), and the other the operand (corresponding to the traditional term head), the assignment being as in the following table:

OPERATOR	OPERAND
Object	Verb
Adjective	Noun
Genitive	Noun
Relative clause	Noun
Noun phrase	Adposition
Standard of comparison	Comparative adjective

The assignment of operator (adjunct) and operand (head) status is in most instances uncontroversial, though some linguists have been less comfortable with declaring the head of an adpositional phrase to be the adposition, rather than the noun (phrase). However, this assignment can be justified, for many languages, by the usual structuralist syntactic test of substitution: in English, for instance, the prepositional phrase of *John is in the house* can be substituted by *in* but not by *the house*, cf. *John is in*, but not, as a similar construction, **John is the house*, and the traditional term prepositional phrase attests to the view that the preposition is the head (just as the noun is head of a noun phrase, the verb of a verb phrase). For present purposes, at any rate, we may assume this assignment of operator and operand to individual constructions, bearing in mind that these assignments have been made by other linguists working independently of the particular correlations that Vennemann wishes to establish.

It is then clear what the general principle underlying types (e) and (f) above is: in languages of type (e), the operator is placed consistently after the operand, whence our suggestion above, following Vennemann, that they be called operand–operator languages; in languages of type (f), the operator consistently precedes the operand, thus giving rise to the operator–operand type. For languages which are typologically consistent in this regard, we need only specify whether they are operator–operand or operand–operator, and this one specification will then predict each of the individual word order parameter values. For languages which are inconsistent, i.e. which do not follow type (e) or (f), the language may be describable as being in general operator–operand or operand–operator, in terms of predominance of one or other ordering among the parameters, but even so special mention will have to be made of those parameters on which the language is exceptional. In the case of Persian, for instance, we would say that Persian is an operand–operator language (prepositions, postnominal adjectives, relative clauses, and possessors), but exceptionally it has OV word order. Thus the deviation of a language from one of the consistent types can be measured in terms of the number of special statements that need to be made about its word order.

We can now profitably contrast this position, or more specifically Vennemann's, with Greenberg's work discussed in section 4.2.1. Vennemann presents us with a schema that is conceptually very simple and very elegant; however, in order to establish this schema, certain liberties have to be taken with the data, as we will see in more detail in section 4.2.3. Greenberg's approach, on the other hand, is truer to the data, but ends up rather with a series of specific universals that do not fit together as a coherent conceptual whole.

4.2.3 CRITIQUE OF THE GENERALIZATIONS

The generalizations by Lehmann and Vennemann discussed in section 4.2.2 can clearly only stand, if they stand at all, as tendencies, since there are numerous counterexamples to them as absolute universals. Being satisfied with universal tendencies is sometimes necessary, forced upon one by the data, but it also brings with it the danger that one will cease to look further for absolute, or stronger, universals. One can see this even by a comparison of Greenberg's work with that of Lehmann or Vennemann. Greenberg did succeed in establishing some absolute universals, for instance the claim that VSO languages invariably have prepositions; however, within Vennemann's operator–operand schema, this exceptionless generalization is stated no differently from one with very low validity, for instance the correlation between SOV word order and adjective–noun order, since almost as many SOV languages have the adjective after the noun as have it before.

One way of comparing Vennemann's schema more directly with Greenberg's universals is to reformulate Vennemann's as a network of implicational universals, thus making them more directly comparable in form to Greenberg's. When reformulated in this way, it becomes clear that Vennemann's universal principles of word order are all expressed as bilateral implications: thus if it is the case that OV order predicts postpositions, then it is equally the case that postpositions predict OV order. Nearly all of Greenberg's universals, however, are unilateral. Thus Greenberg is saying that some word order parameter values are good predictors for some other parameter values, but that this cannot be generalized to all parameters, some of which do not show any good correlation with anything else. Adjective order can serve as a good example here: from knowing that adjectives usually precede or follow the noun in a given language, one can tell virtually nothing about other word order parameter values. More generally, the over-generalization of Greenberg's universals with which we were concerned in section 4.2.2 fails to make any distinction as to the

reliability of individual implications, effectively treating them all as equivalent. Applied to Lehmann's generalization, the criticism would be rather
different, because Lehmann does claim that one word order parameter is
more important than any other, namely the relative order of O and V. But
again, the earlier, more detailed work of Greenberg should have demonstrated that while clause word order is sometimes a good predictor of
other word order parameter values, it is not always so (almost as many OV
languages have postnominal as have prenominal adjectives), and there are
many instances where other parameters have better predictive value (e.g.
adpositions are good predictors of genitive order).

In reaction to the simplifying schema discussed in section 4.2.2, Hawkins has suggested that, even basing ourselves essentially on Greenberg's
original data, it is possible to come up with a set of universals which are
exceptionless, and which moreover are significant in that they tie together
the various logically independent parameters used in word order typology.
This can therefore be regarded as in some sense a compromise between
Greenberg's position and that of Lehmann and Vennemann: further generalizations beyond those claimed by Greenberg are posited, but the claims
are stronger than Lehmann's or Vennemann's in that they are said to have
no counterexamples. On Vennemann's schema, for instance, over half the
world's languages turn out to be exceptions, although, admittedly, some of
them deviate only minimally from the norms of operator–operand or
operand–operator languages, so that some kind of norm does still exist.

Hawkins's universals, like Greenberg's, are unilateral implications.
However, they differ from most (not all) of Greenberg's universals by
looking not just at correlations between two word order parameters, but
rather at more complex implicational relationships using three or more
parameters. The first proposed universals are reproduced as (13) and (14)
below:

$$SOV \rightarrow (AN \rightarrow GN) \tag{13}$$

$$VSO \rightarrow (NA \rightarrow NG) \tag{14}$$

Let us make explicit the claims contained in these universals. First, it is
claimed that clause order is a good predictor of certain other word order
parameters, but only if the basic word order is SOV or VSO, i.e. SVO
word order is not a good predictor, at least not in this case. (Word orders
other than SOV, SVO, and VSO are not considered.) Once we know that a
language has one of these two word orders, then we can make a further
prediction, but this further prediction is itself in the form of an implication: if a language has SOV word order, then if it also has adjectives
before the noun, it will necessarily also have genitives before the noun;

likewise, if a language has VSO word order, then if it also has adjectives after the noun, it will necessarily also have genitives after the noun. The two universals are clearly related formally to one another. It is possible to take these implicational universals and set out all the logical possibilities, then seeing which of these possibilities are in fact disallowed, although we will not carry out this task here. Suffice it to say that the excluded types are, by (13), SOV languages with AN and NG, and, by (14), VSO languages with NA and GN.

The second set of universals is given by Hawkins in two forms. First, there is a weak form, which does have some counterexamples:

$$Pr \rightarrow (NA \rightarrow NG) \tag{15}$$

$$Po \rightarrow (AN \rightarrow GN) \tag{16}$$

Like Greenberg, these claim that the difference between prepositional and postpositional languages can be a significant predictor of other word order parameters, effectively (given the close similarity between the implicata of (13) and (16), and (14) and (15)) as good a predictor as clause word order. The excluded language types are (a) those with prepositions, postnominal adjectives, and prenominal genitives – in Greenberg's list, Arapesh is a counterexample; and (b) languages with postpositions, prenominal adjectives, and postnominal genitives – in Greenberg's sample, some Daghestan languages are exceptions. The number of exceptions, relative to the overall sample, is very small, so that one might let (15)–(16) stand as universal tendencies. However, Hawkins notes further that the exceptions are all SVO languages. As we have indicated several times, SVO is a much less good predictor of other word order parameters than either of SOV or VSO, and we can build this observation into the universals by requiring as implicans, in addition to the appropriate kind of adposition, that the languages be either SOV or VSO, thus giving Hawkins's final formulations:

$$Pr \& (VSO \lor SOV) \rightarrow (NA \rightarrow NG) \tag{17}$$

$$Po \& (VSO \lor SOV) \rightarrow (AN \rightarrow GN) \tag{18}$$

Although these universals may look quite complex in their final formulation, the preceding discussion should have made it clear how these formulations are built up from more basic observations.

Within Hawkins's over-all view of word order typology, then, the above implicational universals would stand as absolute universals. Skewings in the distribution of languages among the permitted types could be described, as for Greenberg, by means of universal tendencies (which Hawkins slightly reformulates as distributional universals). But crucially, in opposition to Lehmann and Vennemann, a distinction will be made between those absolute universals that rigidly delimit possible variation across languages, and those that are only tendencies as seen in skewings in the cross-linguistic distribution of attested types.

4.3 THE VALUE OF WORD ORDER TYPOLOGY

As we have emphasized at several points in this chapter, one of the main roles of word order typology in the recent study of language universals and typology has been methodological–historical: the work originated by Greenberg demonstrated that it is possible to come up with significant cross-linguistic generalizations by looking at a wide range of languages and without necessarily carrying out abstract analyses of these languages; in addition, there were a number of more specific methodological lessons, such as improvements in techniques for language sampling (see section 1.1.2). However, the question does arise as to just how far-reaching word order typology is in terms of the over-all typology of a language. In Greenberg's original work, relatively few correlations between word order and other parameters were drawn. In Vennemann's work, essentially no further correlations are drawn, and as we have seen even the elegance of Vennemann's account of over-all word order typology is in certain respects questionable. Hawkins's work demonstrates that if word order typology is to be rigorous, then it must forsake the extreme elegance of Lehmann's or Vennemann's schemata. At present, the main proponent of word order typology as the basis of a holistic typology is Lehmann, but it has to be acknowledged that, in addition to qualms about the degree of generalization made in his account of word order itself, most of the detailed correlations between word order and other phenomena, including even phonology, remain in need of establishment on the basis of data from a wide range of languages.

NOTES AND REFERENCES

The seminal paper by Greenberg referred to throughout this chapter is Greenberg (1966b); his universals are listed in Appendix III of this article (pp. 110–13). For discussion of Malagasy as a VOS language, see Keenan (1976a); for Hixkaryana as an OVS language, see Derbyshire (1977) and, more generally, Derbyshire (1979). The Kpelle example is from Givón (1975b, 50). On the lack of adpositions in Australian languages, see Dixon (1980, 272).

The discussion in section 4.2.2 is based on Lehmann (1973) and Venne-mann (1972). Section 4.2.3 relates primarily to Hawkins (1980); Hawkins's universals are set out on page 203 of this article.

Some of Lehmann's more wide-ranging typological correlations are included in Lehmann (1978a); for some criticism, see Smith (1980).

See also the notes and references for chapter 10 for work on word order change. Li (1975) is a collection of articles relevant to both chapters 4 and 10.

5

SUBJECT

5.1 THE PROBLEM

In section 3.3, we mentioned some of the problems inherent in working with grammatical relations, including subject, and some of the possible approaches towards a solution to these problems. In the present chapter, we will look in considerably more detail at one particular aspect of this problem, namely the definition of subject cross-linguistically. Subject is an important notion, used frequently, both in traditional grammar and in more recent linguistic work, both in the descriptions of individual languages and in stating cross-linguistic generalizations. If linguists were invariably in agreement in stating which noun phrase, in each construction in each language, is the subject, then we could, perhaps, accept this inter-subjective agreement, and devote correspondingly less energy to trying to find an explicit definition of subject. However, it turns out that, in a wide range of cases, this inter-subjective agreement is lacking, so that the need does arise as a serious empirical problem to establish criteria for declaring a given noun phrase to be or not to be a subject.

One particular instance of lack of agreement among linguists on subject-hood is illustrated by competing analyses of the ergative construction. We shall return below, in sections 5.3 and 6.2.2 to a more detailed discussion of ergativity, and for present purposes we may simply give some illustrative examples of the kind of problem that arises, using Chukchi as our example:

ɣəm   *tə-yet-ɣʔek.*   (1)
I-ABSOLUTIVE came-1SINGULAR
' I came.'

ɣəm-nan   *ɣət*   *tə-lʔu-ɣət.*   (2)
I-ERGATIVE thou-ABSOLUTIVE saw-1SINGULAR-2SINGULAR
' I saw thee.'

Analyses of English agree that, in the English versions of these two sentences, *I* is subject both of the intransitive construction of (1) and of the transitive construction of (2); moreover, English morphology, at least for pronouns, exactly mirrors this distribution: the subjects are in the nominative, the direct object in the accusative. In Chukchi, as in English, there are two cases used for these three noun phrases, but their distribution is quite different: the absolutive case is used to translate *I* (intransitive subject) of (1), and to translate *thee* (direct object) of (2), whereas a separate case, the ergative, is used to translate *I* (transitive subject) of (2). The question therefore arises whether, in Chukchi, one should not rather group together the absolutive noun phrases as subject, following the morphology, rather than simply following the distribution that turns out to be relevant for English. Although in early periods many linguists working on ergative languages tried to solve this problem a priori, by fiat – and in either direction, by relying on the morphology or by disregarding it – the question is in fact an empirical question, and in sections 5.3–4 we will see that its answer is much less simple than either of these solutions. For the moment, however, we may simply note that the problem exists.

Of course, in addition to criteria of case marking in establishing subjecthood, it will be clear from the discussion of section 3.3 that syntactic criteria are also important in establishing subjecthood. In English, for instance, we can note the following two syntactic criteria of subjecthood. First, verbs agree in person and number with their subject; although English verb morphology is fairly atrophied, this distinction is still maintained consistently in the difference in the present tense between third person singular and all other forms, and in a few other instances with irregular verbs, so that we have the third person singular form in *he sees you* but the non-third person singular form in *I see you*. Secondly, in the kinds of constructions called subject-to-object raising by many transformational-generative grammarians, we find that the subject of a *that*-clause, and only the subject, can, after certain verbs, appear in an alternative construction of type (4):

 I believe that Max is an accountant.   (3)

 I believe Max to be an accountant.   (4)

In the vast majority of sentence-types, these two syntactic criteria coincide, i.e. there is agreement between logically independent criteria as to the subject in English. There are, however, some sentence types where this agreement is not found, such as sentences introduced by *there is/are*:

 There are unicorns in the garden.   (5)

 There is a unicorn in the garden.   (6)

In such examples, at least in the standard language, verb agreement is determined by the noun phrase that follows *there is/are*. Subject-to-object raising, however, treats *there* as the subject, giving:

I believe there to be a unicorn/unicorns in the garden.   (7)

And, indeed, in such instances we find disagreement as to which noun phrase, in (5) and (6), should be considered the subject: different weighting of different criteria gives different results. So even in English there are some construction types where there is no agreement among linguists as to which noun phrase is subject.

Faced with such problems surrounding the characterization of the notion subject, there are two possible approaches. On the one hand, one could claim that the notion of subject is misleading from the outset, and should be banished from linguistic theory. On the other hand, one could try and work out a definition of subjecthood which, while corresponding to linguists' inter-subjective intuitions in the clear cases, would also make insightful claims about the unclear cases. In the present chapter, we follow the second of these paths. Before embarking on the details of the definition, however, we should make some further preliminary remarks. First, we are not committed a priori to the view that subject is a necessary descriptive category in the grammar of every language: there may well be languages where it is not appropriate, though equally there are languages (including English) where it is appropriate. Secondly, we are not committed to the view that, even in a language where subject is generally valid, every sentence will necessarily have a subject. Thirdly, we are not committed to the view that the translation of a sentence from language X where a certain noun phrase is subject will necessarily have that same noun phrase as subject in language Y. Examples of all of these points will occur below.

Finally, although we will argue that the notions of topic and agent must play a role in the definition of subject, we argue that, even in English, it is clear that the notion of subject cannot be identified with either of these notions. If we take, for instance, our criterion of verb-agreement, then it is clear that in the passive sentence *the men were hit by the boy*, the plural verb *were* does not agree with the agent; and it is equally clear that in the topicalized sentence *John I know* the non-third person singular verb is not in agreement with the topic. However close the connection may be among grammatical relations, semantic roles, and pragmatic roles, they cannot be identified with one another.

5.2 ON DEFINITIONS AND CATEGORIES

Before turning specifically to the definition of subject, it is necessary for us to make some preliminary remarks on the nature of definitions, in par-

ticular on the nature of definitions of linguistic categories, in order to avoid
certain later misunderstandings. The kind of definition of subject towards
which we will be working is the following: the prototype of subject represents the intersection of agent and topic, i.e. the clearest instances of
subjects, cross-linguistically, are agents which are also topics. There are
two important characteristics of this definition: first, it is multi-factor;
second, it is stated in terms of prototypes, rather than in terms of necessary
and sufficient criteria for the identification of subjects. The second point is
particularly important, given that many subjects in many constructions in
many languages are not topic, or are not agent, or are neither.

The use of a multi-factor definition is unlikely to raise any eyebrows,
since such definitions are quite widespread in linguistics and other areas,
as for instance if we define preposition in terms of the intersection of
adposition and position in front of the governed noun phrase. However,
the attempt to use definitions in terms of prototypes for linguistic categories has met with an inordinate amount of opposition and prejudice, so that
it is worth spending some time on discussion of this issue. Rather than
discussing the problem directly in terms of subject properties, we will use
some other examples, where the use of prototypes is much more clearly
justified. Note that the use of these analogies does not in itself justify the
use of a prototype-based definition of subject, but it does demonstrate that
we cannot a priori reject this kind of definition, but must rather weigh up
the pros and cons in terms of their fit with the data and their evaluation
relative to alternative definitions.

In chapter 2, we illustrated one very clear area where definitions of
categories in terms of prototype seem to be required, namely with colour
terms, where humans seem to recognize a central, focal value for a colour
term, rather than clear-cut boundaries. What this means is that there is no
set of necessary and sufficient conditions that an object must satisfy in
order to be called, for instance, red. But equally, this does not mean that
we can state no restrictions on the use of the term red: this term is most
appropriate for the focal value, and less and less appropriate as one moves
away from this focal area and approaches the foci of other colour terms.
This example thus establishes that there is at least one area where humans
do categorize in terms of prototypes, thus opening up this kind of definition as a real possibility.

Similar examples can also be found using more clearly linguistic categories, and the example we will use here concerns the distinction between
nouns and adjectives in Russian, in particular the relation of numerals to
these two. In Russian, in general, the distinction between nouns and adjectives is clear-cut, so that we can establish criteria that correlate with the
focal values (prototypes) of noun and adjective. Numerals, however, fall in
between these two prototypes, in a way that makes impossible any estab-

lishment of non-arbitrary cut-off points. In distinguishing adjectives from nouns, we may take two comparable construction types, the first being a noun phrase consisting of an attributive adjective and head noun (e.g. *xorošij mal'čik* ' good boy '), the second being a quantity phrase consisting of a head noun defining the quantity and a dependent genitive defining the entity being measured (e.g. *stado ovec* ' flock of sheep ').

The following criteria characterize the adjective in the attributive construction: (a) the adjective agrees in number with its head noun, on a singular/plural opposition, e.g. *xorošij mal'čik* 'good boy', *xorošije mal'čiki* 'good boys'; (b) the adjective agrees in case with its head noun throughout, e.g. nominative *xorošij mal'čik*, but dative *xorošemu mal'čiku*, instrumental *xorošim mal'čikom*; (c) the adjective agrees in gender with its head noun, following a three-way masculine/feminine/neuter distinction (though only in the singular), e.g. *xorošij mal'čik* 'good boy', *xorošaja devočka* 'good girl', *xorošeje okno* 'good window'; (d) many nouns have distinct accusative forms depending on whether or not they are animate, and adjectives agree with their head noun in terms of this distinction, e.g. inanimate accusative *xorošij stol* 'good table', animate accusative *xorošego mal'čika* 'good boy', even though both *stol* and *mal'čik* are masculine singular. Head nouns in the quantitative construction have none of these properties. Thus we have *stado ovec* 'flock of sheep' where *ovca* 'sheep' is feminine, and *stado gusej* 'flock of geese' where *gus'* 'goose' is masculine. For number, we have *massa benzina* 'a mass of petrol' and *massa ljudej* 'a mass of people'. For case, we find that the head noun changes in case, but the dependent noun remains in the genitive, e.g. nominative *stado ovec*, dative *stady ovec*, instrumental *stadom ovec*. Finally, the head noun does not change depending on the animacy of the dependent noun, cf. accusative *massu ljudej* 'mass of people' and *massu karandašej* 'mass of pencils'.

On the other hand, the head noun of a quantitative construction has a number of properties that are not shared by the adjective in the attributive construction, as follows: (e) the head noun can vary in number independently of the dependent noun, e.g. *stado ovec* 'flock of sheep', *stada ovec* 'flocks of sheep'; (f) the head noun in the quantitative construction can take an attribute agreeing with it, e.g. *xorošeje stado ovec* 'good flock of sheep', where *xorošeje* is neuter singular nominative, agreeing with *stado*, while *ovec* is genitive plural; (g) the noun dependent on the head noun is invariably in the genitive, and if countable in the genitive plural – contrast the attributive construction under point (c), where adjective and head noun must be in the same case.

In terms of their adherence to the above seven criteria, we find that we can divide Russian numerals into several classes. First, the numeral ' one ' has all the properties of an adjective and none of those of a head noun: it can even agree in number, with *pluralia tantum*, e.g. *odni* (PLURAL) *nožnicy* 'one (pair of) scissors'. At the other extreme, the numeral *million* 'million', and also all higher numerals, have all the properties of a noun and none of those of an adjective. Intermediate numbers have a varying number of adjectival and nominal properties, as illustrated in the table. In this table, A means that the numeral has the appropriate adjectival property, N that it has the appropriate substantival property; A/N means that either property can be used, A/(N) indicating that there is clear preference for adjectival behaviour; (A) means that the numeral has the adjectival property, but in a restricted form, in particular the numeral 'two' has only a two-way gender opposition, distinguishing feminine *dve* from masculine-neuter *dva*; (N) indicates a similar restriction on a substantival property, as with the plural of *sto* 'hundred', which has only a few restricted uses. In the table, note that 'four' behaves like 'three', and that non-compound numerals between 'five' and 'ninety' inclusive behave like 'five'.

ADJECTIVAL AND SUBSTANTIVAL PROPERTIES OF RUSSIAN NUMERALS

Property	*odin* '1'	*dva* '2'	*tri* '3'	*pjat'* '5'	*sto* '100'	*tysjača* '1000'	*million* '1,000,000'
(a)	A	N	N	N	N	N	N
(b)	A	N	N	N	N	N	N
(c)	A	(A)	N	N	N	N	N
(d)	A	A/(N)	A/(N)	N	N	N	N
(e)	A	A	A	A	(N)	N	N
(f)	A	A	A	A	A	N	N
(g)	A	A	A	A	A	A/N	N

If we now ask the question whether Russian numerals are adjectives or nouns, it becomes clear that there is no straightforward answer, except in the case of 'one' (adjective) and 'million' (noun): in particular, we cannot establish a cut-off point between adjectives and nouns, except arbitrarily, i.e. by deciding arbitrarily that we are going to take one, rather than another, of the seven criteria as definitive – and even then, some of the individual criteria are not definitive, as indicated by alternative entries separated by a slash or entries in parentheses. The situation is rather that we have clear prototypes, and a continuum separating those prototypes from one another, much as with colour terms, even though here we are clearly dealing with grammatical categories.

Actually, the continuum-like nature of the distinction between adjectival and substantival properties finds an even stronger manifestation in

Russian numerals if we also take into account statistical preferences where alternatives are possible. For instance, after the numerals 'two', 'three', and 'four', an adjective may be in either the nominative plural (as would be expected if these numerals were adjectives) or the genitive plural (as would be expected if these numerals were nouns). If one counts the occurrences of either possibility in text, it turns out that the preference for the adjectival type is greatest with 'two' and lowest with 'four', i.e. even as between adjacent numerals one can establish that the lower is more adjective-like than the higher.

In conclusion, definitions based on prototypes must be allowed as a possibility.

5.3 ERGATIVITY

In section 5.1, we posed a general problem for the syntactic analysis of any sentence, namely: what is the subject of the sentence? In view of the discussion of section 5.2, we can slightly reformulate that question. Implicit in the original question was that the question would have a clear-cut, discrete answer, i.e. a given noun phrase either would or would not be a subject. However, in terms of our characterization of subject as the intersection of agent and topic, and given that agent and topic are logically independent notions and need not coincide in a given sentence, it is clear that the answer to our question may well be less than clear-cut: it may be the case that a given noun phrase has certain subject properties, but not all, i.e. instead of simply saying that a noun is or is not a subject we will characterize it as being a subject to a certain degree. Similarly, it is possible that subject properties in a sentence will be distributed among several noun phrases, or at least between two, rather than all characterizing a single noun phrase. In many instances, then, it is as pointless to expect a clear-cut answer to the question 'what is the subject of this sentence?' as it is to expect a clear-cut answer to the question 'is Russian *pjat'* 'five' a noun or an adjective?' In the present section we will examine implications of this further, with particular regard to ergativity.

In section 5.1, we also posed the more specific question of identifying the subject of the ergative construction. In order to discuss this construction adequately, especially in terms of its similarities to and differences from the nominative–accusative construction, it is necessary to have a set of terms that is neutral between the two systems. The following is the set that we propose: The single argument of an intransitive predicate we will symbolize as S; this is clearly mnemonic for subject, and in general there is little or no controversy concerning the subject status in most intransitive (single-argument) constructions across languages, so the mnemonically suitable symbol is also suitable in terms of its content. In the transitive construction, there are two arguments, and in order to avoid circularity we shall label neither of these with the symbol S. In the prototypical transitive situation, the participants are an agent and a patient, and this remains constant irrespective of the morphological or syntactic behaviour of the sentence in any individual language. We may therefore, starting originally with transitive predicates describing actions, label the agent as A, and the patient as P, so that in the sentence *I hit you*, or in its translation into Chukchi, irrespective of the case marking of the various noun phrases *I* will be A and *you* will be P. The labels are again clearly mnemonic, for agent and patient, respectively. However, the advantage of having arbitrary labels A and P rather than actually using agent and patient is that we can continue to use the arbitrary symbols even when we pass beyond prototypical transitive situations (i.e. actions) to other constructions in the language that have similar morphology and syntax. In English, for instance, the transitive verb *see* behaves morphologically and syntactically just like the action transitive verb *hit*, so that although in *I saw you* the pronoun *I* is not, in terms of semantic role, an agent, we can still symbolize it as A. A and P are thus syntactic terms, whose prototypes are defined in semantic terms.

In discussing examples (1) and (2) introduced at the beginning of this chapter, then, we can say that in (1) Chukchi *yəm* and English *I* are Ss; in (2) Chukchi *yəmnan* and English *I* are As, while Chukchi *yət* and English *thee* are Ps. Moreover, in English one case is used to encode S and A – a case of this kind is called nominative; and another case is used to encode P – a case of this kind is called accusative. In Chukchi, one case is used to encode S and P – a case of this kind is called absolutive; another case is used to encode A – a case of this kind is called ergative. The discussion thus far has related essentially to morphology, and we return to ergative–absolutive and nominative–accusative case marking in chapter 6. It is now time to turn to syntactic properties of subjects.

From the remarks made hitherto about subjects in English, it should be clear that English treats S and A alike as subjects for syntactic purposes, certainly for those syntactic points discussed so far, and indeed for most others. We can illustrate this by means of examples using coordination, in particular coordination of clauses that share a noun phrase in common and where that noun phrase is omitted in the second conjunct. If we try and conjoin sentences (8), (9), and (10), taking a transitive clause and an intransitive clause, in that order, then it is clear that we can conjoin, with omission of the second occurrence of the coreferential noun phrase, only (8) and (9), and not (8) and (10):

The man hit the woman. (8)

The man came here. (9)

The woman came here. (10)

The man hit the woman and came here. (= (8) + (9)) (11)

Even though sentence (11) contains no overt S for the intransitive predicate *came here*, it is absolutely clear to the native speaker of English that the only possible interpretation for this sentence is that the man came here, even though the alternative interpretation 'the man hit the woman and the woman came here' would make perfect sense. In other words, in order to permit omission of a noun phrase from a second conjunct, English makes two requirements: (a) the semantic requirement that the two noun phrases be coreferential; (b) the syntactic requirement that the two noun phrases be either S or A. For syntactic purposes, English treats S and A alike, so subject in English means S or A.

We may contrast this situation with the situation that obtains in Dyirbal, with the translations of our three English sentences (8)–(10):

Balan dʸugumbil   baŋgul yaṛaŋgu   balgan. (12)
    woman-ABSOLUTIVE   man-ERGATIVE hit
'The man hit the woman.'

Bayi yaṛa   baninʸu. (13)
    man-ABSOLUTIVE came-here
'The man came here.'

Balan dʸugumbil   baninʸu. (14)
    woman-ABSOLUTIVE came-here
'The woman came here.'

Balan dʸugumbil baŋgul yaṛaŋgu balgan, baninʸu.
    (= (12) + (14)) (15)
'The man hit the woman, and the woman came here.'

(In Dyirbal, nouns are usually accompanied by a classifier agreeing in class, including gender, and case with the noun; in the above examples, these are *balan*, *baŋgul*, and *bayi*.) Note in particular that (15) does not, and in Dyirbal cannot, have the meaning of English sentence (11): the two sentences in the two languages are crystal-clear in their interpretations to native speakers, though the interpretations happen to be different in the two languages. Dyirbal, like English, has two restrictions on coordination with omission of a noun phrase, but while the semantic restriction is as in

English (the two noun phrases must be coreferential), the syntactic restriction is different: in Dyirbal, the coreferential noun phrases must be S or P. Thus for syntactic purposes, Dyirbal treats S and P alike, as opposed to A, so that in Dyirbal the appropriate grammatical relation is one that groups S and P together, in other words subject in Dyirbal means ' S or P '.

Although it might seem that the syntactic difference follows the morphological difference between nominative–accusative morphology in English and ergative–absolutive morphology in Dyirbal (as can be seen by comparing examples (12)–(14)), it is important to emphasize that this is not the case. In English, the syntactic identification of S and A proceeds even with non-pronominal noun phrases, which do not have a morphological nominative–accusative distinction. In Dyirbal, personal pronouns of the first and second persons happen to have nominative–accusative case marking, a fact to which we return in chapter 6, but this does not affect the ergative–absolutive basis of the coordination construction:

ŋadʸa ŋinuna balgan. (16)
I-NOMINATIVE you-ACCUSATIVE hit
' I hit you '

ŋadʸa baninʸu. (17)
I-NOMINATIVE came-here
' I came here.'

ŋinda baninʸu. (18)
you-NOMINATIVE came-here
' You came here.'

ŋadʸa ŋinuna balgan, baninʸu. (19)
' I hit you, and you/*I came here.'

We should also note that not all languages pattern either like English or like Dyirbal. In Chukchi, for instance, in coordinate constructions the omitted S of an intransitive verb can be interpreted as coreferential with either the A or the P of the preceding verb:

ətləɣ -e talayvənen ekək
father ERGATIVE he-beat-him son-ABSOLUTIVE
 ənkʔam ekvetɣʔi. (20)
 and he-left
' The father beat the son, and the father/the son left.'

In Yidiny, as we saw in section 3.4, the preferred interpretation for an omitted S follows the morphology (coreferential with an absolutive or nominative noun phrase in the transitive clause), thus combining aspects of nominative–accusative and ergative–absolutive syntax, whereas Chukchi is completely neutral as between them, in this instance. One important point that the Yidiny material illustrates particularly clearly is that it is misleading to classify a language as being either ergative or not, rather one must ask: to what extent, and in what particular constructions is the language ergative, i.e. where does its syntax operate on a nominative–accusative basis and where does its syntax operate on an ergative–absolutive basis. In Yidiny, then, in the transitive construction, in some instances the A will have subject properties under coordination (example (44) of chapter 3), in other instances the P will have subject properties (example (43) of chapter 3), in yet other instances subject properties will be distributed between the two noun phrases (example (45) of chapter 3).

In common with many, but not all, languages, both English and Dyirbal have different syntactic means of encoding the same semantic roles, i.e. different voices. In English, for instance, we can take the transitive sentence (8), with *the man* as A and *the woman* as P, and rephrase it as a passive, an intransitive construction, in which *the woman* appears as S and *the man* as an oblique object (i.e. neither S, A, nor P):

> *The woman was hit by the man.*   (21)

Since *the woman* is S of (21), and also S of the intransitive sentence (10), it is possible to coordinate these two sentences together, omitting the coreferential S from the second conjunct, to give (22), which has exactly the same meaning as Dyirbal sentence (15):

> *The woman was hit by the man and came here.*   (22)

In Dyirbal, it is possible to take a transitive sentence like (12) (or, for that matter, (16)) and rephrase it so that 'the man' appears as an S, and 'the woman' as an oblique object, adding the suffix -*ŋay* to the verb. This kind of voice, whereby the A of the basic voice appears as an S, has in recent work on ergativity come to be called the antipassive voice:

> *Bayi yaṛa*   *bagun dʸugumbilgu*
>   man-ABSOLUTIVE   woman-DATIVE
> *balgalŋanʸu.*   (23)
>   hit-ANTIPASSIVE
> 'The man hit the woman.'

In Dyirbal, it is then possible to conjoin (23) with the intransitive sentence (13), of which 'the man' is also S. For reasons that go beyond our concerns here, the only order in which this particular conjunction is possible is with the intransitive clause first:

Bayi yaṛa baninʸu, bagul dʸugumbilgu balgalŋanʸu.   (24)
'The man came here and (he) hit the woman.'

Thus we see that one of the functions of different voices in languages is to redistribute subject properties: in English, to enable what would otherwise be a P noun phrase to have subject properties (as an S); in Dyirbal, to enable what would otherwise be an A noun phrase to have subject properties (as an S).

We may close the discussion of this section by recapitulating the main points, and driving them home with one further example. While the assignment of subject is clear in most intransitive constructions, especially those that are literally one-place predicate constructions, in transitive constructions we may find subject properties assigned either to the A, in which case we have nominative–accusative syntax, or to the P, in which case we have ergative–absolutive syntax. Some languages show strong preference for one or the other – e.g. English is largely nominative–accusative, Dyirbal largely ergative–absolutive – while other languages are more mixed. In Chukchi, the infinitive construction works on the nominative–accusative system, with omission of the S or A of the infinitive, with the suffix -*(ə)k*:

ɣəmnan   ɣəː   tite
I-ERGATIVE you-ABSOLUTIVE sometime
   məvinretɣət   ermetvi-k.   (25)
   let-me-help-you to-grow-strong
'Let me help you to grow strong.'

Morɣənan   ɣət   mətrevinretɣət
we-ERGATIVE you-ABSOLUTIVE we-will-help-you
   rivl-ək   əmalʔo   ɣećeyot.   (26)
   to-move all   gathered-things-ABSOLUTIVE
'We will help you move all the gathered items.'

In (25), the S of 'grow strong' is omitted; in (26), the A of 'move' is omitted. In the negative participial construction, with the suffix -*lʔ* on the verb in the participial form, the construction may be used to relativize either the S or the P of the participial clause, but not its A (unless the clause is antipassivized, as in (29), with relativization then effectively of the S):

E -tip?eyŋe-kə   -l?   -in
NEGATIVE sing   NEGATIVE PARTICIPLE ABSOLUTIVE
    ŋevəćqet   raɣtəɣ?i.   (27)
    woman-ABSOLUTIVE she-went-home
'The woman who was not singing went home.'

$Iɣər a$ -yo? -kə   -l?   -etə
now NEGATIVE reach NEGATIVE PARTICIPLE ALLATIVE
    enm -etə   mənəlqənmək.   (28)
    hill ALLATIVE let-us-go
'Now let us go to the hill which (someone) didn't reach.'

En -aɣtat-kə   -l?   -a
ANTIPASSIVE chase NEGATIVE PARTICIPLE ERGATIVE
    qaa   -k   ?aaćek-a   vinretərkəninet
    reindeer LOCATIVE youth ERGATIVE he-helps-them
    ŋevəćqetti.   (29)
    women-ABSOLUTIVE
'The youth who does not chase the reindeer
is helping the women.'

(Note that in (29) the object of the antipassive verb stands in the locative case.)

5.4 SEMANTIC AND PRAGMATIC FACTORS

So far, we have not related splits between nominative–accusative and ergative–absolutive syntax to the distinction between those properties that are more properly correlated closely with agent, and those that are more closely correlated with topic, and it is to this discussion that we now proceed, although our discussion will necessarily involve only exemplification of a limited number of properties.

We may start off with subject properties that correlate more closely with agent properties. In many languages, in imperatives it is possible to omit reference to the addressee if that addressee is an A or an S, but not if it is a P; indeed, many languages have an even stricter requirement, namely that the S or A of an imperative construction must be second person (addressee), i.e. they only have second person imperatives. This can be illustrated for English by the examples *come here!* (i.e. *you come here!*) and *hit the man!* (i.e. *you hit the man!*), where it is possible to omit the addressee pronoun, in contrast to *let/may the man hit you!*, where it is not possible to do so. Interestingly enough, in Dyirbal, precisely the same constraint holds: despite the widespread prevalence in this language of syntactic constructions where S is identified with P, in imperative addressee deletion S is identified with A, as in English:

> *(ŋinda)*   *bani.*   (30)
> you-NOMINATIVE come-here-IMPERATIVE
> 'Come here!'

> *(ŋinda)*   *bayi yaṛa*   *balga.*   (31)
> you-NOMINATIVE   man-ABSOLUTIVE hit-IMPERATIVE
> 'Hit the man!'

The motivation for this distribution is not hard to find. For an instruction to be felicitous, the person to whom the instruction is addressed must have control over the resultant situation. In general, S and, especially, A are the participants who have most control over the situation, whereas P rarely has much control, so that it is more natural that the recipients of instructions should be encoded linguistically as an S or an A than as a P. Imperative addressee deletion simply provides a more compact means of expression for the more expected situation, i.e. addressees can be deleted when they are the more agentive S or A, but not when they are the less agentive P. This is thus a clear instance of a subject property that correlates with an agent property. Note that we are not saying that subject and agent are identical with respect to this property, or that the syntactic rule can be stated in terms of agents rather than in terms of subjects. For English, this is clearly untrue, since one can form passive imperatives where the addressee is not an agent but can be deleted, or where the agent is addressee but cannot be deleted (although the resultant sentences are very unnatural):

> *Be amazed by the world's greatest lion-tamer!*   (32)

> *Let/may this problem be solved by you!*   (33)

What we are claiming is that this subject property has a high correlation with an agent property, and therefore the S/A identification is more natural, even in a language like Dyirbal where the S/A identification otherwise plays little or no role in the language.

Moreover, we are not claiming that a language will necessarily have S/A identification for a subject property that correlates highly with an agent property, only that there will be a strong tendency for this to be the case (i.e. a universal tendency rather than an absolute universal). In Dyirbal, for instance, one might expect the same nominative–accusative syntax to carry over to indirect commands, deleting the S or A of the indirect command if coreferential with the recipient of the command. In fact, however, the A of an indirect command cannot be deleted in that form, rather the antipassive must be used, presenting that noun phrase as an S, which can then be deleted by the general rule allowing deletion of either an S or a P:

ŋana   yabu   gigan ŋumagu
we-NOMINATIVE mother-ABSOLUTIVE told   father-DATIVE
   buṛalŋaygu.   (34)
   see-ANTIPASSIVE-INFINITIVE
'We told mother to watch father.'

(Note that the dative is one of the possible cases for the patient in the antipassive construction.) If the unmarked voice is used for a transitive verb in the infinitive, then only a coreferential P may be omitted, as in (35):

ŋaḏ'a   bayi yaṛa   gigan
I-NOMINATIVE   man-ABSOLUTIVE told
   gubiŋgu   mawali.   (35)
   doctor-ERGATIVE examine-INFINITIVE
'I told the man to be examined by the doctor.'

The example of imperative addressee deletion involved a natural identification of S and A, i.e. natural nominative–accusative syntax. We may now turn to an example of natural ergative–absolutive syntax. In Nivkh, there is a resultative construction, i.e. a construction referring to a state that has come about as the result of a previous event, using the suffix -*yəta*. With intransitive verbs, this involves simply the addition of the suffix to the verb:

Anaq yo   -d'.   (36)
iron rust
'The iron rusted.'

Anaq yo -yəta   -d'.   (37)
iron rust RESULTATIVE
'The iron has rusted.'

(The verb-final suffix *-d'* is an indicator of finiteness.) If, however, we take a transitive verb, then a number of changes take place relative to the non-resultative form:

> *Umgu t'us tʰa -d'*.   (38)
> woman meat roast
> 'The woman roasted the meat.'

> *T'us řa -γəta   -d'*.   (39)
> meat roast RESULTATIVE
> 'The meat has been roasted.'

First, for the majority of transitive verbs in most circumstances, the A of the transitive verb must be omitted in the resultative construction. Secondly, the P of the transitive verb has the property that it conditions consonant-initial alternation in the verb (cf. the initial *tʰ*- of (38)), and the absence of such alternation in the resultative verb suggests that this noun phrase is no longer P. Whatever the precise details of the syntactic analysis, we can say that the resultative verb has a single argument, and that this argument corresponds to the S of a non-resultative intransitive verb, but to the P of a non-resultative transitive verb. In other words, S and P behave alike, as opposed to A.

The explanation this time is to be sought in the pragmatic structure of resultative constructions. Any such construction attributes a change of state to a certain entity. With intransitive predicates, the change of state is necessarily attributed to the S: in sentence (37), it is the iron that has undergone a change of state. With transitive predicates, although it is in principle possible for the change in state to characterize the A, as in *John has climbed the mountain*, it is more usual, especially with the prototypical transitive predicates describing an action involving a change of state, for the change of state to be attributed to the P. If we say *the woman has roasted the meat*, then we are necessarily talking about a change of state in the meat, and whether or not there is any change of state in the woman is simply left open. What Nivkh does is to grammaticalize this natural topicalization of S or P in the resultative construction, by allowing only S or P to be expressed.

Again, we are not claiming that a language must make this identification in the syntax of resultative constructions. English, for instance, does not, so that *the woman has roasted the meat* is perfectly acceptable as the resultative of *the woman roasted the meat*. We are claiming, however, that languages will tend to show a bias towards ergative–absolutive syntax in resultative constructions.

In many constructions, unlike imperatives and resultatives, there seems, a priori, to be no expected bias towards identifying S with either of A or P, for instance with coordination omission of noun phrases, and it is in these constructions that we find most variation across languages: with coordination, for instance, English has nominative–accusative syntax, Dyirbal has ergative–absolutive syntax, Yidiny has both, and Chukchi has neither. However, our present understanding of the cross-language distribution in such cases suggests that nominative–accusative syntax is in fact more widespread than ergative–absolutive syntax, and we might ask why this is so. Moreover, if we take a piece of natural nominative–accusative syntax like imperative addressee deletion, there are few or no languages that go against it by having ergative–absolutive syntax. However, if we take a piece of natural ergative–absolutive syntax, like resultative constructions, then we do find a wide range of languages that go against the natural syntax by having nominative–accusative syntax. In other words, there seems to be a general bias in language, interacting with naturalness of identification of S with A or P, towards nominative–accusative syntax. This general bias, in turn, has an explanation: as we shall see in a slightly different context in chapter 9, humans have a strong tendency to select more agentive entities as topics of discussion, which means that there is a natural correlation between agent and topic: other things being equal, one would expect agent and topic to coincide. The notion of subject then simply reflects the grammaticalization of this expected coincidence, and explains why so many languages do have a grammatical relation of subject definable in its core as the intersection of agent and topic, whereas few languages similarly define grammatical relations reflecting the intersection of, say, patient and topic.

While preference for equating agent and topic does seem by far the most prevalent identification across languages, there are some languages that do not show this particular identification. In Dyirbal, for instance, subject properties that are not agent-bound, and even some of those that are (cf. indirect commands), adhere to the P rather than to the A. In Dyirbal, then, it seems that agentivity is virtually irrelevant to the establishment of subjecthood, preference being given to P, i.e. P is more natural as a topic than A. In a number of Austronesian languages, especially in Philippine languages, a similar, though somewhat less extreme, situation seems to obtain, with some syntactic processes being conditioned by the agentivity (semantic role) of the noun phrases involved, and other syntactic processes – including most of those where no bias would be expected a priori – being controlled by the topic, with preference for a patient rather than an agent to be topic. The following examples are from Tagalog.

If we take the situation of someone borrowing money from a bank, then in Tagalog if the P is definite, it must be topic, irrespective of the defi-

niteness of the other noun phrases, as in (41). Only otherwise is it possible
for the A to be topic, as in (40):

> Humiram   siya   ng pera   sa   bangko.   (40)
> borrowed-ACTIVE he-TOPIC P money DATIVE bank
> 'He borrowed money from the bank.'

> Hiniram   niya ang   pera   sa   bangko.   (41)
> borrowed-PASSIVE he-A TOPIC money DATIVE bank
> 'He borrowed the money from the bank.'

If we embed this construction under a verb meaning 'to hesitate', then this is
a construction which, a priori, favours S/A identification – one can only
hesitate about something under one's own control – and here Tagalog
allows deletion of the A, irrespective of whether it is topic or not:

> Nagatubili   siya   -ng humiram ng pera sa bangko.   (42)
> hesitated-ACTIVE he-TOPIC
> 'He hesitated to borrow money from the bank.'

> Nagatubili siya-ng hiramin ang pera sa bangko.   (43)
> 'He hesitated to borrow the money from the bank.'

(In the last two examples, the suffix -ng is a clause-linker; hiramin in (43) is
the nonfinite equivalent of hiniram.)
   If, however, we take a construction that is neutral as between identification
of S with A or P, then Tagalog treats the topic as subject. For instance, in
Tagalog relative clauses, the noun relativized can only be topic of the relative
clause. Compare the following sentences:

> Bumili   ang   babae   ng baro.   (44)
> bought-ACTIVE TOPIC woman P dress
> 'The woman bought a dress.'

> Binili   ng babae   ang   baro.   (45)
> bought-PASSIVE A woman TOPIC dress
> 'A/the woman bought the dress.'

If we want to relativize 'woman', then the active construction of (44) must
be used, but if we want to relativize 'the dress', then the passive construction of (45) must be used; no other alternatives are possible:

Iyon ang   babae-ng bumili   ng baro.   (46)
that TOPIC woman   bought-ACTIVE P dress
'That is the woman who bought a dress.'

Iyon ang baro-ng binili ng babae.   (47)
'That is the dress that the woman bought.'

To conclude this chapter, we note that treating subject as a diffuse, rather than a discrete, notion, while perhaps seeming at first to weaken the notion of subject, does in fact provide us with a powerful tool which, in conjunction with independently established correlations with agent and topic properties, enables us to describe in a unified way, with a large measure of explanation, disparate phenomena across a wide range of languages.

NOTES AND REFERENCES

The idea of defining prototypical subject as a multi-factor concept is developed initially by Keenan (1976b), although I do not use his classification of properties here. The strongest criticism of this approach comes from Johnson (1977a), but unfortunately Johnson begs the question by assuming that a definition must be in terms of necessary and sufficient conditions. My discussion of the continuum ('squish') from adjective to noun in Russian numerals is based closely on Corbett (1978).

The discussion of ergativity in section 5.3 is based on Comrie (1978b). Very similar ideas, though with certain differences in terminology, emphasis, and concept, are given independently by Dixon (1979); note in particular that Dixon uses O for my P, uses subject for a natural grouping of S and A, and uses pivot for a grouping of S with A or S with P in a particular language. The Dyirbal examples derive originally from Dixon (1972), though they reappear in almost every subsequent discussion of ergativity; example (35) was expressly collected for me by R. M. W. Dixon, who thereby earns a particular debt of gratitude, the more so since this example requires slight modification of pages 128–9 of Dixon (1979). Numerous studies on ergativity are gathered in Plank (1979); the Chukchi examples are from the contributions to this volume by Comrie (1979c, 226, 227, 229) and Nedjalkov (1979, 242).

Splitting subject properties between agent (role) and topic (reference) properties is developed, especially for Philippine languages, by Schachter (1976, 1977); the Tagalog examples are taken from the second of these. The Nivkh examples are from Nedjalkov *et al.* (1974). Factors controlling the distribution of nominative–accusative and ergative–absolutive syntax are discussed by Moravscik (1978b). The discussion of imperative addressee deletion is based on Dixon (1979, 112–14), that of resultative constructions on Comrie (1981a).

6

CASE MARKING

6.1 THE DISCRIMINATORY FUNCTION OF CASES

In this chapter, we are going to look at one way in which consideration of data from a wide range of languages has enabled us to gain important new insights into a general linguistic phenomenon, insights that would probably not have been obtained solely by the investigation of a single language, and certainly not from the detailed, abstract analysis of English. If one looks at the accounts given of the uses of cases in traditional, and many non-traditional, grammars, there is usually the assumption – in many instances, justified – that the use of a given morphological case will correlate highly either with a given semantic role, or with a given grammatical relation. Thus the locative case is said to be the case for expressing location, the ablative for expressing motion away from, and so on; the nominative is described as being the case for the subject, the accusative for the direct object (or, in frameworks that eschew the distinction between semantic and syntactic cases, nominative correlates with agent and accusative with patient). In addition to case marking systems based on semantic and/or syntactic criteria, recent linguistic research has also uncovered languages where pragmatic criteria are important in assigning case, as in Japanese and Tagalog, for instance.

In addition, however, to languages where some or all of the cases can be accounted for in this way, there remains a set of recalcitrant data, where on the basis of semantic roles or grammatical relations or pragmatic roles there remain some cases that do not correlate directly with any syntactic or semantic or pragmatic role, but rather seem to be used for a given role, but only in certain, limited circumstances. The aim of this chapter is to investigate some of these examples, in particular examples concerned with subjects and direct objects (or, more accurately, with S, A, and P). The reason why this discussion fits well into our general discussion of universals and typology is that the kinds of non-correspondence that we shall be looking at are found to recur in a wide variety of languages from different genetic and areal groupings, i.e. we are dealing with a significant phenomenon from the viewpoint of language universals. Moreover, not only can we establish a general pattern of similar distribution across languages, we can actually go a long way towards finding an explanation for this cross-language similarity.

We shall begin our discussion by considering the nominative–accusative and ergative–absolutive case marking systems, already introduced in passing in chapter 5. If we take S, A, and P as our primitives, and assume for the moment that we are restricting ourselves to languages that treat each of these three relations homogeneously, i.e. do not have different cases for different types of S, etc., then it is clear that there are not just two logically possible kinds of case marking system, but five. The nominative–accusative system groups S and A (nominative) together against P (accusative). The ergative–absolutive system groups S and P (absolutive) together against A (ergative). Both of these systems are widespread across the languages of the world. The neutral system would have the same form for all three primitives, but since this is tantamount to lack of case marking for these relations, it is not directly relevant to our considerations: as a system, it is, of course, widespread in the languages of the world, but most languages with this system have other means, such as verb agreement or word order, to indicate which noun phrase is A and which is P in the transitive construction. The fourth possible type, tripartite, would have distinct cases for each of the three primitives. The fifth type would group A and P together as against S.

The tripartite system is found, but is very rare. In a number of languages, as we shall see in more detail below, it is found with a subset of the noun phrases in a language, namely where nominative–accusative and ergative–absolutive systems co-existing in a language intersect. But there is only one language for which it has been reported that this tripartite system exists for all noun phrases in the language, namely Wanggumara. Thus we can say with confidence that this system is very rare across the world's languages. The last type, with A/P–S alignment, seems to be equally rare: the only reliable attestations known to us are for certain classes of noun phrases in certain Iranian languages, where it represents an intermediate diachronic stage in the breakdown of an earlier ergative–absolutive case marking system in the direction of a nominative–accusative system. The question arises immediately why, of four logically possible case marking systems, two should account for almost all the languages of the world that have a case marking system that consistently distinguishes among S, A, and P. If we compare the noun phrase arguments of intransitive and transitive constructions, as in (1)–(2) (irrespective of word order), then a possible motivation for this distribution emerges:

S $\quad$ V$_{\text{intransitive}}$ $\hfill$ (1)

A $\quad$ P $\quad$ V$_{\text{transitive}}$ $\hfill$ (2)

In the intransitive construction, there is only a single argument, so there is no need, from a functional viewpoint, to mark this noun phrase in any way to distinguish it from other noun phrases. In the transitive construction, on the other hand, there are two noun phrases, and unless there is some other way (such as word order) of distinguishing between them, ambiguity will result unless case marking is used. Since it is never necessary, in this sense, to distinguish morphologically between S and A or S and P (they never cooccur in the same construction), the case used for S can be used for one of the two arguments of the transitive construction. The nominative–accusative system simply chooses to identify S with A, and have a separate marker for P; while the ergative–absolutive system chooses to treat S the same as P, with a separate marker for A. The tripartite system is unnecessarily explicit, since in addition to distinguishing A from P, it also distinguishes each of these from S, even though S never cooccurs with either of the other two. The A/P – S system is, from a functional viewpoint, singularly inefficient, failing to make the most useful distinction (between A and P), and making a useless distinction (between A and S, likewise between P and S). Whatever may be the value of functional explanations in general in linguistics and language universals in particular, here we do have a good example where the predictions of the functional approach appear to fit in very well with the observed distribution of case marking systems across the languages of the world.

In fact, the functional approach makes a further prediction that is borne out by actual distribution. In a case system where one of the two cases used for indicating these three primitives is formally less marked than the other, for instance where one of the forms is simply the stem of the noun in question whereas the other has some overt affix, it is nearly always the case that the formally unmarked item is used to indicate S, whence also A in the nominative–accusative system and P in the ergative–absolutive system. This is Greenberg's universal number 38: 'where there is a case system, the only case which ever has only zero allomorphs is the one which includes among its meanings that of the subject of the intransitive verb', although a very few counterexamples to this generalization have since been uncovered, all with a nominative case more marked than the accusative, e.g. in Yuman languages, where the nominative takes the suffix -č and the accusative has no suffix. If, however, we restrict ourselves to the more general pattern, then we can see that in the nominative–accusative system, a special marker is added to P to distinguish it from A, which like S is unmarked. In the ergative–absolutive system, a special marker is added to A to distinguish it from P, which like S is unmarked. The functional explanation of these two case marking systems may also explain why there is so often a discrepancy between the case marking system and the syntactic orientation of the language in question, as discussed in chapter 5: the cases do not relate directly to grammatical relations, but rather directly to distinguishing between A and P.

We would emphasize one point before proceeding further with the functional model of case marking and its implications. We are not claiming that the sole function of case marking is discriminatory in this sense, since there is a whole host of instances where the function of a given case can be correlated with semantic parameters. What we are claiming is that there do exist many instances where this functional approach is necessary in order to guarantee a full understanding of the role of case marking.

6.2 NATURAL INFORMATION FLOW IN THE TRANSITIVE CONSTRUCTION

From section 6.1, it emerges that the discriminatory function of case marking will show itself most clearly in the transitive construction, where there is a need to distinguish between A and P, rather than in the intransitive construction, where S alone occurs. Where one finds different cases used for different occurrences of S in a language, the conditioning factor is usually semantic (to the extent that it is not lexically idiosyncratic): for instance in Bats, as discussed in chapter 3 (sentences (1)–(2)), the distinction between the ergative and absolutive cases for intransitive subject is dependent on the degree of control exercised by the S over the situation described. There are also instances where differential case marking on A and/or P can be readily handled in semantic terms without appeal to functional factors. For instance, in Finnish the P stands in the partitive case if only partially affected by the action (e.g. if only some of an entity is affected), but in a non-partitive case if totally affected:

> *Hän otti rahaa* (PARTITIVE).   (3)
> 'He took some money.'
>
> *Hän otti rahan* (ACCUSATIVE).   (4)
> 'He took the money.'

In this section, however, we will be concerned with formal case distinctions that do not correlate this closely with a combination of semantic or syntactic factors, in particular trying to account for the following facts: a large number of languages have special cases for animate and/or definite Ps, distinct from the cases used for other Ps, and also not used elsewhere as markers of definiteness; conversely, many languages have a special case used only for As of low animacy, and not otherwise used as indicators of either A or low animacy.

Before proceeding to the data here, we will outline the explanation, following on from the discussion of the preceding section, that we will be appealing to, as this will make the citation of the individual pieces of data more comprehensible. In the transitive construction, there is an information flow that involves two entities, the A and the P. Although in principle either of A and P can be either animate or definite, it has been noted that in actual discourse there is a strong tendency for the information flow from A to P to correlate with an information flow from more to less animate and from more to less definite. In other words, the most natural kind of transitive construction is one where the A is high in animacy and definiteness, and the P is lower in animacy and definiteness; and any deviation from this pattern leads to a more marked construction. This has implications for a functional approach to case marking: the construction which is more marked in terms of the direction of information flow should also be more marked formally, i.e. we would expect languages to have some special device to indicate that the A is low in animacy or definiteness or that the P is high in animacy or definiteness. This is precisely what we will try to document in the remainder of this section.

In the immediately preceding discussion, we have introduced the two terms animacy and definiteness. We will return to definiteness in more detail later on in this chapter, but for the moment we can work with the general definition of definiteness as the presupposition that the referent of a definite noun phrase is identifiable by the hearer; in terms of English structure, a definite noun phrase will either be a pronoun, a proper name, or a common noun introduced by the definite article or a demonstrative or other determiner. Animacy is a much more complex phenomenon, to which we return in chapter 9. For the moment, suffice it to say that a noun phrase is higher in animacy if it is to the left on a continuum some of whose main points are: first/second persons pronouns > other human noun phrases > animal noun phrases > inanimate noun phrases.

If a given transitive construction has to be marked to show that it does not correspond to the normal direction of flow of information, then there are (at least) three ways in which this marking could be made. First, one could mark the construction as a whole, say by marking the verb, to indicate an unexpected constellation of A and P; we examine this possibility in section 6.2.1. Secondly, one of the noun phrases (or both of them) could be marked, say by having a special marker for unexpected As (those low in definiteness or animacy) and/or for unexpected Ps (those high in definiteness or animacy); such examples are discussed in section 6.2.2.

6.2.1   INVERSE FORMS

A number of languages have special verb forms to indicate whether the transitive action is initiated by an A higher in animacy than the P or lower in animacy than the P (with the third possibility, A and P equal in animacy, being treated arbitrarily as the one or the other). Perhaps the most famous instance of this in the linguistic literature is in the Algonquian languages, where one set of verb forms, the so-called direct forms, are used when the A is higher in animacy than the P, while the so-called inverse forms are used where the P is higher than the A. The actual animacy hierarchy of Algonquian languages takes the form: second person > first person > third person proximate > third person obviative. The distinction between two subtypes within third person, proximate and obviate, the former higher in animacy than the latter, guarantees that there will never, in fact, be a transitive construction where A and P are equal in animacy.

The examples below are from Fox, though the general principle holds for Algonquian languages as a whole. The suffix *-aa* in these examples indicates the direct form, while *-ek* indicates inverse form. The prefix *ne-* indicates first person: this illustrates another important property of the Algonquian verb forms, namely that the prefix invariably encodes the participant higher in animacy, irrespective of its grammatical role:

ne	*-waapam-aa*	*-wa.*	(5)
1SINGULAR see	DIRECT	3	

' I see him.'

ne	*-waapam-ek*	*-wa.*	(6)
1SINGULAR see	INVERSE	3	

' He sees me.'

6.2.2   DIFFERENTIAL MARKING OF A AND P

The most widespread indication of unnatural combinations of A and P across languages, however, is not by marking the verb, but rather by marking one or both of the noun phrase arguments. The following patterns in particular are found: (a) mark a P high in animacy, i.e. the accusative case is restricted to Ps that are high in animacy; (b) mark a P high in definiteness, i.e. the accusative case is restricted to definite Ps; (c) mark an A that is low in animacy, i.e. the ergative case is restricted to noun phrases that are low in animacy. Somewhat embarrassing is the absence of clear attestations of the fourth expected type, namely marking of an indefinite A; languages seem rather to avoid this particular construction by outlawing or discouraging transitive sentences with an indefinite A, either recasting them as passives or by using a presentative construction (like English *there is/are ...*). In English, although the sentences *a bus has just run John over* and *a bird is drinking the milk* are surely grammatical, more natural ways of expressing these pieces of information would be *John has just been run over by a bus* and *there's a bird drinking the milk*. In most languages that use the three methods outlined above for indicating less natural combinations of A and P, the case marking of A and P is determined independently, i.e. any A below a certain degree of animacy is marked ergative, irrespective of the P; conversely, any P above a certain degree of definiteness or animacy is marked accusative, irrespective of the A. This contrasts with the inverse verb forms discussed in section 6.2.1, where it is usually the relation of A to P that is important. Finally, before proceeding to detailed exemplification, we should note that there are some languages where the occurrence of the special ergative or accusative marker is conditioned not by any specific rigid cut-off point on the animacy or definiteness hierarchies, but rather by a more general condition of the kind: use the special marker only if there is likelihood of confusion between A and P; the assessment of likelihood of confusion is left to the speaker in the particular context. Hua is an example of a language of this type.

For the relevance of animacy, particularly clear data are provided by Australian languages, almost all of which have split case marking determined by the animacy hierarchy. As would be expected from our discussion above, a special accusative case is often restricted to noun phrases towards the top of the animacy hierarchy: thus in Dyirbal it is found only with first and second person pronouns; in Arabana only with human noun phrases; and in Thargari only with animate noun phrases. Conversely, the special ergative case is found only towards the bottom of the hierarchy, though usually, in fact, in these languages extending quite high up the hierarchy: thus most Australian languages have a separate ergative case for all non-pronominal noun phrases (e.g. Dyirbal), sometimes extending further up the hierarchy into the pronouns. Since the determination of the case of A and P is independent, it sometimes happens that accusative and ergative case marking meet neatly in the middle of the hierarchy without any overlap or gap, but quite frequently there is overlap in the middle of the hierarchy, which means that some noun phrases have a tripartite case marking system; and it sometimes happens that there is a gap in the middle of the hierarchy, some noun phrases having the neutral case marking system. Thus Ritharngu, for instance, has a nominative–accusative case marking system for pronouns; the tripartite system for humans and intelligent animals; and ergative–absolutive case marking for other nouns, i.e. for non-intelligent animals and inanimates. In some languages, the middle ground in the hierarchy may be shared by both the tripartite and neutral case marking systems, as was discussed in section 3.4 for the Saibai dialect of Kalaw Lagaw Ya, which thus combines within one language nominative–accusative, ergative–absolutive, tripartite, and neutral case marking.

One result of the split case marking pattern is that a single sentence, in addition to having a nominative A and an accusative P, or an ergative A and an absolutive P, can also have one of the patterns: ergative A and accusative P; nominative A and absolutive P. These possibilities were often effectively discounted in earlier work on ergativity, with its rigid distinction between nominative and ergative constructions. The following illustrations are from Dyirbal:

Balan dʸugumbil   *baŋgul yaṛaŋgu*   *balgan.*   (7)
  woman-ABSOLUTIVE   man-ERGATIVE hit
'The man hit the woman.'

Ŋadʸa   *ŋinuna*   *balgan.*   (8)
I-NOMINATIVE you-ACCUSATIVE hit
'I hit you.'

Ŋayguna   *baŋgul yaṛaŋgu*   *balgan.*   (9)
I-ACCUSATIVE   man-ERGATIVE hit
'The man hit me.'

Ŋadʸa   *bayi yaṛa*   *balgan.*   (10)
I-NOMINATIVE   man-ABSOLUTIVE hit
'I hit the man.'

Although the most spectacular evidence for the relevance of animacy in the A does seem to come from Australian languages, it is also found in other languages. For instance, in some North-East Caucasian languages (e.g. Lak), nouns have an ergative–absolutive case marking system, but personal pronouns have a neutral system. This is particularly interesting in that it goes against an otherwise largely valid generalization that pronouns tend to distinguish more categories than do nouns.

The restriction of accusative marking to nouns that are high in animacy is very widespread across the languages of the world, and we will limit ourselves to a few examples. Even English provides relevant data here, since it has a nominative–accusative distinction with (many) pronouns, e.g. *I – me*, whereas it does not have any comparable distinction for other noun phrases. A particularly clear set of instances is provided by the Slavonic languages, where animacy is one of the key parameters determining whether a noun phrase will have a separate accusative case or not. In Russian, for instance, masculine singular nouns of the declension Ia have a separate accusative case (with the ending *-a*) if animate, but not otherwise:

Ja videl mal'čik-a/begemot-a/dub/stol.   (11)
' I saw the boy/hippopotamus/oak/table.'

In Russian, all animate nouns in the plural have a separate accusative case, while no inanimate nouns do. In Polish, only male human nouns have a special accusative case in the plural, instantiating a different cut-off point on the animacy hierarchy:

Widziałem chłopców/dziewczyny/psy/dęby/stoły.   (12)
' I hit the boys/girls/dogs/oaks/tables.'

The forms of the last four nouns are identical with the nominative plural, whereas the nominative plural of ' boys ' is *chłopcy*.

There are data from a wide range of languages for special marking of definite direct objects: again, a few examples will suffice. In Turkish, only definite direct objects take the special accusative case suffix *-ı* (or its vowel harmony variants), all other direct objects being in the same suffixless form as is used for subjects (A or S):

Hasan öküz-ü   aldı.   (13)
Hasan ox   ACCUSATIVE bought
' Hasan bought the ox.'

Hasan bir öküz aldı.   (14)
Hasan a   ox   bought
' Hasan bought an ox.'

(In Turkish, *Hasan öküz aldı* is also possible, although it leaves open how many oxen were bought, i.e. ' Hasan bought an ox or oxen '.) In Persian, the suffix *-rā* is used to indicate definite direct objects:

> *Hasan ketāb-rā   did.*   (15)
> Hasan book ACCUSATIVE saw
> 'Hasan saw the book.'

> *Hasan yek ketāb did.*   (16)
> Hasan a   book saw
> 'Hasan saw a book.'

(As in Turkish, Persian also allows *Hasan ketāb did* 'Hasan saw a book or books'.)

What is particularly interesting in this respect is that some languages, in determining whether or not a P is to take the special accusative form or not, use both parameters of animacy and definiteness. In Hindi, for instance, a human direct object will normally take the postposition *ko* whether or not it is definite; only occasionally, and with affective value, does one find indefinite human noun phrases without *ko* in P position. Non-human, especially inanimate, Ps, however, never take *ko* if they are indefinite, though they may, and usually do, take *ko* if they are definite:

> *Aurat   bacce ko   bulā   rahī   hai.*   (17)
> woman child ACCUSATIVE calling PROGRESSIVE is
> 'The woman is calling the/a child.'

> ?*Aurat baccā bulā rahī hai.*   (18)

(The oblique form *bacce*, of *baccā*, is automatic before a postposition.)

> *Un   patrõ ko   paṛhie.*   (19)
> those letters ACCUSATIVE read-POLITE
> 'Please read those letters.'

> *Ye   patr   paṛhie.*   (20)
> these letters read-POLITE
> 'Please read these letters.'

> *Patr   likhie.*   (21)
> letters write-POLITE
> 'Write letters please.'

Thus, in order to know whether to assign *ko* to a P in Hindi, one must weigh against one another its position on both animacy and definiteness hierarchies, and even then there is room in the middle for subjective judgement.

A somewhat similar situation is observed in Spanish, in connection with the use of *a* to mark certain direct objects. Normally, this preposition is only used for human Ps, but such Ps must moreover be high in definiteness: in particular, human Ps that are non-specific occur without the preposition:

> *El director busca el carro/al empleado/a un*
> *empleado/un empleado.*   (22)
> 'The manager is looking for the car/the
> clerk/a (certain) clerk/a clerk.'

In this example, the difference between *a un empleado* and *un empleado* in P position is that the former implies that there is some specific individual that the manager is seeking, whereas the second implies simply that he needs any clerk.

Although we have treated animacy and definiteness as if they were unproblematic categories in the brief preceding discussion, this is in fact far from the case. In chapter 9, we return to examining animacy in more detail, but to conclude the present chapter we will turn to some problems concerning definiteness. One problem when we compare categories across languages is that we should have some basis on which to identify the same category in different languages. Thus, if we say that definite direct objects go into the accusative case in both Turkish and Persian, then we should be able to justify using the same term definite in referring to both these languages, and also to English, where the category definiteness exists but does not condition case marking. Failure to ensure this cross-language comparability would mean that we are not doing language universals research, but are simply analysing each language as an independent unit – and, unlike those linguists who maintain that this is the only way to study languages, we would be doing so surreptitiously by pretending, through use of the same term, that our results are comparable across languages. We will show below that a problem of this kind seems to arise in connection with definiteness, but that a solution to this problem is in fact forthcoming, a solution which, moreover, actually strengthens the universal base of our discussion.

The problem is that certain Ps in Persian and Turkish stand in the accusative case even though they are clearly not definite. In Persian, for instance, if one wants to say 'give one of them to me', then although the noun phrase 'one of them' is clearly, by definition, indefinite, yet still Persian here requires the definite marker *-rā*:

> *Yeki az ānhā -rā   be man bedehid.*   (23)
> one of them ACCUSATIVE to me   give

In sentences (14) and (16) we illustrated the absence of the accusative marker in Persian and Turkish with the indefinite article *yek* or *bir*. However, although the direct object introduced by the indefinite article is clearly indefinite, both languages allow the accusative suffix here, so that the full range of data is actually:

Hasan bir öküz aldı. (24)

Hasan bir öküz-ü aldı. (25)

Hasan yek ketāb did. (26)

Hasan yek ketāb-rā did. (27)

The existence of the second example in each language might seem to quash any possibility of identifying the concept called definite in these languages with that called definite in the discussion of English.

An indication of the route out of this dilemma is, however, indicated by our discussion of animacy. Animacy is clearly not a single dichotomy between animate and inanimate, but rather a continuum along which we can range entities according to their degree of animacy, so that for instance people are more animate than animals, and animals more animate than inanimate objects. In describing definiteness cross-linguistically, we can make use of a similar notion of continuum, i.e. a continuum of definiteness (or specificity). Definiteness in the highest degree means, as in English, that the speaker presupposes that the hearer can uniquely identify the entity being spoken of. In Persian example (23) we are clearly not dealing with definiteness in this extreme degree, rather what is at issue is that the referent of the noun phrase has been delimited by specifying a certain set, which can be identified (namely *ānhā* 'them'), and then indicating that the entity which is to be given, while not uniquely identifiable, must still be a member of this identifiable set. This can be described by the term definite superset, meaning that the identity of the entity is not determinable absolutely, but some headway can be made in identifying it because it must be a member of a delimited set.

Turkish example (25) and Persian example (27) represent a different realization of the notion degree of definiteness/specificity. Although both members of each pair of sentences in (24)–(27) are translated the same way into English, they are far from equivalent in the original languages. The versions with the accusative marking on the P noun phrases suggest that the reference of the noun phrase in question is important, relevant for the discourse as a whole. In other words, in a discourse that started with (25) or (27) we would expect the ox or the book to recur in the discourse. The versions without the accusative suffix, however, are quite neutral in this respect, and could be used, for instance, in simply relating the various events that happened to Hasan, without any particular interest in the ox or the book. We can refer to this distinction as relevance of referent identification. The absence of the accusative suffix advises the hearer not to bother about identifying the referent, while presence of this suffix advises him that the referent of this noun phrase, though not yet determinable by the hearer, will be of relevance to the ensuing discourse. So all uses of the accusative case can be linked together in terms of a hierarchy of definiteness: at one extreme we have complete identifiability of the referent; further down the hierarchy we have partial identifiability (definite superset); and further down still we have indication that identification of the referent is relevant; at the bottom, identification of the referent is neither possible nor relevant. If we then compare accusative case marking in Persian and Turkish with definiteness (say, the occurrence of the definite article with common nouns) in English, then we see that the same parameter is involved throughout, only the cut-off points are different in the various languages.

6.3 SUMMARY

To conclude this chapter, we may note that case marking, which has so often been viewed as an area of language-specific idiosyncrasy, often lacking in generalization even internal to a single language, can be the subject of fruitful language universals, fruitful not only in the sense that they involve cross-language generalizations about case marking, but also because they point the way to more adequate analyses of other areas of language structure.

NOTES AND REFERENCES

The discussion of the five homogeneous systems for case marking of S, A, and P is taken from Comrie (1978b, 330–4). The Wanggumara data are discussed by Blake (1977, 11). The A/P – S system, considered unattested by Comrie (1978b), is documented by Payne (1979, 443) for Roshani. My information on Yuman languages is from Pamela Munro (University of California, Los Angeles).

The presentation in section 6.2 stems from some of the ideas contained in Comrie (1978b, 384–8), as modified by the similar results obtained independently by Silverstein (1976). The explanation has been modified slightly in the direction of ideas presented in DeLancey (1981). In particular, as noted by DeLancey, and also by Hopper & Thompson (1980), it is misleading to claim that Ps are typically inanimate/indefinite, rather than just less animate/definite than As. The structure of the verb in Fox is discussed by LeSourd (1976).

Much of the discussion in section 6.2.2 follows Comrie (1977b, 1978c, 1979b); many of the data are taken from these articles and sources cited there. The ergative in Hua is discussed by Haiman (1979, 59–61). The Australian data are from Silverstein (1976), Heath (1976) (for Ritharngu), Blake (1977, 13–15), and Dixon (1972, 59–60). For the closing remarks on a continuum of definiteness, see further Comrie (1978a).

7

RELATIVE CLAUSES

7.1 SOME TYPOLOGICAL CHARACTERISTICS OF ENGLISH RELATIVE CLAUSES

In this section, the aim is to indicate some of the ways in which the study of relative clauses has been biased, until quite recently, by concentration on data from English and the construction of abstract analyses to account for these characteristics. We shall not be criticizing these analyses *qua* analyses of English, but the discussion of later sections of this chapter, in which we examine relative clause equivalents in a wide range of languages, will demonstrate some of the limitations of trying to build a universal syntactic theory solely on the basis of English data and abstract analyses thereof.

One of the distinctions that has attracted considerable attention is that between restrictive and non-restrictive relative clauses in English. An example of a restrictive relative clause would be *the man that I saw yesterday left this morning*, more specifically the relative clause *that I saw yesterday* within this sentence. This clause serves to delimit the potential referents of *the man*: the speaker assumes that the sentence *the man left this morning* does not provide the hearer with sufficient information to identify the man in question (the hearer would probably have to ask *which man?*), so the additional information *that I saw yesterday* is added to indicate specifically which man is being talked about. Non-restrictive relative clauses are illustrated by the following examples: *the man, who had arrived yesterday, left this morning*, or *Fred, who had arrived yesterday, left this morning*. In these sentences, it is assumed by the speaker that the hearer can identify which man is being talked about, and that it is one particular, identifiable Fred that is being talked about, and the relative clause serves merely to give the hearer an added piece of information about an already identified entity, but not to identify that entity. In English, non-restrictive relatives (also called: appositive, descriptive, explanatory) require the relative pronoun *who* or *which*, or

131

their inflected forms (*whom, whose*), and are also set off intonationally from the main clause, indicated orthographically by commas. Restrictive relatives allow, in addition to *who* and *which*, the relative pronoun (or conjunction?) *that* in most instances, or even suppression of the relative pronoun/conjunction, as in *the man I saw yesterday left this morning*; moreover, it is not necessary, or usual, for the restrictive relative clause to be set off intonationally from the main clause, indicated orthographically by the absence of commas.

Despite the similar syntactic constructions for restrictive and non-restrictive relative clauses, they are radically different in semantic or pragmatic terms, in particular in that the restrictive relative clause uses presupposed information to identify the referent of a noun phrase, while the non-restrictive relative is a way of presenting new information on the basis of the assumption that the referent can already be identified. In typological terms, however, this distinction seems to be almost completely irrelevant. Formal distinction between restrictive and non-restrictive relatives is found sporadically across languages, but probably most languages have either no formal distinction, or only an intonational distinction where the relative clause follows the head noun. To give just one further example of a language with a formal distinction, in Persian the suffix *-i* is required on the head of a restrictive relative, but not on the head of a non-restrictive relative:

> *Mardhā-i* [*ke   ketābhārā be ānhā dāde budid*]   *raftand.*   (1)
> men   that books   to them you-had-given went
> 'The men that you had given the books to went.'

> *Mo'allef* [*ke   nevisandeye xubi -st*] *in*
> author   that writer   good is this
>
>   *sabkrā exteyār karde ast.*   (2)
>   style   has-chosen
> 'The author, who is a good writer, has chosen this style.'

In English, the semantic distinction applies equally to prenominal adjectives, as in *the industrious Japanese*, meaning (a) those Japanese that are industrious (but not those that are lazy), or (b) all Japanese, who are (incidentally) industrious; here, however, there is no formal distinction corresponding to the potential *who/that* distinction, or different intonation patterns, in the fully-fledged relative clause.

The second characteristic of work on relative clauses, especially within the transformational-generative framework (though also continuing some ideas of traditional grammar) can be seen by comparing relative clauses with the closest corresponding independent sentences. For the sake of simplicity, we will for the most part give examples with the *wh-* relative forms. If we compare the relative clause *whom I saw yesterday* of *the man whom I saw yesterday left today* with the independent sentence *I saw the man yesterday*, then it is clear that there is a difference in the order of grammatical relations: in the independent sentence, as usually in English, the direct object follows the main verb; in the relative clause, however, the relative pronoun occurs clause-initially, and indeed the general principle of English relative clause formation is that the relative pronoun must occur clause-initially, or at least as part of the clause-initial noun or prepositional phrase (to allow for relative clauses like *with whom I arrived, the roof of which I repaired*). In transformational terms, relative clause formation in English involves a movement transformation, moving the *wh-* word from its normal position in the clause to clause-initial position. For present purposes, although we shall continue to use the terminology of movement, this can be understood more neutrally as a way of referring to the difference between the word order of the independent sentence and that of the relative clause, without any necessary commitment as to the most appropriate formal means of describing this difference.

In fact, we can be even more specific about this property of English relative clauses: they involve movement without any overt trace being left behind in the position moved out of. In non-standard English, it is sometimes possible to move the *wh-* element while leaving an overt trace, in the form of a pronoun, as in *this is the road which I don't know where it leads*, compared to *I don't know where the road leads*: in the relative clause the *wh-* element *which* has been moved to clause-initial position, but the pronoun *it* has been left behind. This latter construction can be referred to as a copying transformation (movement with copying), while the kind discussed earlier is known technically as a chopping transformation (movement without an overt copy).

As described so far, English might seem to permit movement of any noun phrase to clause-initial position in the formation of relative clauses. In fact, however, there are several restrictions on this process in English. One such restriction is that it is impossible to move the subject of an embedded clause with an overt conjunction in this way, so that if we start from *I don't know where the road leads*, it is impossible to move *the road*, as subject of the embedded clause *where the road leads*, by a chopping transformation to give **this is the road which I don't know where leads*. At least, this is impossible using a chopping transformation. As we saw above, for those varieties of English where at least some relative clauses can be formed by copying, rather than chopping, relativization of such a noun phrase is possible, to give *this is the road which I don't know where it leads*.

On the basis of the English data, then, one might be led to posit that constraints on relative clause formation are constraints on movement transformations, more specifically constraints on chopping transformations. The fact that some varieties of English allow relativization of certain otherwise inaccessible positions provided a pronoun is retained would seem to reinforce this impression: the constraint is on chopping, rather than copying, so copying enables one to override the constraint.

Examination of data from a wider range of languages, however, suggests that, however adequate this may be as an analysis of relative clause formation in English, it is not adequate as a general syntactic account of relative clause formation cross-linguistically, or even of constraints on relative clause formation cross-linguistically. First, many languages quite regularly use pronoun-retention as a means of forming relative clauses (see further section 7.2.3). If constraints were simply constraints on chopping, then one would expect such languages to relativize freely any noun phrase. However, this is not the case. For instance, Zürich German requires pronoun-retention for relativization of most noun phrases, but in Zürich German it is just as impossible as in English to relativize a noun phrase which is itself within a relative clause, i.e. to start from *John saw the man that gave me the book* and relativize *the book* to give **I'm going to sell the book that John saw the man that gave me (it)*. On the other hand, Persian, which also has pronoun-retention, does allow the formation of such relative clauses. So constraints on chopping are not sufficient to characterize cross-language accessibility to relative clause formation.

Secondly, there are many languages in which relative clause formation does not seem to involve any movement at all, but where still there are constraints on relativization. Even for English, it is arguable that the relative clause introduced by *that* or zero involves no movement, since *that* can be analyzed as the general subordinating conjunction *that* rather than as a relative pronoun. Thus the ungrammatical relative clause **this is the road (that) I don't know where leads* would involve no movement, but would still violate a constraint on relativization. The following Basque examples show that Basque has no movement in the formation of relative clauses; in these examples, *-k* indicates a (transitive) subject (ergative case) and *-ri* an indirect object (direct objects take no suffix), while the suffix *-n* on the auxiliary verb *dio* indicates that it is in a relative clause:

> *Gizona-k emakumea-ri liburua eman dio.*   (3)
> man   woman   book   has-given
> 'The man has given the book to the woman.'

> *[emakumea-ri liburua eman dio-n] gizona*   (4)
> 'the man who has given the book to the woman'

[*gizona-k emakumea-ri eman dio-n*] *liburua*   (5)
'the book which the man has given to the woman'

[*gizona-k liburua eman dio-n*] *emakumea*   (6)
'the woman to whom the man has given the book'

Nonetheless, the range of noun phrases that can be relativized in Basque is highly restricted; in particular it is not possible to relativize on possessives, to give a literal translation of *the boy whose book the man has given to the woman*.

All of this material goes to show that, before having a reasonable chance of coming up with cross-linguistically valid generalizations about relative clause formation, it is necessary to investigate some of the different types of relative clause constructions that are found across the languages of the world. This problem is addressed in the remainder of this chapter.

7.2   TYPES OF RELATIVE CLAUSE

7.2.1   DEFINING THE NOTION RELATIVE CLAUSE

Given that the constructions which we have, so far informally, been calling relative clauses differ quite considerably in their syntactic structures across languages, it is essential that we should have some reliable way, independent of language-specific syntax, of identifying relative clauses (or at least, prototypical relative clauses) cross-linguistically. We can illustrate this by contrasting the English relative clause, discussed in section 7.1, with one type of Turkish relative clause:

[*Hasan-ın   Sinan-a   ver   -diğ-ı*]
   Hasan of Sinan to give   his
   patates-i   *yedim.*   (7)
   potato ACCUSATIVE I-ate
'I ate the potato that Hasan gave to Sinan.'

In terms of its syntactic structure, (7) differs considerably from its English translation. The verb form *ver-diğ-* is a non-finite form of the verb *ver* 'give', with the nominalizing suffix *-diğ*; like other nominalized verb forms in Turkish, it requires its subject (*Hasan*) in the genitive and the appropriate possessive suffix (here *-ı* 'his') on the verb noun. Thus a literal translation of the head noun and relative clause *Hasanın Sinana verdiği patates* would be 'the potato of Hasan's giving to Sinan'. In

English traditional grammar, the term clause is often restricted to constructions with a finite verb, so in terms of this definition the Turkish
construction is not a clause, therefore not a relative clause. However, this
terminology simply reflects a general property of English syntax: subordination is carried out primarily by means of finite clauses; whereas in
Turkish subordination is in general by means of non-finite constructions.
The claim found in some discussions of Turkish that Turkish does not
have relative clauses is thus in one sense correct, but from a wider perspective, it is clear that the Turkish construction illustrated in (7) fulfils
precisely the same function as the English relative clause: thus, in its
restrictive interpretation, there is a head noun *patates* 'potato', and the
relative clause restricts the potential reference of that head noun by telling
us which particular potato (the one that Hasan gave to Sinan) is at issue.
The lesson of this comparison is thus that we need a functional (semantic,
cognitive) definition of relative clause, on the basis of which we can then
proceed to compare relative clauses across languages, neglecting language-
specific syntactic differences in our over-all definition of relative clause,
but using them as the basis of our typology – for instance, the distinction
between finite and non-finite relative clauses is one typological parameter.

We can now be somewhat more specific about the definition of relative
clause, bearing in mind that, as so often, what we are giving is a characterization of the prototypical relative clause, rather than a set of necessary and
sufficient conditions for the identification of relative clauses. We will
assume that restrictive relative clauses are more central to the notion of
relative clause than are non-restrictives, and construct the definition accordingly. A relative clause then consists necessarily of a head and a restricting clause. The head in itself has a certain potential range of referents,
but the restricting clause restricts this set by giving a proposition that must
be true of the actual referents of the over-all construction. Taking (7) as an
example, whether in its English or Turkish form, this is a relative clause
because it has a head with a range of potential referents, namely 'potato';
however, the actual set of referents is limited to the potatoes (in this case,
to the one potato) of which the proposition 'Hasan gave the potato to
Sinan' is true.

In one sense, this definition is somewhat narrower than the traditional
concept of relative clause, for instance by excluding non-restrictive relatives, and also certain, arguably marginal, constructions of the type *John is
no longer the man that he used to be*, where the function of the relative clause
(if such it is) is hardly to restrict the range of reference of *the man*. In
another sense, however, it is much broader. In English, for instance, it will
include not only finite relative clauses of the kind already discussed, but
also non-finite (participial) constructions like *passengers leaving on flight*

738 should proceed to the departure lounge, and even restrictive attributive adjectives, like *good* in *the good students all passed the examination.* We would argue that this is not a disadvantage: note that these latter constructions have straightforward paraphrases as relative clauses in the traditional sense (*passengers who are leaving, the students who are good*); moreover, none of the generalizations made in the discussion to follow on universals of relative clause formation is affected by either including or excluding such constructions.

One requirement on the definition of relative clause is that, in order to say that a language has relative clauses, it should be the case that there is some construction or constructions correlating highly with the definition given above. In this sense, it may well be that some languages do not have relative clauses. In Walbiri, for instance, the usual translation of ' I speared the emu that was drinking water' would be:

Ŋatʸulu-ḷu   -ṇa   yankiri pantuṇu kutʸa
I   ERGATIVE AUXILIARY emu   speared CONJUNCTION
-ḷpa   ŋapa ŋaṇu.   (8)
AUXILIARY water drank

However, this Walbiri sentence is equally the most natural translation of ' I speared the emu while it was drinking water', i.e. the Walbiri could be used in answer to either 'which emu did you spear?' or 'when did you spear the emu?' In Walbiri, then, this is a fairly general subordination construction, and not a construction whose sole, or even prototypical, function is to encode meanings in accordance with our definition of relative clause. We therefore leave open the possibility that some languages do not have relative clauses, and if this possibility does have to be accepted, then such languages are irrelevant to (though not counterexamples to) generalizations made with regard to languages that do have relative clauses.

7.2.2 WORD ORDER AND RELATIVE CLAUSE TYPES

In chapter 4, in discussing word order typology in general, we noted the two most widespread types of relative clause with respect to word order, namely the postnominal type where the relative clause follows its head (as in English), and the prenominal type where the relative clause precedes its head (as in Turkish example (7) above). In addition to these, however, there is a third type, in which the head actually occurs inside the relative clause, and it is this type that we will illustrate in this section.

In the clearest examples of the internal-head type of relative clause, the head noun remains expressed within the relative clause, in the usual form for a noun of that grammatical relation within a clause, and there is no overt expression of the head in the main clause. The following example is from Bambara:

N ye   so   ye.   (9)
I PAST house the see.
'I saw the house.'

Tyɛ   be   [n ye   so   mìn ye] dyɔ.   (10)
man the PRESENT I PAST house   see build
'The man is building the house that I saw.'

In this construction, the whole clause *n ye so mìn ye* functions as direct object of the main clause, but the sense is clearly that of a relative clause. Bambara has SOV basic word order, therefore the main clause of (10) has the order subject – auxiliary – direct object – verb. The fact that a clause is functioning as a noun phrase referring to the head is even clearer in Diegueño, where the clause in question can take the appropriate suffix to indicate its syntactic role in the main clause, in example (13) being in the locative:

Tənay   Pəwa :Pəwu :w.   (11)
yesterday house I-saw
'I saw the house yesterday.'

Pəwa :-pu   -Lʸ   Pciyawx.   (12)
house DEFINITE LOCATIVE I-will-sing
'I will sing in the house.'

[*Tənay   Pəwa : Pəwu :w*]-*pu   -Lʸ*
yesterday house I-saw   DEFINITE LOCATIVE
  Pciyawx.   (13)
  I-will-sing
'I will sing in the house that I saw yesterday.'

Here, the suffixes -*pu*-*Lʸ* are attached to the end of the embedded clause.

In this construction, unlike most kinds of relative clause, there is no problem in processing the relative clause syntactically – it has basically the structure of a simplex sentence – but there are potential problems in working out which of the noun phrases within the relative clause is to be interpreted as its head, and therefore also its function within the main clause. In Bambara, this problem is solved by placing the relative marker *min* after the noun phrase within the relative clause that is head of that construction, as in (9)–(10). In some languages, however, there is no such marker, and relative clauses can therefore be ambiguous as to which noun phrase within them is to be interpreted as head, as in this example from Imbabura Quechua:

[*Kan kwitsa-man kwintu-ta   villa-shka*]
you girl   to   story ACCUSATIVE tell   NOMINALIZER
-*ka   sumaj -mi.*   (14)
  TOPIC pretty VALIDATOR

'$\begin{Bmatrix} \text{The girl to whom you told the story} \\ \text{The story that you told to the girl} \end{Bmatrix}$ is pretty.'

A second kind of relative clause construction that is sometimes referred to as having an internal head is the following correlative construction from Hindi:

Ādmī ne   jis   cākū se   murgī   ko
man ERGATIVE which knife with chicken ACCUSATIVE
   mārā thā, us   cākū ko   Rām ne   dekhā.   (15)
   killed   that knife ACCUSATIVE Ram ERGATIVE saw
'Ram saw the knife with which the man killed the chicken.'

The literal translation of (15) would be: 'with which knife the man killed the chicken, Ram saw that knife.' Although, in (15), the noun phrase of the first clause is repeated in the second clause, it would be possible to have a coreferential pronoun in the second clause instead of the repeated noun phrase. In one sense, this construction does have an internal head, since the relative clause *ādmī . . . thā* contains a full noun phrase *jis cākū* referring to the head. Alternatively, one could argue that the head is actually the noun phrase (with a full noun, or just a pronoun) that occurs in the second clause, in which case this kind of construction would be a subtype of the prenominal relative clause. Both classifications are found in the literature, and perhaps it would be more accurate to say that this correlative construction combines features of both prenominal and internal-head types, i.e. these two types are not necessarily mutually exclusive.

7.2.3 THE ROLE OF THE HEAD IN THE RELATIVE CLAUSE

It is clear from the definition given of relative clause in section 7.2.1 that the head of a relative clause actually plays a role in two different clauses in the over-all relative clause construction: on the one hand, it plays a role in the main clause (traditionally, the term head is often restricted to the noun phrase in question as it occurs in the main clause), but equally it plays a role in the restricting clause, i.e. the relative clause in the sense of the embedded (subordinate) clause. This is particularly clear in the correlative construction, as in (15), where an overt noun phrase appears in both clauses. More commonly, however, cross-linguistically, the head noun appears in a modified or reduced form, or is completely omitted, in one of the two clauses. The first kind of internal-head relative clause discussed in section 7.2.2 illustrates omission of the head noun from the main clause. In this section, we shall be concerned with the expression of the role of the head noun within the embedded clause. Although, a priori, this might seem no more important than the role of the head in the main clause, it turns out that, from the viewpoint of typological variation, the encoding of the role in the embedded sentence is, cross-linguistically, one of the most significant parameters. Below, we distinguish four major types along this parameter: non-reduction, pronoun-retention, relative-pronoun, and gap.

The non-reduction type simply means that the head noun appears in full, unreduced form, in the embedded sentence, in the normal position and/or with the normal case marking for a noun phrase expressing that particular function in the clause. This type is illustrated by the Bambara (10), Dieguño (13), and Hindi (15) examples above, i.e. by the internal-head type in its widest sense (including correlatives).

In the pronoun-retention type, the head noun remains in the embedded sentence in pronominal form. We have already noted, in passing, that this type is found in non-standard English, as when from the sentence *I know where the road leads* one forms the relative clause *this is the road that I know where it leads*. In this construction, the pronoun *it* indicates the position relativized, i.e. enables retrieval of the information that relativization is of the subject of the indirect question clause. In English, this type has a rather marginal existence, but in many languages it is a major, in many circumstances obligatory, means of forming relative clauses, without any stylistically pejorative overtones. In Persian, for instance, pronoun-retention must be used for relativization of all grammatical relations other than subject and direct object; with direct objects, pronoun-retention is optional; with subjects, it is unusual, though examples are attested. The following examples illustrate relativization on subject, direct object, and indirect object, respectively:

Mard-i [*ke   (*u) bolandqadd bud*] *juje*
man   that   he tall   was chicken

-rā   košt.   (16)
ACCUSATIVE killed
'The man that was tall killed the chicken.'

Hasan mard-i-rā   [ke   zan   (u   -rā)
Hasan man   ACCUSATIVE that woman he ACCUSATIVE
zad] mišenāsad.   (17)
hit   knows
'Hasan knows the man that the woman hit.'

Man zan   -i-rā   [ke   Hasan be u
I   woman   ACCUSATIVE that Hasan to her
sibe zamini dād] mišenāsam.   (18)
potato   gave I-know
'I know the woman to whom Hasan gave the potato.'

In (18), it would be impossible to omit *be u* 'to her', or *u* 'her' on its own.

Before going on to the next type, we should note two points that emerge from the presentation so far. The first is that a given language may have more than one type of relative clause construction in its over-all battery of relative clause formation possibilities. Thus (16)–(18) illustrate both gap (see below) and pronoun-retention types within Persian, to some extent in complementary distribution (only the gap type with subjects, only pronoun-retention with non-direct objects), but also sometimes overlapping (as with direct objects). The same can, of course, apply also to other typological parameters, so that languages may have both finite and non-finite types (as does English, cf. the non-finite participial construction mentioned above), or both prenominal and postnominal types, as in Tagalog:

babae   -ng [nagbabasa ng diyaryo]   (19)
woman   that   reads   P newspaper

[nagbabasa ng diyaryo-ng] babae   (20)
'the woman that reads the newspaper'

The distribution of types within a language, however, is not completely arbitrary, as we shall see in section 7.3.3. The second general point to note is that the order of types being presented here proceeds from most explicit to least explicit, with regard to encoding of the role of the head noun within the relative clause. The non-reduction type is as explicit as it is possible to be; the pronoun-retention type is less explicit, since it is necessary to establish the appropriate anaphoric relation for the pronoun before the relative clause construction as a whole can be interpreted.

The next type is the relative-pronoun type, and is that found most frequently in European languages, although it is not particularly frequent as a type across the world's languages as a whole. As with the pronoun-retention type, there is a pronoun in the relative clause indicating the head, but instead of being in the usual position, in terms of linear word order, for a pronoun expressing that grammatical relation, it is moved to clause-initial position (occasionally preceded by, for instance, prepositions). For the pronoun in question to encode the role of the head noun within the relative clause, given that this cannot be done by order (the pronoun must be clause-initial), it is essential that the pronoun be case marked, at least to the same extent that noun phrases in main clauses are, to indicate its role. In English, those varieties of the language that distinguish nominative *who* from accusative *whom* thus count as having a relative-pronoun type of relative clause, but clearer examples can be found from languages with a richer case system, for instance Russian:

Devuška   prišla.   (21)
girl-NOMINATIVE arrived
'The girl arrived.'

devuška, [kotoraja   prišla]   (22)
girl   who-NOMINATIVE arrived
'the girl who arrived'

Ja videl devušku.   (23)
I   saw   girl-ACCUSATIVE

devuška, [kotoruju   ja videl]   (24)
girl   who-ACCUSATIVE I   saw
'the girl whom I saw'

Ja dal   knigu devuške.   (25)
I   gave book girl-DATIVE
'I gave the book to the girl.'

devuška, [kotoroj   ja dal knigu]   (26)
girl   who-DATIVE I   gave book
'the girl to whom I gave the book'

In each of the relative clause examples for Russian, the relative pronoun *kotor-*, though invariably in clause-initial position, unequivocally encodes the role of the head noun in the relative clause. In comparison with the pronoun-retention type, however, this relative-pronoun type involves greater deformation of the structure of the embedded sentence: instead of appearing in the basic word order position for a subject, direct object, or non-direct object, the relative pronoun must appear clause-initially. It is for this reason that we describe this type as somewhat less explicit than the pronoun-retention type.

In some languages, unstressed pronouns, as clitic pronouns, gravitate towards sentence-second position, irrespective of their grammatical relation. This can give rise to a type of relative clause that can be classified as representing simultaneously both the pronoun-retention and the relative-pronoun types, as for instance in colloquial Czech. The normal word order is subject – verb – object:

> To   děvče uhodilo toho muže.   (27)
> that girl hit   that man
> 'That girl hit that man.'

If the object is a pronoun, it appears as a clitic immediately following the first major constituent, so that pronominalizing *toho muže* 'that man' to *ho* 'him' necessarily involves a change of word order:

> To   děvče ho   uhodilo.   (28)
> that girl   him hit
> 'That girl hit him.'

One way of forming relative clauses in Czech uses the invariable conjunction *co*, with a clitic pronoun referring back when relativization is of the direct or indirect object:

> muž, [co   ho   to   děvče uhodilo]   (29)
> man   that him that girl hit
> 'the man that that girl hit'

In principle, this could be regarded as pronoun-retention (the pronoun occupies the position normal for a clitic pronoun), or as relative-pronoun (the pronoun gravitates towards sentence-initial position, giving rise to a single phonological word *co-ho*, marked as accusative case). While we are not aware of any crucial typological generalizations that depend on the assignment in this particular instance, it seems reasonable to restrict the term relative-pronoun type to examples where the movement is specific to relative clauses, thus excluding examples such as the Czech example where the movement is determined by other principles.

A similar problem, which does have implications for universals of relative clause formation (see section 7.3), occurs where a language requires or
allows pronouns to be present in a simplex sentence coreferential with full
noun phrases, and also allows or requires the same in relative clauses. In
Hausa, for instance, in simplex sentences the subject must be taken up by a
coreferential pronoun:

> Yūsufù yā zō.   (30)
> Joseph he came
> 'Joseph came.'

*Yūsufù zō is ungrammatical. It is therefore no surprise that, when rela-
tivizing a subject, a pronoun must be retained in the relative clause:

> dōkìn [dà   ya mutù]   (31)
> horse that it died
> 'the horse that died'

Since the pronoun is required independently of relative clause formation,
we would not classify this as an example of pronoun-retention, thereby
restricting this term to examples where there is a pronoun in the relative
clause in addition to possibilities of pronoun occurrence in main clauses.

Common to all of the types discussed so far has been overt indication –
by a full noun phrase, pronoun, or moved relative pronoun – of the role of
the head noun within the relative clause. The next major type, the gap
type, simply does not provide any overt indication of the role of the head
within the relative clause. In English, at least in those varieties that do not
have a *who/whom* distinction, this type is used to relativize subjects and
direct objects:

> the man who/that gave the book to the girl   (32)

> the book which/that the man gave to the girl   (33)

In some other languages, this type is much more widespread, and can be
used to relativize a variety of even non-direct objects, as in the Korean
prenominal example below:

> [Hyənsik-i   kɨ kä -lɨl
> Hyensik NOMINATIVE the dog ACCUSATIVE
>   ttäli-n]   maktäki   (34)
>   beat RELATIVE stick
> 'the stick with which Hyensik beat the dog'

Given that this type lacks any explicit means of encoding the role of the head noun within the relative clause, the question naturally arises of how it is possible for such constructions to be interpreted reliably. In practice, a number of strategies can be invoked, ranging from strategies based on syntactic properties of the language in question to knowledge of real-world properties. In English, for instance, given that the basic, and for most purposes only, word order is subject – verb – object, a relative clause construction like *the man that saw the girl* can only be interpreted as relativizing the subject: the direct object position is already filled by *the girl*, while the subject position preceding *saw* is empty. Indeed, given the rigid word order of English, it is difficult to construct examples that are ambiguous, though it is possible to find examples such as *the model that the artist helped to paint* (cf. either (a) *the artist helped the model to paint*, or (b) *the artist helped to paint the model*). In languages with freer word order, this strategy is not available, although unequivocal interpretation will often be possible where an obligatory argument of a verb is missing. Thus in Turkish example (7), the verb of the relative clause, 'give', would normally take three arguments (subject, direct object, and indirect object); its subject and indirect object are expressed in the relative clause, so by elimination the position relativized must be the direct object. The interpretation of each of the Basque relative clauses (4)–(6) is determined likewise: this is particularly clear in differentiating between 'the man who gave the book to the woman' and 'the woman to whom the man gave the book', where the alternative interpretations 'the man to whom the woman gave the book' and 'the woman who gave the book to the man' would still make sense.

In some instances, however, neither of these structurally based strategies will work, and recourse must be had to common sense: thus in Korean example (34), the most likely relation, in the real world, between the act of someone's hitting a dog and a stick is that of instrument, so that the only natural interpretation is 'the stick with which Hyensik beat the dog', rather than 'the stick for which Hyensik beat the dog' or 'the stick behind which Hyensik beat the dog'. In yet further instances, even this strategy will fail, and the resulting relative clause will simply be ambiguous, as in the following example from Imbabura Quechua:

[*Kan shamu-shka*   *llajta-ka*] *uchilla-mi.* (35)
  you come NOMINALIZER town TOPIC small VALIDATOR
'The town you are coming to/from is small.'

Since one can come either to or from a place, either interpretation is permissible. In some languages, restrictions are sometimes placed on the range of interpretations of such potentially ambiguous constructions, so that in Korean, unlike Imbabura Quechua, example (36) can refer to the place Hyensik came to, but not the place he came from:

[*Hyənsik -i*   *o*   *-n*]   *mikwuk*   (36)
Hyensik NOMINATIVE come   RELATIVE United-States
'the United States, to which Hyensik came'

Such restrictions apparently have to do with less versus more marked interpretations, but we are not aware of any detailed wide-ranging cross-language study of such instances.

Some further ways in which the range of interpretations can be restricted within the gap type of relative clause are discussed below, with respect to the equi type (section 7.2.4) and constraints on accessibility to relativization (section 7.3).

7.2.4   THE ROLE OF THE HEAD IN THE MAIN CLAUSE

In most of the world's languages, it seems that the role of the head noun in the main clause makes little or no difference to the possibility of forming relative clauses or to the particular relative clause construction that is used. However, there are some exceptions, which we will discuss in this section.

One phenomenon that is found sporadically is that known to traditional grammarians of Latin and Greek as attraction, whereby the case marking of the head noun in one clause is attracted into that of the other clause. Persian provides particularly clear exemplification of attraction from the relative clause. Without attraction, we would have (37) and (38) for relativization of subject and direct object respectively:

Ān zan   -i-rā   [ke diruz   āmad] didam.   (37)
that woman   ACCUSATIVE   that yesterday came   I-saw
'I saw that woman who came yesterday.'

Zan   -i [ke   didid]   injā -st.   (38)
woman   that you-saw here is
'The woman that you saw is here.'

As an alternative to (37), however, one can have (39), where *-rā* is omitted from the direct object (though definite) of the main clause because the head also functions as subject of the relative clause:

Ān zan-i [ke diruz āmad] didam.   (39)

Likewise, since the head is not only subject of the main clause in (38) but also direct object of the relative clause, it can be marked with the direct object marker *-rā* in subject position too:

Zan-i-rā [*ke didid*] *injā-st*.   (40)

In Ancient Greek, attraction usually works the other way round, an expected accusative relative pronoun in the relative clause being attracted into the case of its antecedent:

ek   tōn póleōn   [*hōn   éxei*]   (41)
from the cities-GENITIVE   which-GENITIVE he-has
'from the cities which he has'

The preposition *ek* requires the genitive case, so the genitive case of *tōn póleōn* is as expected in the main clause; the verb *éxei* 'he has', however, would be expected to have an accusative object, but instead the relative pronoun has been attracted into the case of the noun phrase within the main clause.

A more deep-rooted interaction between main clause and embedded clause roles is found in languages that have the equi type of relative clause, whereby the head noun must fulfil the same role in both clauses in order for a relative clause, or at least a relative clause within a certain range, to be grammatical. In some Australian languages, the general requirement that noun phrases can only be omitted if both clauses have the same subject (defined, as will be recalled from section 5.3, as P of a transitive construction or S of an intransitive construction) leads more particularly in the case of relative clause constructions with omission of the head noun in one clause to the requirement that the head be subject of both clauses. Note that since omission of the noun phrase destroys encoding of its role within that clause, the equi type is actually a subtype of the gap type of relative clause. A somewhat more widespread use of the equi type is found in Modern Hebrew: if a position that would normally require a preposition is relativized, and if moreover the same preposition also occurs on the head noun in the main clause, then the preposition (and accompanying pronoun) may be omitted, at least for many speakers, as in:

Natati sefer le oto   yeled [*še   Miriam natna* (*lo*)   *sefer*]. (42)
I-gave book to same boy   that Mary   gave   to-him book
'I gave a book to the same boy that Mary gave a book to.'

Although the equi type of relative clause does occur in languages that are otherwise very different genetically, areally, and typologically, it is always a very restricted type. No language seems to have only the equi type of relative clause and also the possibility of relativizing on a wide range of syntactic positions, and it is easy to see why this should be so, from a functional point of view: in such a language it would be very easy to express such unlikely pieces of information as 'the crops prospered notwithstanding the rain notwithstanding which the excursion still went ahead', but impossible or difficult to say 'the man that you saw has already sold his house'. The equi type seems only to exist as a marginal means of shortening expressions in languages where some other type(s) is the basic relative clause type, or in languages where there are also severe restrictions on the positions that can be relativized in the relative clause. Moreover, although examples such as those of the present section do occur where the role of the head in the main clause is relevant to relative clause formation, this is always in conjunction with its role within the relative clause, i.e. the actual constraint is on the relation between main clause and embedded clause roles. Since there are many instances, discussed in sections 7.2 and 7.3, where the role of the head in the relative clause is important, this justifies the observation made at the beginning that the role of the head noun in the subordinate clause is a major typological parameter for cross-language comparison.

7.3   ACCESSIBILITY TO RELATIVE CLAUSE FORMATION

7.3.1   SIMPLEX SENTENCES

In section 7.3, we shall return to one of the problems discussed in our brief treatment of English in section 7.1, namely constraints on accessibility of noun phrase positions to relative clause formation. In the light of the discussion of section 7.2.3–4, it is clear that we will be concerned primarily, indeed exclusively, with the role of the head noun within the embedded clause. In the present section, we will restrict ourselves to relativizing constituents of simplex sentences. Here, English presents essentially no evidence of any kind of restriction, since it is possible to relativize on, for instance, subject, direct object, non-direct object, and possessor in the possessive construction as in:

the man [*who bought the book for the girl*]   (43)

the book [*which the man bought for the girl*]   (44)

the girl [*for whom the man bought the book*]   (45)

the boy [*whose book the man bought for the girl*]   (46)

In many languages, however, there are heavy restrictions on relativization on these positions. For the purposes of the present section, we will limit the discussion to precisely the four positions just mentioned, since these positions seem to form a cross-linguistically valid hierarchy with respect to relativization. Certain other positions, such as locatives and temporals, do not seem to fit into this hierarchy: in some languages they are very easy to relativize, in other languages very difficult to relativize.

The intuition that underlies the discussion of the present section is a very simple one: the hierarchy subject > direct object > non-direct object > possessor defines ease of accessibility to relative clause formation, i.e. it is, in some intuitive sense, easier to relativize subjects than it is to relativize any of the other positions, easier to relativize direct objects than possessors, etc. Clearly, however, this intuition requires much more substantiation before it can be tested out rigorously. And the particular instantiation of the intuition that seems to be borne out as a language universal is the following: if a language can form relative clauses on a given position on the hierarchy, then it can also form relative clauses on all positions higher (to the left) on the hierarchy; moreover, for each position on the hierarchy, there is some possible language that can relativize on that position and all positions to the left, but on no position to the right. In fact, in order to provide evidence for the second of these two points, we need at least one actual language to illustrate each cut-off point on the hierarchy; fortunately, however skewed the set of actual languages may be in other respects, it does provide us with the actual examples that we need.

Thus there are languages that can only relativize subjects, such as Malagasy. Starting from a simplex sentence like (47), the only possible relative clause is (48):

> *Nahita ny vehivavy ny mpianatra.* (47)
> saw the woman the student
> 'The student saw the woman.'

(It will be recalled that Malagasy has verb – object – subject basic word order.)

> *ny mpianatra* [*izay nahita ny vehivavy*] (48)
> the student that saw the woman
> 'the student who saw the woman'

Sentence (48) cannot mean 'the student whom the woman saw', nor is there any way of translating this English relative clause literally into Malagasy (we shall see below how this information can be encoded in Malagasy).

Likewise, there are languages where relativization is possible only of subjects and direct objects, such as Kinyarwanda:

N-a   -bonye umugabo [w   -a   -kubise abagore].   (49)
I   PAST see   man   RELATIVE PAST strike women
'I saw the man who struck the women.'

Nabonye abagore [Yohani yakubise].   (50)
I-saw   women John   he-struck
'I saw the women that John struck.'

It is not, however, possible to take an instrument like n-ikaramu 'with the pen' in (51) and form a relative clause directly corresponding to 'the pen with which John wrote the letter':

Yohani yanditse ibaruwa n   -ikaramu.   (51)
John   wrote   letter   with pen
'John wrote the letter with the pen.'

Continuing down the hierarchy, we find languages that allow relativization on the first three positions of the hierarchy, but not on possessors, such as the Fering dialect of North Frisian. Finally, there are languages like English which can relativize on all four positions.

In the sample of some fifty languages investigated by Keenan and Comrie in the article referenced at the end of this chapter, nearly all were in accordance with this generalization. However, there were a small number of counter-examples, in particular a number of Austronesian languages (and, even more specifically, West Indonesian languages) which, typically, allow relativization of subjects, do not allow relativization of direct objects, but then do allow relativization of non-direct objects and/or genitives, thus clearly violating the generalization given above as an absolute universal. In Malay, for instance, (52) illustrates relativization of a subject, and (53) relativization of a possessor; it is not possible to relativize on direct objects, or on (most) non-direct objects:

Gadis [yang duduk di atas bangku] itu kakak   Ali.   (52)
lady   that sit   on top bench   the elder-sister Ali
'The lady who sat on the bench is Ali's elder sister.'

Orang [yang abang   -nya memukul saya] itu   (53)
person that elder-brother his hit   me   the
'the person whose elder brother hit me'

Faced with a small number of counterexamples to an otherwise valid universal, there are, as always, two ways of proceeding. On the one hand, one could simply say that the universal is a tendency, rather than an absolute: the number of exceptions is small relative to the over-all sample, moreover the fact that most of the exceptions belong to a single genetic and areal grouping serves only to accentuate their exceptional nature. The alternative would be to try and reformulate the universal, effectively weakening it, so that the counterexamples are no longer counterexamples; this is the strategy adopted by Keenan and Comrie in the work cited. They argue that, if one distinguishes different strategies of forming relative clauses, in particular if one distinguishes between (a) prenominal, postnominal, and internal-headed relative clauses, and (b) between relative clauses where the role of the head noun in the relative clause is encoded ([+ case]) versus those where it is not ([− case]), then the more general universal can be replaced by two more specific universals: (a) every language can relativize on subjects; (b) any relative clause strategy must cover a continuous segment of the accessibility hierarchy.

Given this reformulation, nearly all of the counterexamples disappear, in particular those from West Indonesian languages. One counterexample does still remain, namely Tongan, where a [+ case] strategy is used for (some) subjects and all non-direct objects and genitives, but not for direct objects, which use a [− case] strategy; however, it is possible, perhaps, to circumvent this counterexample by taking note of the relatively high degree of ergativity in Tongan, with consequent split of subject properties between A and P of the transitive construction. Let us, for the sake of argument, assume that under the reformulation there are no counterexamples. Then we have clearly succeeded in replacing a universal tendency by an absolute universal, which, other things being equal, is clearly meritorious. In the process, however, an essential part of the original intuition has been lost. The reformulation no longer corresponds to the original intuition that positions higher on the hierarchy are easier to relativize than positions lower down, since in Malay, for instance, it is clearly easier to relativize genitives than direct objects (it is in fact impossible to relativize the latter). Here we shall simply point out the advantages and disadvantages of both ways of treating counterexamples to the original generalization: there is no obvious solution to selecting which is the better, but for present purposes it is essential that the issue involved should be understood, even if its resolution is not to hand.

Given that we are using grammatical relations such as subject in stating the universal restrictions on accessibility to relative clause formation, one question that might naturally arise is whether the relevant grammatical relations are those of surface structure, or whether more abstract syntactic analysis is required. In fact, it turns out that the relevant grammatical relations are those of surface structure: this particular piece of work thus provides evidence in favour of stating at least some universals in terms of more concrete levels of analysis. The evidence here is most easily seen in languages that have heavy constraints on relativization, such as Malagasy (only on subjects) or Kinyarwanda (only on subjects and direct objects).

In Malagasy, in addition to the active voice illustrated in (47), there are also other voices which enable other arguments of the verb to appear as surface structure subject. For instance, in the examples below, (54) is in the active; (55) is in the so-called passive, with the direct object of the active as surface subject; (56) is in the so-called circumstantial voice, with a non-direct object (here, benefactive) as surface subject:

> *Nividy ny vary ho an'ny ankizy ny vehivavy.*   (54)
> bought the rice for   the children the woman
> 'The woman bought the rice for the children.'

> *Novidin'   ny vehivavy ho an' ny ankizy ny vary.*   (55)
> was-bought the woman   for   the children the rice
> 'The rice was bought for the children by the woman.'

> *Nividianan'   ny vehivavy ny vary ny ankizy.*   (56)
> was-bought-for the woman   the rice the children
> 'The children were bought rice by the woman.'

In (54), only the subject, *ny vehivavy* 'the woman' can be relativized. However, if one wants to convey the information of English relative clauses like 'the rice that the woman bought for the children' or 'the children for whom the woman bought the rice', then it is possible to do so provided one uses the appropriate non-active voice, with the relativized noun phrase in subject position. From (55) we can thus form (57), and from (56) we can form (58):

> *ny vary [izay novidin'ny vehivavy ho an'ny ankizy]*   (57)
> 'the rice that was bought for the children by the woman'

> *ny ankizy [izay nividianan'ny vehivavy ny vary]*   (58)
> 'the children who were bought rice by the woman'

Likewise in Kinyarwanda, in addition to sentence (51), there is an alternative construction where the semantic instrument appears as a direct object:

> *Yohani yandikishije ikaramu ibaruwa.*   (59)
> 'John wrote the letter with the pen.'

In this instance, a literal translation into English is not possible; note that the change in voice is indicated by the suffix -*ish* on the verb. In this version, 'pen' can be relativized, just like any other direct object, to give a sentence with the same information content as 'I saw the pen with which John wrote the letter':

Nabonye ikaramu [*Yohani yandik̇ishije ibaruwa*].   (60)

Note that nothing in the discussion of these Malagasy and Kinyarwanda derived sentences has required any additional principles: the behaviour of these sentences follows perfectly straightforwardly from the generalization that relativization in these languages is constrained in the way it is by surface structure grammatical relations, plus the knowledge that these languages have these voices in addition to the basic voice. Thus although it would be possible to recognize here a further type of relative clause, namely a verb-coding type (the verb form encodes what position is being relativized), it seems unnecessary to do so. One can, however, venture the further observation that heavy restrictions on relativization tend to correlate with the existence of a wide range of voices, so that positions that are not relativizable directly can be made more accessible by using a different voice. This generalization seems to be borne out, although it is a statistical correlation rather than an absolute linking of accessibility possibilities to range of voices: for instance, English has a passive voice, but this does not increase accessibility to relativization, since direct objects can be relativized directly. We may note further that in the West Indonesian languages discussed above that have a gap in relativization possibilities as defined by the hierarchy, the missing position(s) can usually be relativized indirectly by the use of a derived voice, so that the possibility of conveying this information is not lacking. In Malay, for instance, a direct object can effectively be relativized by using the passive voice, so that the noun phrase in question appears as a subject and can then be relativized:

kawan saya [*yang dipukul   oleh Ali*]   (61)
friend my   that hit-PASSIVE by   Ali
'my friend who was hit by Ali'

7.3.2 COMPLEX CONSTRUCTIONS

In section 7.3.1, we looked only at simplex sentences, and only at a single position at a time. However, one might venture to claim that the kinds of generalization made in section 7.3.1 can be extended if one also considers more complex constructions. In the present section, we shall examine two instances where this does indeed seem to be the case, but also some examples where there are as yet unsolved problems.

One obvious extension would be to arguments of subordinate clauses as well as those of simplex sentences. An extension that seems to be valid is that it will never be easier to relativize a given constituent of a subordinate clause than to relativize the same constituent of a main clause, e.g. it would not be easier to relativize the direct object of a subordinate clause than the direct object of a main clause. We could reformulate this as an implicational universal: if a language can relativize a subordinate direct object, then it can relativize a main clause direct object. There are languages where one can relativize both, such as English. There are languages where one can relativize neither, such as Malagasy. And there are languages like Russian where one can relativize main clause direct objects but not subordinate clause direct objects:

> devuška, [kotoruju   ja ljublju]   (62)
> girl   who-ACCUSATIVE I   love
> 'the girl that I love'

> *devuška, [kotoruju   ty   dumaješ', čto ja ljublju]   (63)
> girl   who-ACCUSATIVE you think   that I   love
> 'the girl that you think (that) I love'

In the absence of languages that can relativize subordinate direct objects but not main clause direct objects, the universal seems to hold.

A similar extension would hold with possessive constructions. In section 7.3.1, we simply asked in general whether it was possible to relativize possessors, without asking about the role of the whole noun phrase of which the possessor is a part, e.g. whether it is easier to relativize a possessor that is part of a subject noun phrase than one that is part of a direct object noun phrase. Again, there is evidence from languages in favour of this: for instance, in Malay, it is possible to relativize the possessor of a subject, but not the possessor of a non-subject:

> orang [yang abang   -nya memukul saya] itu   (64)
> person that elder-brother his hit   me   the
> 'the person whose elder brother hit me'

> *orang [yang saya memukul abang   -nya] itu   (65)
> person that I   hit   elder-brother his   the
> 'the person whose elder brother I hit'

However, there are also problems in generalizing these extensions, indicating that further work needs to be done in some of these areas. For instance, a reasonable extension would be to claim that subjects of subordinate clauses should be more accessible to relativization than non-subjects (just as subjects of main clauses are more accessible than non-subjects). However, all the evidence suggests just the opposite. In English, non-subjects of subordinate clauses are freely relativizable, while subjects can be relativized only if there is no conjunction:

the girl [*that you think (that) I love*]   (66)

the girl [*that you think (*that) loves me*]   (67)

In Hungarian, quite irrespective of conjunctions, subordinate subjects cannot be relativized, whereas non-subjects often can:

a   pénz,   [*amit*   *mondtam, hogy a*   (68)
the money   which-ACCUSATIVE I-said   that the
  fiú   elvett]
  boy took-away
'the money that I said (that) the boy took away'

*a   fiú, [*aki mondtam, hogy elvette   a   pénzt*]   (69)
  the boy who I-said   that took-away the money-ACCUSATIVE
'the boy that I said took away the money'

(*Elvette* is used with a definite direct object, otherwise *elvett*.) In Imbabura Quechua, it is possible to relativize a non-subject of an embedded clause using the gap type, but not the subject of an embedded clause:

[*Marya Juan wawa -ta   riku-shka*
  María Juan child   ACCUSATIVE see   NOMINALIZER
    -ta   ni -shka]   *llugshi-rka.*   (70)
    ACCUSATIVE say NOMINALIZER leave   PAST-3SINGULAR
'The child that María said that Juan saw left.'

*[*Marya warmi   Juan-ta   riku-shka*
  María woman Juan ACCUSATIVE see   NOMINALIZER
    -ta   ni -shka]   *llugshi-rka.*   (71)
    ACCUSATIVE say NOMINALIZER leave   PAST-3SINGULAR
'The woman that María said saw Juan left.'

There is thus good cross-linguistic evidence for the surprising generalization that subordinate non-subjects are easier to relativize than subordinate subjects, but apparently no good explanations as to why this should be so.

7.3.3 THE DISTRIBUTION OF RELATIVE CLAUSE TYPES

In section 7.2, we noted that it is often the case that a given language has more than one relative clause type, usually with at least some non-overlap between them. It has been observed that, in such instances, the distribution of relative clauses is not arbitrary. For instance, where the choice is between a pronoun-retention and a gap relative clause, it is nearly always the case that the pronoun-retention type is used lower down the accessibility hierarchy (or, more generally, in positions that are, cross-linguistically, less accessible), while the gap strategy is used higher up. As already mentioned, Persian uses the gap type on subjects and direct objects, the pronoun-retention type on direct objects, non-direct objects, and genitives (and also constituents of subordinate clauses and coordinate constructions). In Malay, the gap type is used for subject, the pronoun-retention type for genitives (and some non-direct objects, which are constructed basically as genitives). In English, pronoun-retention is marginal, but is used in some varieties for one of the least accessible positions, namely subject of a subordinate clause with an overt conjunction. This observation can probably be generalized somewhat: wherever a language has both a more explicit and a less explicit way of forming relative clauses (in the sense of section 7.2.3), then the more explicit type will be used lower down the hierarchy and the less explicit type higher up the hierarchy.

The generalization thus has a functional basis: the more difficult a position is to relativize, the more explicit indication is given of what position is being relativized, to facilitate recovery of this information. This is, of course, simply a generalization of the functional explanation already suggested in section 1.3.3.

NOTES AND REFERENCES

A useful source of information on relative clauses in a variety of languages is Peranteau *et al.* (1972). The Persian data are from Lambton (1957, 75–8).

The major work on constraints on movement transformations in English is Ross (1967). The critique of stating such constraints purely as constraints on movement (chopping), with discussion of the Zürich German and Persian examples, is from Keenan (1975, 406–10). Relative clauses in Basque are discussed by de Rijk (1972).

The characterization of relative clauses proposed in section 7.2 is based on Keenan & Comrie (1977, 63–4). The Walbiri example is from Hale (1976), which also discusses similar constructions in other Australian languages.

In section 7.2.2, the Bambara examples are from Bird (1968), and the Diegueño examples from Larry Gorbet (University of New Mexico, Albuquerque). The Imbabura Quechua examples here and below are from Cole (1982, 47–60). The classification in section 7.2.3 follows closely that of Maxwell (1979), itself based on Givón (1975a). The Korean examples here and below are from Tagashira (1972). In section 7.2.4, the Ancient Greek example is from Goodwin (1894, 220). The Hebrew example is discussed by Cole (1976, 244).

The discussion of section 7.3.1 is a simplified and revised rendering of Keenan & Comrie (1977); examples cited or referenced in this work or its companion (Keenan & Comrie, 1979) are not referenced again here. The positions indirect object and object of comparison, for which there is less cross-linguistic evidence, are omitted here. In the original, the hierarchy constraints are presented as absolute universals (with reservations over Tongan). The Kinyarwanda examples are from Gary & Keenan (1977). My understanding of the Malay examples has benefited greatly from discussion with Chiang Kee Yeoh (Universiti Sains Malaysia, Minden, Penang), and the examples are from Yeoh (1979); the discussion of Malay by Keenan & Comrie (1977, 1979) contains some unfortunate slips. The ungrammaticality of sentences like (67) (with *that*) is discussed by Perlmutter (1971, 99–122), but unfortunately his solution generalizes to neither Hungarian nor Imbabura Quechua, neither of which requires overt unstressed pronominal subjects.

8

CAUSATIVE CONSTRUCTIONS

Causative constructions have played an important role in the recent history of linguistics, not only from a typological viewpoint, and also represent an important area of convergence between linguistics and such adjacent disciplines as philosophy (the nature of causation) and cognitive anthropology (human perception and categorization of causation). Internally to linguistics, causative constructions are important because their study, even within a single language, but perhaps more clearly cross-linguistically, involves the interaction of various components of the over-all linguistic description, including semantics, syntax, and morphology. Outside typology, the study of causative constructions has been crucial in, for instance, the development of generative semantics. In the present chapter, however, our concern will be primarily with universals of causative constructions and typology of causative constructions, although this study does on occasion indicate why some of the questions posed by generative semanticists, on the basis usually of English data alone, remained unresolved within this framework.

In this chapter, we are concerned with various linguistic expressions of causation, and a useful starting point is a characterization of the causative situation (event) as a whole. Any causative situation involves two component situations, the cause and its effect (result). Let us imagine the following scene: the bus fails to turn up; as a result, I am late for a meeting. In this simple example, the bus's failing to turn up functions as cause, and my being late for the meeting functions as effect. These two micro-situations thus combine together to give a single complex macro-situation, the causative situation. In this case, it would be natural to express the macro-situation in English by combining the two clauses together, e.g. as *the bus's failure to come caused me to be late for the meeting*, or *the bus didn't come, so I was late for the meeting*, or *I was late for the meeting because the bus didn't come*. Very often, however, the expression of one of the micro-situations, usually the cause, can be abbreviated, giving rise to sentences like *John caused me to be late*: here, the effect is clearly that I was late, but the expression of the cause has been abbreviated, so that it is not clear what particular piece of behaviour by John caused me to be late. We may therefore generalize our definition of cause somewhat to allow that *John* in such a sentence can be treated as an instance of cause.

The characterization of cause given above is essentially independent of structural parameters, and there are in fact a number of ways of expressing such a causative situation in English and other languages, such as the use of causative or resultative conjunctions (*because*, *so that*) or prepositions (*because of*, *thanks to*), the use of a separate predicate of causation (e.g. the verb *to cause* or *to bring it about that*), or of a predicate that includes within itself the notion of cause, as in *John killed Bill* (which can be decomposed into a cause – some action of John's, not further specified – and an effect – Bill's death). Linguistically, however, it turns out that certain of these causative expressions are of greater interest than others, largely independently of whether the interest is primarily typological or not. In particular, most attention has been devoted to causative constructions where the notion of causation is contained in the predicate, either with a separate predicate of causation like English *cause* or French *faire* 'to make', or with causation as one semantic component of the predicate, as with English *kill* or Turkish *öl-dür* 'kill, cause to die' (cf. *öl* 'die'). It is with predicational causation of these kinds that we will be concerned in the present chapter.

As indicated above, one of the reasons for the recent intense interest in causative constructions is that their study involves the interaction of formal syntax and semantic analysis, and in many instances the correlation of formal and semantic parameters. In section 8.1 we will outline the major relevant parameters, turning in section 8.2 to their interaction on the basis of examples from a range of languages.

8.1 PARAMETERS IN THE STUDY OF CAUSATIVE CONSTRUCTIONS

8.1.1 FORMAL PARAMETERS

One of the main formal parameters, indeed often the only one found in early discussions of causative verbs, is the formal relationship between the expression for the causative macro-situation and the resultant micro-situation, i.e. the relationship between, for instance, *cause to die* and *die*, or between *kill* and *die*. On this morphological parameter, we can make a three-way typological distinction, although, as with many typological distinctions, forms in languages do not always fit neatly into one or other of these three types, rather a number of intermediate types are found. The continuum as a whole ranges from analytic causatives through morphological causatives to lexical causatives.

The prototypical case of the analytic causative is where there are separate predicates expressing the notion of causation and the predicate of the effect, as in English examples like *I caused John to go*, or *I brought it about that John went*, where there are separate predicates *cause* or *bring it about* (cause) and *go* (effect). Although such constructions are widely used by linguists, especially in glossing other construction types, in terms of frequency of occurrence cross-linguistically and even in terms of naturalness of use within individual languages, such pure analytic causatives are relatively rare. In Russian, for instance, it would be possible to say *ja sdelal tak, čtoby Džon ušel*, literally 'I did thus, so that John left', but this would be a very unnatural construction; the nearest natural constructions all express much more than simple causation, e.g. *ja zastavil Džona ujti* 'I forced John to leave', which implies direct coercion, and would be inappropriate, for instance, if *John* were to be replaced by an inanimate noun phrase.

Turning now to morphological causatives, the prototypical case has the following two characteristics. First, the causative is related to the non-causative predicate by morphological means, for instance by affixation, or whatever other morphological techniques the language in question has at its disposal. A simple example is provided by Turkish, where the suffixes -*t* and -*dır* (the latter with vowel harmony variants) can be added to virtually any verb to give its causative equivalent, e.g. *öl* 'die', *öl-dür* 'kill', *göster* 'show', *göster-t* 'cause to show'. The second characteristic of the prototypical morphological causative is that this means of relating causative and non-causative predicates is productive: in the ideal type, one can take any predicate and form a causative from it by the appropriate morphological means. Turkish comes very close to this ideal, since as indicated above one take pretty well any verb and form a causative from it, and can even form causatives of causatives: from *öl* 'die' we can form *öl-dür* 'kill', but we can then take *öl-dür* as the basis for this same process and form *öl-dür-t* 'cause to kill'. However, there are limitations on the iterativity of this process, so that long chains of causative suffixes, though occasionally found illustrated in manuals, are of marginal acceptability in the language. In this sense, there is probably no language that illustrates the pure prototypical morphological causative, with unrestricted iterativity of the relevant morphological process.

In the examples given in the previous paragraph, it was invariably the case that the causative predicate was formed from the non-causative, in the particular Turkish examples chosen by suffixation. However, it is also possible to find examples with the inverse derivational relation, where the predicate expressing the effect has more morphological material than the causative predicate, as in Russian *lomat'* 'to break' (transitive) versus *lomat'sja* 'to break' (intransitive), in which the suffix *-sja/-s'* derives the non-causative from an inherently causative simplex verb. Such derived non-causatives are sometimes referred to as anti-causatives. In Russian, then, we have pairs of sentences like the following:

Palka slomala-s'. (1)
'The stick broke.'

Tanja slomala palku. (2)
'Tanya broke the stick.'

In yet other cases, it is difficult or impossible to speak of any direction of morphological derivation. In Swahili, for instance, the intransitive verb 'boil' is *chem-k-a*, while the transitive verb, 'cause to boil', is *chem-sh-a*: here the effect verb and the causative verb simply have different suffixes, so that both are, in a derivational morphological sense, equally complex. Similar lack of directionality is found with suppletive pairs like English *die* and *kill*: while one may argue whether *kill* should be derived syntactically from *die* or not, morphologically the two forms are completely unrelated. In terms of the relation between expression of the effect micro-situation and the causative macro-situation, however, all of these subtypes can be treated together, although they will differ in degree of productivity (for instance, while the genuine derived causative may be a productive process, the derived anti-causative will not be, since one cannot iteratively reduce the degree of transitivity of a predicate: once it is intransitive, that is necessarily the end of the process).

Introducing the *die/kill* relationship in the preceding paragraph has brought us to the third type of causative in morphological terms, namely the lexical causative, i.e. examples where the relation between the expression of effect and the expression of causative macro-situation is so unsystematic as to be handled lexically, rather than by any productive process. The clearest examples here are of suppletive pairs, like English *kill* as the causative of *die*, or Russian *ubit'* 'to kill' as the causative of *umeret'* 'to die'. Suppletion forms the clearest instance of lexical causatives in that there is, by definition, no regularity to the formal relationship between the two members of the pair.

Although there are many instances in languages that instantiate these ideal types, or come very close to doing so, there are also many constructions that fall between the adjacent types on the continuum. An excellent example of a type intermediate between analytic and morphological is the French construction with *faire*, as in *j'ai fait courir Paul* ' I have made Paul run '. At first sight, this would seem to be a straightforward analytic causative, since we have separate predicates *faire* expressing cause and *courir* ' to run ' expressing the effect. However, as soon as one compares this construction with other constructions where there are clearly two predicates, the apparent clarity of this example dissolves. In general, where there are two predicates in French, each will take its own set of noun phrase arguments, as in *j'ai demandé à Paul de courir* ' I have asked Paul to run ' or *j'ai demandé à Paul de manger les pommes* ' I have asked Paul to eat the apples '. The verb *demander* ' to ask ' takes, in addition to its subject, an indirect object with the preposition *à*. In the infinitive construction, as usually in such constructions in French, the subject of the infinitive is omitted, but any objects required or allowed by the verb in the infinitive remain: *courir* is intransitive, but with the transitive verb *manger* ' to eat ' we find the direct object *les pommes* ' the apples ' in the above example. The *faire* construction is very different in that, despite the presence of two words *faire* and the dependent infinitive, this complex behaves for most purposes as a single compound predicate. For most speakers, it is not possible to insert noun phrases between the two components, so that even though one might expect a priori that *Paul* of *j'ai fait courir Paul* would be either object of *faire* or subject of *courir*, this noun phrase cannot intervene between *faire* and *courir*, even though an object of *faire* would be expected immediately to follow it, and a subject of *courir* immediately to precede it. In our example, the phrase *faire courir* behaves as a single complex, and *Paul* is the direct object of this whole complex, therefore quite naturally follows the complex as a whole. This becomes even clearer, as we shall see in more detail in section 8.2, when we consider transitive infinitives after *faire*, because the grammatical relation of the causee (the entity caused to do something) has to adjust to accommodate to the valency of the compound predicate *faire* plus infinitive as a whole. Since a transitive verb already has a direct object of its own, the causee in fact appears as an indirect object, as in *j'ai fait manger les pommes à Paul* ' I made Paul eat the apples '. Contrast this with the behaviour of the *demander* construction, where the person asked to carry out the action is invariably an indirect object, as required by the valency of the main clause verb *demander*.

In purely morphological terms, as we saw in section 2.3, the distinction between analytic and synthetic is a continuum rather than a clear-cut distinction, and here we see that even where, in purely formal terms, a construction may seem to belong clearly to one or the other type, further investigation of its behaviour may show it rather to be intermediate. More generally, one could typologize causative constructions in terms of the degree of reduction of the two separate predications (cause and effect) into a single predication, ranging from such pedantically explicit renderings as *I brought it about that John left* via *I caused John to leave* via *I had John leave* to French constructions of the *faire* type and so on to morphological causatives in the strict sense.

Likewise, there are constructions intermediate between the ideal morphological type and the ideal lexical (suppletive) type, in particular examples where there is a clear formal relationship between the predicates used to express effect and to express causation, but no regularity to this formal relationship. A good illustrative example here is Japanese, which has both canonical morphological causatives and causatives using a less productive morphological relationship. The canonical morphological causative uses the suffix *-(s)ase*, as in *sin-ase-* 'cause to die' (cf. *sin-* 'die'), *tomar-ase-* 'cause to stop' (cf. *tomar-* 'stop', intransitive), *ori-sase-* 'cause to come down' (cf. *ori-* 'come down'). In addition, however, many verbs also have a non-productively related causative, so that alongside *tomar-ase-* there is also *tome* 'stop' (transitive), and alongside *ori-sase-* there is also *oros-* 'bring down'. In Japanese, such non-productive causatives behave like canonical lexical causatives, e.g. like *koros-* 'kill' as a lexical causative of *sin-* 'die'. In other languages, however, there is often a difference in behaviour between suppletive and non-productive non-suppletive causatives. In English, for instance, many causatives can be formed without any morphological change to the verb, as with *melt* (transitive and intransitive). The relation between transitive and intransitive *melt* is not quite the same as that between members of a suppletive pair like *kill* and *die*, as can be illustrated by the following pair of sentences, where (3) is much more natural than (4):

> *John tried to melt the glass, but it wouldn't* (sc. *melt*). (3)

> **John tried to kill Mary, but she wouldn't* (sc. *die*). (4)

Thus the existence of a formal relationship, even though not productive, does facilitate identification of the causative and non-causative members of the pair for purposes of retrieval of omitted information.

As with other lexical relations, the semantic relation between putative causative and non-causative verbs is sometimes idiosyncratic, for instance with English *fall* and *fell*, the latter being much more restricted in meaning than 'cause to fall' – in non-metaphorical usage, *fell* is restricted to causing trees to fall. However, there are sufficient examples cross-linguistically of canonical and close-to-canonical lexical causatives where the meaning relationship is regular to make possible the inclusion of such causatives within a general typological study of causative constructions.

In addition to the classification into analytic, morphological, and lexical causatives, there is one further formal parameter that turns out to be crucial in the cross-linguistic comparison of causative constructions, and this is the grammatical encoding of the semantic relation causee in the causative construction, i.e. of *John/the tree/the vase* in *I caused John/the tree/the vase to fall* and in other ways of expressing the same basic meaning. As this is a fairly complex parameter, interacting closely with parameters to be discussed in section 8.1.2, a whole section, namely 8.2, has been devoted to this area of interaction, and discussion of the encoding of the causee is postponed until then.

8.1.2 SEMANTIC PARAMETERS

In this section, we will be concerned with two major semantic parameters, namely the distinction between direct and indirect causation and the problem of the degree of control retained in the causative macro-situation by the causee. There are also other semantic distinctions that can be made within causative constructions, but on which we will not concentrate here. One such parameter is, however, deserving of mention, namely the distinction between true causation and permission. In English, these two types are kept apart by the use of different main verbs in the usual analytic constructions, as in *I made the vase fall* (true causative) versus *I let the vase fall* (permissive). In many languages, however, especially in languages with a morphological causative, the same construction ranges over both true causative and permissive senses, as in Georgian:

Mama švil-s   *çeril -s*   *a-çer*
father son DATIVE letter ACCUSATIVE   write
-in-eb-s.   (5)
           3SINGULAR
'Father makes/helps/lets his son write the letter.'

(In this example, the prefix *a-* and the suffix sequence *-in-eb* marks the causative.) It is easy to see the relationship between true causative and permissive, in terms of our initial characterization of (true) causative. In both constructions, the anterior event (or its agent) has some control over whether or not the effect is realized: with the true causative, the anterior event/agent has the power to bring the effect about; in the permissive, the anterior event/agent has the power to prevent the effect from coming about. In both types, the realization of the effect is, at least partially, within the control of the causer/permitter.

In discussing semantic distinctions within causative constructions, much as in our earlier discussion of semantic roles in general in section 3.1, we are concerned solely with those semantic distinctions that have grammatical relevance in at least some languages. Since we are thus interested primarily in correlations between semantic and formal parameters, in the discussion below we will frequently refer back to the formal distinctions made in section 8.1.1, and forward to the discussion of formal–semantic interactions in section 8.2.

The distinction between direct and indirect causatives is concerned with the mediacy of the relationship between cause and effect. On the one hand, there are instances where cause and effect are so close to one another temporally that it is difficult to factor the macro-situation physically into cause and effect, even though it remains possible to do so conceptually. Thus if I am walking past the sideboard and catch the vase with my hand, thus causing it to fall from the sideboard, the relation between cause (my catching the vase) and effect (the vase's falling off the sideboard) is very direct. In other instances, however, the relation between cause and effect may be much more distant, as in the following scenario: the gunsmith, knowing that the gunfighter has a crucial fight coming up, ensures that the gun, which has been entrusted to him for repair, will fail to fire; some hours later, the gunfighter goes out for his fight and, since his gun has been tampered with, he is killed. The relation between cause and effect is very indirect, although nonetheless, there is an inevitable flow of events between the cause (the gunsmith's tampering with the gun) and the effect (the gunfighter's death).

Many languages have a formal distinction correlating with this distinction between direct and indirect causatives. Moreover, the kind of formal distinction found across languages is identical: the continuum from analytic via morphological to lexical causative correlates with the continuum from less direct to more direct causation. Thus if one were forced to establish different situations correlating with the difference between English *Anton broke the stick* and *Anton brought it about that the stick broke*, or their Russian equivalents *Anton slomal palku* and *Anton sdelal tak, čtoby palka slomalas'*, then one would probably do so by inventing, for the second example in each language, a situation where Anton's action is removed by several stages from the actual breaking of the stick. Similarly, in Nivkh, the lexical and morphological causatives of the verb *če-* 'dry' (intransitive) can be distinguished semantically:

If lep   seu-d'.   (6)
he bread dry

If lep   če -gu   -d'.   (7)
he bread dry   CAUSATIVE

In Nivkh, the morphological causative has the suffix -*gu*; in this particular example, the lexical causative involves a non-productive derivational process of initial consonant alternation. Example (6) simply states that he dried the bread, and would be most appropriate for a situation where the person in question deliberately set about drying the bread, for instance by putting it in the oven. Example (7), however, corresponds rather to 'he caused the bread to get dry' or even 'he let the bread get dry', implying, for instance, that he forgot to cover the bread, as a result of which the bread dried.

It must be emphasized that the distinction between direct and indirect causation is one of degree along a continuum. It is very difficult, and perhaps even impossible, to construct examples which clearly allow only a direct causation or only an indirect causation interpretation. But when one contrasts different causative constructions that differ on the analytic – morphological – lexical continuum, then it becomes clear that the construction closer to the analytic end is more appropriate for the distant (indirect) causative, while the one closer to the lexical end is more appropriate for the direct causative. Failure to recognize this engendered much unnecessary controversy within the generative semantics debate over the relation between English *kill* and *die*, with participants arguing back and forth as to whether *kill* and *cause to die* are or are not synonymous. To be sure, it is difficult to invent situations where one or other of these expressions would be excluded, but it is easy to invent situations, and more especially pairs of situations, where one of the two variants is more appropriate than the other.

The second semantic parameter that we wish to discuss is the degree of control retained by the causee in the causative construction. Since this semantic parameter interrelates in particular with the formal expression of the causee in the causative construction, most of the discussion of the formal–semantic interaction will be retained until section 8.2. Where the causee is an inanimate entity, as in *John caused the tree to fall*, this causee in general has no potential for exercising any control over the macro-situation, so that the question of control does not arise. Where, however, the causee is animate, there is the potential for a continuum of degree of control retained by that causee. If one takes an English sentence like *I brought it about that John left*, then this leaves quite unexpressed whether I got John to leave by direct coercion (e.g. by knocking him unconscious and carrying him out when he was in no position to resist), or whether I subtly played upon his deeper psyche in an attempt, ultimately successful, to persuade him to leave – in either case, I did something (cause) which had as its ultimate result that John left (result). Of course, in English it is possible to express such distinctions, by suitable choice of matrix verb, as in the difference between *I compelled John to leave, I made John leave, I imposed on John to leave, I persuaded John to leave*. In many languages, however, differences along this continuum can be expressed by varying the case of the causee. For the moment, we will content ourselves with an illustrative example, from Hungarian:

Én köhögtettem a gyerek-et. (8)
I caused-to-cough the child ACCUSATIVE

Én köhögtettem a gyerek-kel. (9)
I caused-to-cough the child INSTRUMENTAL

Example (8), with the accusative of the causee, implies low retention of control, and would be appropriate, for instance, for a situation where I slapped the child on the back, thereby inducing him to cough whether he wanted to or not. Sentence (9), with the instrumental, leaves greater control in the hands of the causee, implying, for instance, that I got the child to cough by asking him to do so. We leave open the philosophical question of whether the causee does in fact retain more of his own free will when he is persuaded to do something, rather than being forced to do it: at least, language does make this distinction concerned with degree of retention of control.

8.2 VALENCY CHANGES IN MORPHOLOGICAL CAUSATIVES

From a typological viewpoint, perhaps the property of causative constructions that has most interested linguists in recent years has been the valency of morphological causatives, in particular the grammatical encoding of the causee. There are two basic viewpoints that can be opposed on this question, although, as we shall suggest below, an over-all analysis of causative constructions seems to require aspects of both of these opposing viewpoints. The first viewpoint can be referred to as syntactic, and would argue that all, or at least much, of the problem to hand can be handled in purely syntactic terms, without recourse to semantics. The second viewpoint is semantic, and would argue that all, or at least much, of the problem to hand requires statement in semantic terms, with syntax playing a correspondingly smaller role.

Before turning to evidence for and against each of these opposing viewpoints, we may first note some of the universals of causative constructions that these two viewpoints address themselves to. We are concerned here with universal tendencies in the syntax and semantics of causative constructions, rather than with absolutes, but when one considers the logically possible range of variation that one might have found across languages, then the fact that the actual range of variation is so much smaller does stand out significantly.

The morphological causative normally has a valency one higher than that of the corresponding non-causative, since in addition to the arguments of that non-causative predicate there is also the causer. With analytic causatives this introduces no problems, since each of the two predicates, expressing cause and effect, retains its own set of arguments. With the morphological causative, however, the arguments of both semantic predicates have to be combined together into one single set of arguments on a single predicate. Cross-linguistically, this problem of valency increase is almost invariably solved by altering the expression of the causee. One simple solution is simply to omit mention of the causee from the causative construction, and this is particularly frequent as a possibility cross-linguistically in dealing with causatives of transitive verbs, as in the following example from Songhai:

> *Ali nga-ndi   tasu di.*　　　　　　　　　　　　　　　　　(10)
> Ali eat CAUSATIVE rice the
> 'Ali got someone to eat the rice.'

Omission of the causee does, of course, result in loss of information – in (10) it is simply unclear who was made to eat the rice – and no language seems to have this as its only possibility across a wide range of causative sentence types. Rather what happens is that the grammatical exponency of the causee is altered to fit in with the new over-all pattern of valency of the morphological causative predicate.

The pattern that emerges as the norm across languages here can be illustrated with examples from Turkish. In a non-causative Turkish sentence, the noun phrase corresponding to the causee is subject in the nominative, as in examples (11), (13), and (15) below. In the corresponding causative, the subject slot is already occupied by the causer, and since Turkish, like most languages, does not permit two subjects in a single clause, the causee cannot also be subject. Where the non-causative verb is intransitive, as in (11), then the causee appears as a direct object in the accusative, as in (12):

> *Hasan öl -dü.*　　　　　　　　　　　　　　　　　　　　　(11)
> Hasan die PAST
> 'Hasan died.'

Ali Hasan-ı   *öl -dür*   *-dü.*   (12)
Ali Hasan ACCUSATIVE die CAUSATIVE PAST
'Ali caused Hasan to die, killed Hasan.'

Where the non-causative verb is transitive, the direct object slot is already occupied by the direct object of the non-causative verb, so the causee cannot appear as direct object in a language like Turkish that permits only one direct object per clause, rather it appears as an indirect object in the dative:

Müdür mektub-u   *imzala-dı.*   (13)
director letter ACCUSATIVE sign PAST
'The director signed the letter.'

Dişçi mektub-u   *müdür -e*
dentist letter ACCUSATIVE director DATIVE
   imzala-t   *-tı.*   (14)
   sign CAUSATIVE PAST
'The dentist got the director to sign the letter.'

Where the non-causative verb already has an indirect object, then this slot is also unavailable to the causee – with reservations to be made below – and in Turkish, in such instances, the causee appears as an oblique object with the postposition *tarafından*:

Müdür Hasan-a   *mektub-u*   *göster-di.*   (15)
director Hasan DATIVE letter ACCUSATIVE show PAST
'The director showed the letter to Hasan.'

Dişçi Hasan-a   *mektub-u*   *müdür*
dentist Hasan DATIVE letter ACCUSATIVE director
~   *tarafından göster-t*   *-ti.*   (16)
   by   show CAUSATIVE PAST
'The dentist got the director to show the letter to Hasan.'

When the Turkish data are set out in this way, the formal solution to accounting for this distribution is clear. It requires the establishment of a hierarchy of grammatical relations, as follows: subject > direct object > indirect object > oblique object. The grammatical encoding of the causee proceeds as follows: the causee occupies the highest (leftmost) position on this hierarchy that is not already filled. Thus in (14), since subject is already occupied by the causer, and direct object by the direct object of 'sign', the highest remaining position is indirect object, and this is indeed how the causee is encoded. Although we will note below some counterexamples to this generalization, and some points that are not explained by this formal approach, it does still, we would maintain, remain the case that a wide range of properties of morphological causatives are explained by this hierarchy that are not captured by alternative accounts.

The hierarchy is very similar to that proposed in chapter 7, where we noted that accessibility to relative clause formation is determined by a hierarchy: subject > direct object > non-direct object > genitive. Clearly, the genitive is irrelevant to the discussion of valency of causative verbs, since it is an argument of a noun phrase, not of a verb. The only difference would then be the inclusion of indirect object in the causative hierarchy. Moreover, there is some, albeit slight, evidence from relative clause formation that indirect object should be included in the hierarchy, between direct and oblique object, which would then make the relevant parts of the hierarchy identical. (Note that we are using the term non-direct object to subsume both indirect object and oblique object.) There are, however, some problems with establishing this identity between the two hierarchies. First, there is the general problem of establishing indirect object as a valid grammatical relation: in Turkish, as far as we are aware, there is no independent evidence (i.e. other than the behaviour of causative constructions) for separating off indirect objects from the other non-direct objects. In many languages, it seems that causative constructions would be the only ones where indirect object is a relevant grammatical relation, and, as discussed in section 3.3, the language-internal justification of a grammatical relation really requires a number of logically independent parameters. Secondly, even if we assume the existence of a grammatical relation of indirect object, it turns out that the evidence for this position as relevant to relative clause formation is very marginal indeed: hardly any languages have indirect object as a clear cut-off point. Yet, in the cross-linguistic study of causative constructions, indirect object seems to be one of the best justified positions, the use of indirect objects to express the causee in the causative of a transitive verb being extremely widespread across the languages of the world. So, for present purposes, we will take a more cautious line, noting that there are close similarities between the relative clause and the causative hierarchies, without there necessarily being identity between them; moreover, we note that, if it should turn out that indirect object is not a grammatical relation in languages that use this construction for the causative of a transitive, then some other way (i.e. other than as a grammatical relation) must be found of characterizing this position on the hierarchy.

The next problem to consider with regard to the formal approach outlined above is that many languages allow doubling on one of the positions in this hierarchy. In Sanskrit, for instance, it is in fact impossible to express the causee in the causative of a transitive verb in the dative case, rather it must appear either in the instrumental (discussed below) or in the accusative, giving rise to constructions with two accusatives:

Rāmaḥ   *bhṛtyaṁ*   *kataṁ*
Rama-NOMINATIVE servant-ACCUSATIVE mat-ACCUSATIVE
   kārayati.   (17)
   prepare-CAUSATIVE
'Rama makes the servant prepare the mat.'

It turns out, however, that nearly all languages allowing this possibility in causative constructions are languages that otherwise allow clauses to have two accusative objects – it is even conceivable that one should say 'all languages' rather than 'nearly all languages', although there are some languages with this causative construction for which we have been unable to find evidence concerning non-causative constructions with two direct objects. When, however, we turn to indirect objects, then the possibilities for doubling are much more widespread, indeed it seems to be the case that every language that allows the causee to be expressed in the causative of a ditransitive verb construction allows doubling on indirect object in this position, so that even in Turkish we have, as an alternative to (16):

Dişçi müdür-e mektub-u Hasan-a göster-t-ti.   (18)

In some languages, such examples may be ambiguous (though in Turkish, the first dative is interpreted as causee), or stylistically infelicitous for other reasons in certain instances, but there is no doubt that they exist as possible constructions. The possibility of doubling on indirect objects in this way does not correlate with any possibility of having two indirect objects in a single clause, and is thus more directly a counterexample to the formal universal of causative construction formation as an absolute universal.

Although this universal cannot remain as an absolute universal, it does still remain as a strong universal tendency. Indeed, the claim can even be strengthened beyond this. As we noted in the previous discussion, doubling on subjects is unknown in causative constructions; doubling on direct objects is attested, but restricted; doubling on indirect objects is very widespread. In other words, the possibilities for doubling on a given grammatical relation increase as one descends the hierarchy. Presumably, no language that has oblique objects places a restriction of the kind that only one oblique object per clause is permitted.

In the discussion so far, when we have referred to oblique objects we have simply referred to them as a single undifferentiated class, but clearly, even for the restricted purposes of discussing causative constructions, this is inadequate. It is not the case in Turkish, for instance, that the causee in the causative of a ditransitive verb can stand as any arbitrary kind of oblique object, rather it must take the postposition *tarafından*. Likewise in French, such a causee must take the preposition *par* 'by':

> *J'ai fait écrire une lettre au directeur par Paul.*   (19)
> 'I have made Paul write a letter to the director.'

Not only is the choice of oblique not random within a given language, there is also a high degree of correlation across languages: the oblique object chosen is typically that used to express the agent in the passive construction, as with Turkish *tarafından* and French *par*. This obviously suggests an alternative explanation, other than the hierarchy, for the appearance of this particular oblique object in the causative construction, namely that the oblique object arises not through demotion down the hierarchy, but rather by the application of passive in the derivation of the causative construction. Both suggestions have a degree of initial plausibility. In what follows, we will argue that, although the passive analysis may indeed be appropriate for certain languages, it is not a general solution to all such cases, i.e. that demotion down the hierarchy must remain, at least for the present, as a possibility.

The possible validity of the passive analysis can be illustrated by using French data. First, we should note that with the causative of a transitive verb (i.e. even with a verb lacking an indirect object), French allows the causee to be expressed with *par*:

> *Jean a fait manger les pommes par Paul.*   (20)
> 'Jean made Paul eat the apples.'

This is therefore in violation of the formal hierarchy explanation as an absolute universal, which would predict demotion to indirect object only (which is an alternative possibility in French). The passive analysis, however, would predict the existence of sentences like (20), since in general in French any transitive verb can be passivized. The argument would thus run that the subordinate clause *Paul manger pommes* 'Paul to eat apples' is passivized to give *pommes manger par Paul* 'apples to eat by Paul', in which *pommes* is now subject of an intransitive construction. Construction (20) is thus causative of an intransitive, and by the regular demotion procedure the causee, *pommes*, ends up as direct object of the causative construction as a whole. One problem for the passive analysis is that, in French and virtually all languages that have a morphological causative, there is never any trace of passive morphology in the causative verb, i.e. it is impossible to say:

> **Jean a fait être mangées les pommes par Paul.* (21)
> ' Jean has made the apples be eaten by Paul.'

However, in many languages there are close correlations of detail between the passive construction and the possibility of a passive agent-like expression in causative constructions, down to idiosyncratic lexical restrictions on passivization, so that one might be prepared to overlook the morphological problem. And, indeed, for French, at least, the passive solution does have considerable plausibility.

There are, however, also some problems for the passive analysis. First, some languages, such as Hungarian and Finnish, allow the use of an oblique object for the expression of the causee even though they lack any passive constructions, or at least any passive construction that would express the agent in the same case as is used in the causative construction. This would require setting up a passive that occurs only in the causative construction, thus destroying any possible independent motivation for the passive analysis of causative constructions. More damaging to the passive analysis as a universal solution to oblique objects in causative constructions, however, is the fact that in some languages, of which Turkish is an excellent example, the expression of the causee as an oblique object is restricted to causatives of ditransitive verbs, whereas passive applies freely to the whole range of transitive verbs. In Turkish, it is not possible to replace the dative of (14) by a prepositional phrase with *tarafından*:

> **Dişçi mektub-u müdür tarafından imzala-t-tı.* (22)

In Turkish, then, demotion to the bottom position on the hierarchy takes place only when it is required to avoid two occurrences of a given grammatical relation; there is no such constraint on passive, which means that passive cannot be used, on its own, to account for the distribution of grammatical expressions of the causee.

Above, we noted exceptions to the demotion analysis as an absolute universal whereby the causee appeared in a position higher on the hierarchy than predicted, giving rise to doubling on some position. There are also exceptions occasioned by the appearance of the causee lower down the hierarchy than predicted. Some of these we have already noted, for instance French example (20), in connection with the passive analysis. In addition, some languages do not use the indirect object position on the hierarchy, but have a straight choice between direct object and oblique object for the expression of the causee. When we look at other violations of the absolute interpretation of the hierarchy, especially instances where alternative expressions of the causee are possible, then the relevance of semantic considerations becomes much more apparent. Before, therefore, looking at the data in more detail from both a formal and semantic viewpoint, we may outline how a semantic approach to the grammatical encoding of the causee might proceed.

The essential factor involved here is the degree of control exercised by the causee. As we noted in section 8.2, differences of control are most perceptible with animate causees. In many languages, there is, in addition to any correlation between morphological case and grammatical relation, also a fairly high correlation, often mediated by grammatical relations, between morphological cases and semantic roles. For instance, the accusative, as the basic morphological encoding of the direct object, typically refers to an entity with a very low degree of control. On the other hand the instrumental, or whatever case is used for passive agents, is frequently used for an entity with a high degree of control, especially in passive constructions, or elsewhere when the interpretation of the semantic role instrument is excluded. Dative, as the typical exponent of experiencer or recipient, occupies an intermediate position: experiencers are indeed low in control, though they still differ from patients in that they must be sentient; recipients even more clearly are intermediate, since in the situation *John gave the book to Mary*, while Mary clearly has less control than John (since John is the prime initiator), she does have some control, e.g. in being able to refuse the gift, whereas the book has none. One could thus establish a hierarchy: instrumental > dative > accusative, in terms of the degree of control (from greatest to least), a hierarchy which is remarkably similar to the formal hierarchy proposed above (for expository purposes, the two hierarchies are presented in reverse order).

Turning now to the expression of the causee: in general, the subject of a transitive verb has more control than the subject of an intransitive verb; many intransitive verbs express situations over which the subject has no control (e.g. *John is tall*), although there are of course many potentially controllable intransitive actions (e.g. *John went*); conversely, although there are subjects of transitive verbs with low degree of control (e.g. *John underwent an operation*), these are far less typical than those with control exercised by the subject. The fact that causees in causatives of intransitives go into the accusative, whereas causees in causatives of transitives go into the dative (or instrumental, in languages that do not use the dative) at least correlates very highly with the hierarchy given above: for the causee exercising greater control, choose the case higher on the hierarchy.

This viewpoint finds further confirmation when one looks at alternative expressions for the causee independent of the valency of the non-causative verb. The formal explanation based on the syntactic hierarchy has no explanation here: at best, it allows such alternatives as violations of what is, after all, only a tendency rather than an absolute universal. We find this kind of alternation with intransitive verbs, as for instance in the following Hungarian examples, where, as already discussed (see (8)–(9)), use of the instrumental rather than the accusative implies greater retention of control by the causee:

Én köhögtettem a gyerek-et (ACCUSATIVE). (23)

Én köhögtettem a gyerek-kel (INSTRUMENTAL). (24)
'I made the child cough.'

A similar distinction is found in Japanese, where *o* marks the accusative case; since Japanese uses *ni* for both indirect objects and passive agents, no formal distinction is possible here between the two:

Taroo ga Ziroo o ik-ase-ta. (25)
'Taroo made Ziroo go.'

Taroo ga Ziroo ni ik-ase-ta. (26)
'Taroo got Ziroo to go.'

The distinction is also found with transitive verbs in many languages. In Kannada, for instance, we find a contrast between the dative (less control) in (27) and the instrumental (greater control) in (28):

Avanu   nanage   bisketannu tinnisidanu. (27)
he-NOMINATIVE I-DATIVE biscuit   eat-CAUSATIVE
'He fed me a biscuit.'

Avanu nanninda (INSTRUMENTAL) *bisketannu tinnisidanu.* (28)
'He got me to eat the biscuit.'

Examples of this kind, where there is a consistent cross-linguistic correlation between alternative expressions and different meanings concerned with degree of control, make it clear that semantics must play some role in the cross-linguistic study of causative constructions, especially for linguists interested in universals and typology. However, this does not mean that this semantic explanation, at least to the extent that it has been elaborated to date, supersedes the syntactic account of causative constructions given above. There are still many aspects of the syntax of causative constructions that are not accounted for by the semantic explanation. For instance, there are languages like Turkish where semantic factors seems completely irrelevant to the expression of the causee: in the causative of an intransitive verb, it must be accusative; in the causative of a monotransitive verb, it must be dative; in the causative of a ditransitive verb, it may be either dative or with the postposition *tarafından*, though without any apparent difference in degree of control. There are many instances where there is no variation within a given language: for instance, variation between two expressions for the causee in the causative of an intransitive verb, though clearly attested in such languages as Hungarian and Japanese, is by no means a widely available choice in a wide range of languages, and even in these two languages there is no corresponding choice with causatives of transitives: here, Hungarian must use the instrumental for the causee, Japanese must use the postposition *ni*.

Another piece of evidence in favour of retaining at least some of the validity of the formal explanation for tendencies concerning cross-linguistic restrictions on the syntax of causative constructions is that the same morphology as is used to indicate causative in many languages is also used as a general indicator of increase in valency (and, likewise, anti-causative as a general indicator of decrease in valency), without any necessary connection with the semantic parameters of causative constructions. In Wolof, for instance, the suffix *-al* can indicate a causative:

> Di   naa   toog-al   nenne bi.   (29)
> FUTURE 1SINGULAR sit   CAUSATIVE child the
> 'I will make the child sit.'

However, it is also used to increase the valency of a monotransitive verb to ditransitive, e.g. to enable inclusion of an indirect object in the valency of the verb *dyàng* 'read':

> Mungi dyàng-al eleew yi   tééré -ém.   (30)
> he   read   pupil the-PLURAL book his
> 'He is reading his book to the pupils.'

Thus perhaps the main lesson of work on typology of causative constructions, in addition to specific results and methodological indications, is that any detailed approach to language typology, or indeed to any aspect of language, must combine formal and semantic viewpoints if it is to uncover all of the relevant factors.

NOTES AND REFERENCES

Two collections of articles providing a variety of data and viewpoints on causative constructions are Shibatani (1976a) and Xolodovič (1969). The introduction by Shibatani (1976b) in the former is a useful introduction to the whole area.

The general characterization of causative constructions given here is based on Nedjalkov & Sil'nickij (1969a). Discussion and exemplification of the morphological typological parameters is given by Nedjalkov & Sil'nickij (1969b). The Japanese examples are from Shibatani (1976b, 17). The Nivkh example is from Nedjalkov et al. (1969, 183).

The formal syntactic approach to valency change in causative constructions is introduced in Comrie (1975), and elaborated in Comrie (1976); many of the examples cited are from these sources. The importance of the semantic approach has become particularly clear to me through discussion with Peter Cole (University of Illinois at Urbana-Champaign); for Hindi data, see also Saksena (1980), and for more general information Shibatani (1976b). An earlier attempt to synthesize the two approaches, with rather different emphases, is Comrie (forthcoming, a). The Songhai examples are from Shopen & Konaré (1970). The Hungarian examples are from Hetzron (1976, 394). The Kannada examples are from Peter Cole (University of Illinois at Urbana-Champaign) and S. N. Sridhar (State University of New York at Stony Brook); for some discussion, see Sridhar (1976, 137–40) and Cole & Sridhar (1977), the latter arguing in particular against a passive analysis for the instrumental causee. The Wolof examples are from Nussbaum et al. (1970, 390–1).

9

ANIMACY

9.1 INTRODUCTION: THE NATURE OF ANIMACY

The present chapter, the last of those concerned with synchronic study of language universals and typology, is somewhat different from its predecessors, which were concerned for the most part with the examination of some particular construction type or formal phenomenon across a range of languages. In this chapter, the unifying theme is rather an extra-linguistic conceptual property, namely animacy, and we will be drawing together a range of formally quite different ways in which animacy manifests itself in the structure of different languages. Thus, whereas in earlier chapters we essentially worked from linguistic form towards generalizations, some of which have conceptual relevance, the method of the present chapter is largely the reverse. However, from another viewpoint, the material of the present chapter does fit very closely with that of preceding chapters: we argue that the reason why animacy is of linguistic relevance is because essentially the same kinds of conceptual distinction are found to be of structural relevance across a wide range of languages. Even though our initial intuitions about animacy may be non-linguistic – and this is an advantage, as they can be tested independently of linguistic reflections – consideration of a wide range of languages still provides a necessary underpinning to initial speculations or generalizations derived from the study of only a small range of languages.

As an initial characterization of animacy, we define it as a hierarchy whose main components, from highest to lowest degree of animacy, are: human > animal > inanimate, although, as we shall see, some languages in fact make use of less fine distinctions (e.g. human versus non-human, animate versus inanimate), or of finer distinctions. (Throughout, we use the term animal in its ordinary-language, as opposed to biological, sense, excluding humans.) Although most of our data will be from synchronic analysis of various languages, there is also comparable data from diachronic linguistics of animacy being relevant in language change, as we will note in several places in passing. This is particularly important in that animacy can be a relevant parameter in language change even where it is not particularly salient in the synchronic state of the language prior to the change, thus suggesting that animacy is a universal conceptual category that exists independently of its realization in any particular language. The discussion of Slavonic data below will be particularly relevant here, since the sudden emergence of animacy as a major parameter determining the case marking of direct objects is a radical innovation within this branch of Indo-European.

Although we use animacy as the cover-term for the material discussed in this chapter, and although the parameter with which we are concerned is clearly very closely connected with animacy in its literal sense, some of the particular examples discussed will require a slight extension of our notion of animacy in the narrow sense. In chapter 6, we introduced one structural area where animacy is relevant in many languages, namely case marking of A and P in transitive constructions, noting in particular that the existence of a separate accusative case frequently correlates with higher degree of animacy. However, some of the specific distinctions require us to go beyond this. For instance, it is frequent for first and second person pronouns to be treated as more 'animate' by this case marking criterion, although in a literal sense the first person pronoun *I* is no more animate than the common noun phrase *the author of this book*. Likewise, some languages treat proper names as being 'higher in animacy' than common noun phrases, although again strictly speaking there is no difference in literal animacy between *William Shakespeare* and *the author of 'Hamlet'*. For the body of the present chapter, we will simply leave this problem unresolved, to return to it in section 9.4, where we will offer some suggestions for a more accurate characterization of the hierarchy involved. To look ahead somewhat, we will suggest that in fact several different hierarchies are probably involved, although there is so much overlap between them that the similarities far outweigh the dissimilarities.

As has already been suggested in our discussion in chapter 6, for case marking, and indeed many other linguistic reflections of animacy, animacy interacts with other parameters, rather than being relevant entirely on its own, in many languages, so that a single phenomenon in a given language (e.g. the use of the postposition *ko* in Hindi) may require reference to both animacy and, for instance, definiteness, or topicality. This is one of the areas to which we will return in section 9.4. In section 3.1, we introduced the notion of control in our discussion of semantic roles. As indicated there, it is important to distinguish between animacy, which is an inherent property of noun phrases, and control, which is a relation contracted between a noun phrase and its predicate. In the present chapter we are concerned solely with animacy. Although there are some instances of inter-action between animacy and control in formal properties of language – for instance, in Bats (examples (1)–(2) of chapter 3), an ergative intransitive subject is possible only when that noun phrase is high in animacy (first or second person) and high in control – these seem to be relatively rare, and are not directly relevant to the discussion of the present chapter.

Another parameter which can, however, be relevant in the more general consideration of animacy and to which we will work in section 9.4 is that of semantic roles which are fixed as between noun phrase and predicate, as opposed to those like control which are subject to a continuum of in-terpretation. Thus we find many languages, some of them documented below, where the operation of verb agreement, or the interpretation of potentially ambiguous sentences, is determined by the degree of animacy normally assigned to a given grammatical relation, so that agreement is taken to be preferentially with an indirect object rather than with a direct object, preferentially with a benefactive rather than with an indirect object. For the moment we simply register the existence of such cases.

Finally, before turning to consideration of the data themselves, we should note that the correlation between the linguistic phenomena we are to discuss and the concept of animacy is very close, much closer than with many universal tendencies, but still it is not an absolute universal, so we must not be surprised to find individual examples in individual languages that go against the general trend. In many languages, even where a distinc-tion correlates highly with animacy, there is random distribution of some items between the more animate and less animate classes, as in the distri-bution of inanimate nouns in Latin among masculine, feminine (the typi-cally animate classes), and neuter (almost exclusively inanimate). We may find splits within noun phrases of a given degree of animacy that clearly are not themselves determined by animacy, as when, in Warungu, the special accusative case may be used optionally with personal proper names and kin terms, but only if they end in a vowel. And finally, we will find straightfor-ward exceptions, where an item behaves quite unlike noun phrases adjac-ent to it in the hierarchy. In English, the second person pronoun *you* has no nominative/accusative distinction, though this distinction is character-istic of high animacy noun phrases (cf. *I* – *me*), and is found lower down the hierarchy, with third person pronouns (*he* – *him*, and even *they* – *them*, which can have inanimate reference); having distinct singular and plural forms is again a characteristic of noun phrases with high animacy in languages that have a split, but English *you* is again exceptional, although even inanimate nouns have the distinction.

One parameter which, in this regard, participates in a rather ambivalent interaction with animacy is number. We are not prepared to make any generalization as to whether number raises or lowers the animacy of a noun phrase, even in the wider sense of section 9.4, and certainly there is a fair amount of evidence where number is relevant in either direction, suggesting that over all it is randomly, rather than significantly, relevant. Within Slavonic languages, for instance, one finds some languages, like Russian, where plurality increases the likelihood of a noun phrase taking the special animate accusative ending (cf. nominative–accusative singular *mat'* 'mother', nominative plural *materi*, accusative plural *materej*), but also languages like Polish, where plurality decreases the likelihood of a noun phrase taking the special animate accusative ending (cf. nominative singular *pies* 'dog', accusative singular *psa*, nominative–accusative plural *psy*).

9.2 PHENOMENA CONTROLLED BY ANIMACY

In morphology – whether one is talking literally about the actual forms of noun phrases, or including more generally alternative forms that can be used in a given construction – animacy seems to be one of the main parameters determining a split in the morphological system: examples will be cited in the detailed discussion below. Since in many instances the particular oppositions found seem to have no inherent connection with animacy, for example in that there is no reason why in Finnish *hän* should be the pronoun to refer to humans and *se* the pronoun to refer to non-humans, rather than vice versa, we might refer to these as arbitrary structural correlations of animacy. The fact that such arbitrary correlations are so widespread across languages is good testimony to the salience of animacy as a conceptual distinction, forming the basis of classifications even where there is no reason, other than its general salience, why it should.

With this we may contrast instances of splits where there does seem to be some motivation for having animacy as the factor controlling the split. For instance, in chapter 6 we saw that there is a relatively small number of recurrent parameters that control split case marking of subjects and direct objects, especially the latter, and that animacy is one of these; moreover, we provided an explanation, involving the nature of animacy, as to why the split should occur precisely the way round that it does. It is not just that animacy determines whether or not there is a special accusative case, but rather that a high degree of animacy determines that there will be a separate accusative case, never that this opposition will be lacking. In the detailed discussion of this section, we will examine a number of areas where animacy is relevant either as an arbitrary controller or as a motivated controller of a range of distinctions. The classification at the present time is necessarily provisional, since it may well be that with some example that at present seems arbitrary, it will in due course be possible to provide an explanation as to why the distribution should be the way that it is rather than the reverse. There are also some instances where a motivated correlation may be expected, but where we lack sufficient cross-linguistic material to justify this suspicion, to show that we do not have an accidental apparent motivation. One example would be the alternation between the dative and locative cases to express the P in Yidiny in the antipassive construction, where the dative is used with noun phrases of higher animacy, which may correlate with the greater tendency for animate noun phrases to stand in the dative (the case of recipients) than in the locative (the case of locations) in general. For the moment, we leave this open.

Since we have already introduced case marking, both in this chapter and earlier in chapter 6, we may briefly dispose of our discussion of it in this chapter before passing on to other areas. Some of the clearest evidence comes from Australian languages, especially with case marking of P of the transitive construction, where we find languages that have separate accusatives only for first and second person pronouns (e.g. Dyirbal), only for pronouns and proper names and kin terms (e.g. Gumbainggir), only for human noun phrases (e.g. Arabana), only for animate noun phrases (e.g. Thargari), as well as languages that have no accusative (e.g. Yalarnnga) and accusative for all Ps (e.g. Wanggumara). But although the Australian data are so clear, it should not be forgotten that languages in other parts of the world provide equally impressive evidence in favour of some or all of these cut-off points, as well as continua of case marking correlating with degrees of animacy. In Slavonic languages, for instance, either the distinction between human and non-human or that between animate and inanimate is relevant to the existence or not of a special, genitive-like accusative (often in conjunction with other parameters, some of which, like number and declension class, are not directly linked to the animacy hierarchy). In Hindi, the use or non-use of the postposition *ko* correlates with the degree of animacy (and also of definiteness), though with no clear cut-off point between human and non-human.

Continuing with noun phrase morphology, another opposition that correlates closely with animacy is the existence versus non-existence of a number distinction, the split invariably being that noun phrases higher in animacy have the distinction while those lower in animacy do not. This seems therefore to be a motivated correlation, perhaps reflecting greater human concern with entities of higher animacy as individuals, therefore countable, while entities of lower animacy are more readily perceived as an indeterminate mass. In Chukchi, personal pronouns, proper names, and certain kin terms have an obligatory singular–plural number opposition (the plural of a proper name has the meaning 'X and his associates');

non-human nouns have no number distinction in the oblique cases (i.e. other than the absolute, where all noun phrases distinguish singular and plural); other human noun phrases usually show no number distinction in the oblique cases, but they may do so optionally, i.e. they are intermediate between the first and second classes mentioned. In Mandarin Chinese, the personal pronouns necessarily show an opposition of number (e.g. *wǒ* 'I', *wǒmen* 'we', *tā* 'he, she', *tāmen* 'they'), while most other noun phrases do not, although some human noun phrases may (e.g. *péngyou* 'friend(s)', *péngyoumen* 'friends'). In many Austronesian languages, pronouns show number distinctions regularly, often with distinct duals (and occasionally trials) in addition to singular versus plural, whereas most noun phrases do not; within the noun phrases, a small number usually do show number, typically kin terms, and rarely if ever non-human nouns.

Although we are, for the moment, concerned primarily with noun phrase morphology, in connection with number distinction we may note in passing that a number of languages use singular verbs in agreement with plural noun phrases that are low in animacy, but plural agreement when the noun phrase is of high animacy, e.g. Ancient Greek, Persian, Georgian.

Several other specific case choices in languages are determined by the animacy hierarchy, although here it is not always obvious that any non-arbitrary correlation is involved. A particularly interesting set of oppositions is found in Chukchi, where there are three possible morphological encodings for the A of a transitive verb. The A form is always distinct from that for S or P, so the case marking system is consistently ergative–absolutive. With personal pronouns, there is a separate ergative case distinct from all other case forms, with the ending *-nan*, e.g. *yəm-nan* 'I'. For proper names and certain kin terms obligatorily, and for other human nouns optionally (and rarely, especially in the singular), the locative is used, with the ending *-ne* in the singular and *-rək* in the plural (where *-r* is the plural ending and *-k* the locative), e.g. *rintə-ne* 'Rintyn'. All other noun phrases use the instrumental, with the ending *-(t)e*, e.g. *riquke-te* 'ermine'. It will be noted that the distinction here follows exactly the same partition as number marking, mentioned above.

In Chukchi, this choice of different forms has rigid cut-off points, apart from the possibility of using either system with common human nouns. In Yidiny, however, one finds rather a continuum in the choice between dative and locative as the case to encode the P in the antipassive construction. Noun phrases with human reference must stand in the dative, but for all non-human noun phrases either the dative or the locative is possible, though with preference for the dative with noun phrases of higher animacy, and strong preference for the locative with noun phrases of very low animacy (e.g. stones).

More generally, in noun phrase morphology, one often finds different declension types, or different choices of items, correlating with degree of animacy. We have already noted that Finnish has different pronouns for human and non-human referents in the third person, human *hän* 'he, she', non-human *se* 'it', plural human *he*, non-human *ne* 'they'. In fact, only the human forms are genuinely personal pronouns, the non-human forms being demonstratives, a pattern found quite frequently across languages. English, of course, has a similar distinction, though with the added dimension of a gender distinction within human, in the singular *he, she, it* distinction. English likewise distinguishes human *who* from non-human *what* as interrogative pronouns, while Russian distinguishes animate *kto* (which thus includes animals) from inanimate *čto*. In Yidiny, as elsewhere in this language, we find a continuum of choice between two forms rather than an absolute cut-off point: with humans, one set of demonstratives, e.g. *ŋunʸdʸu-* 'that', must be used, while for other noun phrases one may use either set, e.g. *ŋunʸdʸu-* or *ŋuŋgu-* 'that', although the former is preferred the higher the degree of animacy of the noun phrase in question.

Turning now from noun phrase morphology to verb agreement, we find a common, motivated pattern across a wide range of languages: agreement is often carried out in such a way that the verb agrees with noun phrases higher in animacy, and fails to agree with those lower in animacy, even where this overrides, in particular cases or in general, grammatical relations, the usual determiners of agreement cross-linguistically. Above, we have already mentioned the failure of plural inanimate noun phrases to trigger plural verb agreement in a number of languages, and the present discussion can be considered an extension, albeit a considerable extension, of this observation. We return, in section 9.4, to possible explanations for this particular distribution.

In Tangut, verb agreement is optional, and can only be with a first or second person noun phrase. Where a transitive construction contains one first or second person argument only, then the agreement is with this noun phrase, irrespective of its grammatical relation. Grammatical relations become relevant only when there are two noun phrases of the first or second person, in which case agreement is in fact with the P rather than with the A. This illustrates one of the simplest kinds of system where hierarchical relation among noun phrases is more important than grammatical relations.

A more restricted, but equally clear, example is found in Chukchi. In Chukchi, in most tense-aspects, a transitive verb agrees with its A and P (which in Chukchi includes the patient, rather than the recipient, of a ditransitive verb). With ditransitive verbs, however, the situation is slightly more complex than this, but only with the one verb *yəl-* 'give'. If both patient and recipient are in the third person, then the usual P agreement rule with the patient applies, as in *tə-yəl-ɣʔan ərək* 'I gave it to them', where the verb shows first person singular A and third person singular P agreement, and the dative pronoun is third person plural, or *tə-yəl-nat ənək* 'I gave them to him', where the verb agreement shows a first person singular A and a third person plural P, and the dative pronoun is third person singular. If, however, the recipient is first or second person, then P agreement must be with that recipient rather than with the patient, as in *na-yəl-ɣəm* 'they gave it/them to me' (P agreement as with first person singular), *tə-yəl-tək* 'I gave it/them to you-all' (P agreement as with second person plural). Two further points should be noted in connection with these Chukchi examples. First, although agreement is with the recipient if first or second person, the appropriate noun phrase, if expressed, remains in the dative case, rather than being in the absolutive, the usual case for a P – the verb *yəl-* seems to be the only verb that allows P agreement with a noun phrase not in the absolutive. Secondly, in Chukchi it is impossible to have first or second person patients with the verb *yəl-*, so the question of what to do when both patient and recipient are non-third person does not arise.

In the examples of verb agreement looked at so far, the hierarchy of animacy (actually, non-third person versus third person) has overridden grammatical relations. Some languages, however, manage to retain both a rule stating agreement in terms of grammatical relations and have agreement preferentially with the noun phrase of higher animacy, by using voice distinctions to bring the appropriate noun phrase into a position where it can trigger agreement. In Chukchi, for instance, verb agreement in the so-called Present-II tense is on an ergative-absolutive basis, agreement being with S or P only. However, agreement is also with the highest of A or P on the person hierarchy 1, 2 > 3. When A is in fact higher than P, this necessitates application of the antipassive, with the prefix *ine-*, so that agreement can be with a derived S. Compare *nə-lʔu-muri* 'he/they see(s) us' with *n-ine-lʔu-muri* 'we see them', with first person plural agreement suffix *-muri* in both cases.

Related to the above-mentioned phenomenon of using voice so that a noun phrase can trigger agreement without violating correlations between agreement and grammatical relations is a more general phenomenon, found in some languages, whereby voice must be used to bring a noun phrase higher in animacy into subject position – irrespective of agreement possibilities. A neat illustration of this is provided by Southern Tiwa, again in the distinction between non-third and third person. In a transitive construction, if the A is first or second person, and thus higher than or equal to the P in animacy, the active construction must be used, in which case the initial agreement prefix on the verb will encode both A and P (in a fused form):

Bey   -mu -ban.   (1)
2SINGULAR–1SINGULAR see PAST
'You saw me.'

If, however, the P is higher in animacy than the A, i.e. the A is third person and the P is first or second person, then the P must be made subject by the application of passive; since the construction is now passive, agreement is with the S (original P) only:

Seuanide-ba   te   -mu -che   -ban.   (2)
man   INSTRUMENTAL 1SINGULAR see PASSIVE PAST
'The man saw me', literally: 'I was seen by the man.'

Where both A and P are third person, either active or passive may be used. Although the voice alternation does have repercussions for agreement, in that there is no agreement with the A in the passive construction, there is clearly no sense in which agreement can be seen as the sole motivation for the alternation, given that in the active there is agreement with both A and P in the fused prefix.

In Navaho, the passive voice, with the prefix bi- rather than yi-, is used whenever the P outranks the A in animacy, and is optional when they are of equal animacy; only the yi- form can be used when the A is of greater animacy than the P:

Diné 'ashkii y-oo'į.   (3)
man boy   see

'Ashkii diné b-oo'į.   (4)
boy   man   see
'The man sees the boy.'

At'ééd nimasi yi-diíłid.   (5)
girl   potato   burnt
'The girl burnt the potato.'

At'ééd nimasi bi-diíłid.   (6)
girl   potato   burnt
'The potato burnt the girl.'

Most of the clear examples of verb agreement conditioned by animacy given above in fact involved the distinction between non-third and third persons, rather than animacy in the strict sense, except for the observation that plural verb agreement occurs only with animate noun phrases in some languages. Just to demonstrate that other animacy distinctions can be involved in verb agreement, we may cite some data on verb object agreement in the ergative construction in Eshtehardi. The agreement system distinguishes two genders (masculine, feminine) and two numbers (singular, plural), with masculine and singular being unmarked. At least for the older generation of speakers, the gender distinction is quite consistently maintained where the direct object is animate, but is not maintained elsewhere. In the following examples, the object noun *asb* 'horse' is masculine, while *mādiuna* 'mare' and *siva* 'apple' are feminine:

Asb   arāši   -eš.   (7)
horse galloped-MASCULINE he-ERGATIVE
'He galloped a horse.'

Mādiuna arāšia   -š.   (8)
mare   galloped-FEMININE he-ERGATIVE
'He galloped a mare.'

Hasan-e   siva -š   bexārd.   (9)
Hasan ERGATIVE apple he-ERGATIVE ate-MASCULINE
'Hasan ate an apple.'

As regards number, agreement is again found only with animate direct objects, but only sporadically even there. Diachronically, this represents the interesting phenomenon of the loss of agreement being conditioned by the animacy hierarchy.

9.3   CONCEPTUAL ANIMACY DISTINCTIONS

So far, we have looked at various linguistic manifestations of animacy, and now it is time, true to our aim of finding correlations between linguistic and extra-linguistic parameters, to see what generalizations these linguistic data give about the nature of animacy. On the one hand, since we have already observed that there are instances where we have arbitrary exceptions to structural animacy correlations (as with English *you*), we shall disregard such exceptions from consideration in setting up the animacy hierarchy – though clearly, if a putative exception were to recur in a sufficiently large number of unrelated languages, this would suggest that it is not an exception and would cause us to modify the hierarchy accordingly. On the other hand, in order for a distinction on the animacy hierarchy to be made, it must be shown to be relevant in at least one (and preferably more than one) language, in addition to being conceptually valid. Distinctions which have been illustrated in the immediately preceding discussion of section 9.2 will not be illustrated again, though examples will be cited for other distinctions, especially finer distinctions within some of these classes.

One of the clearest distinctions, illustrated several times above and in chapter 6, is that between, on the one hand, first and second person (speech act participants), and third person, and this will turn out to be significant in section 9.4: although the speech act participants are necessarily high in animacy, because human, they are no more animate, in the literal sense, than are other noun phrases with human reference, yet their behaviour is differentiated. Another similar distinction that is found in many languages, and which is even more difficult to relate directly to animacy in its literal sense, is that between all pronouns on the one hand and non-pronouns on the other. This means, in effect, that a pronoun whose referent is low in animacy is actually placed higher than a noun phrase whose referent is high in animacy. One illustration of this was given above for Chukchi, where one class of noun phrases consists of all pronouns, irrespective of animacy in the literal sense. An even clearer example is provided by some Slavonic languages, in particular Russian, in which the special genitive-like accusative is used for all pronouns, including the third person singular neuter pronoun, whose referent will hardly ever be animate, and which replaces a neuter singular noun phrase which can never take the genitive-like accusative, cf. *ja otkryl okno* (accusative = nominative) 'I opened the window' and *ja otkryl ego* (accusative = genitive) 'I opened it'.

This last example, with the distinction being between pronouns and non-pronouns, also illustrates another point that will become relevant in section 9.4: the hierarchy, even as established in purely linguistic terms, is not a single linear parameter on which all individual noun phrases can be arranged. The pronoun/non-pronoun opposition in fact cross-cuts the human/non-human or animate/inanimate opposition.

A common linguistic reflection of animacy is a distinction between human and non-human, already illustrated several times above. In addition to this straightforward dichotomy, one also finds many languages where there is a division within human noun phrases (apart from any possible distinction involving pronouns). One common way for this distinction to work is for proper names and/or (certain) kin terms to be treated as higher in animacy than all other human nouns: individual examples were cited in section 9.2. Again, the referents of such noun phrases are not inherently more animate, in the literal sense, than those of common nouns, indeed frequently the same human being can be referred to either by a proper name/kin term or by a common noun. Chukchi actually makes an even finer distinction here: only kin terms expressing kinship relations to the speaker, and then only those referring to kin older than the speaker, are treated as being higher in animacy. In some instances with proper names, we again find cross-cutting of different features that are relevant in this area, so that, for instance, proper names referring to animals may raise such noun phrases of the hierarchy to be equal to or even higher than common nouns referring to humans. In Chukchi, proper names of reindeer behave like proper names of people, i.e. obligatorily show a number distinction and have a locative-like ergative, even though common nouns referring to humans rarely have these properties and common nouns referring to reindeer never do.

Another parameter which is sometimes found discriminating among human noun phrases is sex, the clearest examples known to us being from Slavonic languages, where male nouns often have the special genitive-like accusative where female nouns do not. In some instances, this has a functional explanation independent of the hierarchy, because in the singular most feminine nouns have an inherited accusative distinct from the nominative, and therefore do not require the separate genitive-like form. In the plural, however, feminine nominative and accusative have been identical since Proto-Slavonic, so here this explanation does not hold. Yet still one finds in, for instance, Polish that the genitive-like accusative is found for male human plural noun phrases, e.g. *widziałem chłopców* 'I saw the boys', whereas female human plural noun phrases have the same form as the nominative, e.g. *widziałem dziewczyny* 'I saw the girls'. In looking back to the emergence of the genitive-like accusative in Slavonic languages, it seems that an even more rigorous socially-based distinction existed in the early period, namely that the new form was used only for male, adult, freeborn, healthy humans, i.e. not for women, children, slaves, or cripples. While the treatment of children as lower in animacy than adults is found in several languages, this particularly restrictive reflection of high animacy is not one that we find widespread. (In early Slavonic, the names of supernatural beings were also treated as non-human, for whatever reason.)

Above, we also gave examples of the straightforward distinction between animate and inanimate noun phrases, but within the over-all class of animals we again find that some languages make finer distinctions. In some instances, these distinctions seem to be clear-cut, as in Ritharngu, where the special accusative pronominal affix is used for humans and higher animals, such as dogs and kangaroos, while this affix is not used for lower animals, such as insects and fish, and inanimates. In Yidiny, as discussed above, instead of there being a clear-cut distinction with animals, there is rather a continuum, with higher animals being treated as animate more often than lower animals, although without any absolute restriction against the more or less animate alternative with any particular animals. With many pairs of animals the distinction is clear, as between most mammals and insects, although for animals that are conceptually close in terms of animacy it might be difficult or impossible to rank them on the hierarchy. Although some animal names occur frequently in lists of higher animals in terms of animacy, such as *dog*, we are not aware of any detailed cross-language study that has been done on this subject.

Finally, we come to inanimates. Most languages seem to leave this as an undifferentiated class, or, if there is any internal distinction, these distinctions tend to be arbitrary (as far as we can see), as in the distribution of inanimate nouns among the three genders in the older Indo-European languages. However, there is one language where a very clear hierarchy of inanimate noun phrases has been found, and that is Navaho. In Navaho, inanimate entities that are capable of spontaneous motion are classified higher than other inanimates, the former including, for instance, wind, rain, running water, lightning. As noted above, when two noun phrases are almost equal in animacy, either the *yi-* or the *bi-* prefix verb form can be used; if we take the example 'the lightning killed the horse', then 'lightning' and 'horse' are considered sufficiently close to permit both variants, whereas with 'old age killed my horse', only the *bi-* version is possible, signalling a P higher in animacy than the A:

> 'Ii'ni'   łįį'   yi-yiisxį.   (10)
> lightning horse   killed

> Łįį' 'ii'ni' bi-isxį.   (11)
> 'Lightning killed the horse.'

> Shi-łįį'   są   bi-isxį.   (12)
> my horse old-age   killed
> 'Old age killed my horse.'

9.4   CONCLUSIONS: THE NATURE OF ANIMACY

Much of the discussion of this chapter has made it clear that animacy in its literal sense, i.e. a parameter extending from human through animal to inanimate, cannot be the entire framework within which our discussion must be carried on. Many of the relevant distinctions, such as between pronoun and non-pronoun, proper name and common noun, are clearly not direct reflections of animacy in its literal sense. In this concluding section, we will attempt – perhaps not too definitively – to give some indication of just what is involved as the conceptual background to the phenomena we have been discussing. Clearly, in many instances, animacy in the literal sense does give us a close approximation to the ranking of noun phrases that we find justified on structural grounds, so that it may well be the case that animacy in the literal sense will remain part of our over-all conceptual schema, rather than being subsumed into some other parameter of which it would be a special case.

We already know, for instance from the discussion of case marking in chapter 6, that it is quite frequent for a given phenomenon to be conditioned by more than one logically independent parameter, as with the combined effect of animacy and definiteness, so it should again not be surprising if this should turn out to be the case with what we have hitherto been calling animacy. In the following reflections, we will consider various alternatives to animacy in the strict sense, noting the strengths and weaknesses of each.

One suggestion might be that the hierarchy in question is not one of animacy but rather one of topic-worthiness. Assuming that we have independent evidence, for instance from analysis of discourse structure, of which noun phrases are more likely to occur as topics, then we can go on to ask whether this correlates closely with the animacy hierarchy as we have been presenting it. The result is a very high degree of correlation indeed. Agreement is almost complete, and can even be carried further in certain instances, for instance in assigning degrees of topic-worthiness to individual grammatical relations and semantic roles, as was suggested in section 9.1. However, there is one major problem for the identification of topic-worthiness and the animacy hierarchy, and this concerns the relation between first and second person pronouns. As presented above, there is no distinction between first and second person within the animacy hierarchy, and indeed this lack of distinction seems to be borne out by the data: if we look, for instance, at the rich array of data on case marking provided by Australian languages, then we find some languages where first person functions as if above second person, some languages with the opposite, and some languages where both are equal. Yet work on topic-worthiness suggests strongly that first person is more natural as a topic than second person, or more generally that selection of topics is egocentric. Thus topic-worthiness makes a distinction that is not justified in discussing linguistic reflections of animacy.

There is a second problem with treating topic-worthiness as the primitive underlying the animacy hierarchy. With animacy in its literal sense, we have extra-linguistic and even extra-conceptual evidence – i.e. scientific knowledge independent, by and large, of particular linguistic or cultural biases – in assigning degrees of animacy to individual entities. With degrees of topicworthiness, however, we have no such independent characterization, and so the question naturally arises: what is the basis of topic-worthiness? The danger here is of answering this question circularly, by citing as the bases of topic-worthiness precisely those parameters which are included in the animacy hierarchy. Thus it seems at least as likely that topic-worthiness is determined by the conceptual basis of the animacy hierarchy as vice versa.

A second possibility would be to try and reduce the animacy hierarchy to a hierarchy of individuation or, what is essentially the same, a hierarchy of salience. Salience relates to the way in which certain actants present in a situation are seized on by humans as foci of attention, only subsequently attention being paid to less salient, less individuated objects. Here we have the possibility of carrying out non-linguistically based perceptual tests, so in one sense, at least, the danger of vicious circularity is avoided. The degree of salience does indeed correlate highly with the degree of animacy on the animacy hierarchy, though again there are certain discrepancies. In particular, work on salience indicates that singular entities are more salient than plural entities, while linguistic reflexes of animacy provide no solid justification for transposing this to linguistic animacy: as we noted above, plurality sometimes facilitates and sometimes hinders linguistic reflexes of animacy.

The problem we found with topic-worthiness also rears its head here again, namely that salience is not treated as a primitive in itself, but rather as the result of the interaction of a number of factors, such as animacy in the strict sense, definiteness, singularity, concreteness, assignability of a proper name. Thus explaining the animacy hierarchy in terms of salience runs the risk of ultimate circularity when salience is itself explained in terms of the various primitives that go to make up the animacy hierarchy.

Our conclusion, then, is that the animacy hierarchy cannot be reduced to any single parameter, including animacy itself in its literal sense, but rather reflects a natural human interaction among several parameters, which include animacy in the strict sense, but also definiteness (perhaps the easiest of the other parameters to extricate from animacy), and various means of making an entity more individuated – such as giving it a name of its own, and thereby making it also more likely as a topic of conversation. The various individual parameters that we have discussed in this chapter are often closely related to one another, but there are also individual irreducible differences, and the over-all pattern is of a complex intertwining rather than of a single, linear hierarchy.

NOTES AND REFERENCES

Most of this chapter represents original ideas, which I have not previously put together in written form, and most of the references are therefore to data sources.

The factors controlling the genitive-like accusative in Slavonic languages, in addition to being described in comprehensive grammars of the individual languages, are summarized in Comrie (1978c). The Australian data on case marking are summarized, with references, by Blake (1977, 13–15). The various reflections of animacy in Chukchi are drawn together in Comrie (1979a). Data on animacy in Yidiny are from Dixon (1977, 110–12). Verb agreement in Tangut is discussed by Kepping (1979).

The Southern Tiwa data are from Allen & Frantz (1978). There is a rich literature on *yi*- and *bi*- in Navaho; the discussion here relies primarily on Frishberg (1972). The data on Eshtehardi are from Yar-Shater (1969, 237, 239). The Ritharngu data are from Heath (1976, 173).

The criteria of individuation are given by Timberlake (1977, 162). The hierarchy of topic-worthiness is discussed by Hawkinson & Hyman (1974).

IO

TYPOLOGICAL AND HISTORICAL LINGUISTICS

IO.I DIACHRONIC DIMENSIONS IN UNIVERSALS AND TYPOLOGY

If we observe similarities between two languages, then there are, in principle, four reasons why these similarities may exist. First, they could be due to chance. Secondly, they could stem from the fact that the two languages are genetically related, and have inherited the common property from their common ancestor. Thirdly, the two languages could be in areal contact: one language could have borrowed the property from the other, or both could have borrowed it from some third language, either directly or through the mediation of yet other languages. Fourthly, the property could be a language universal, either absolute or a tendency. For the linguist who is interested in comparative-historical linguistics, it is important to be able to distinguish among these four bases of similarity, because only in this way will he be able to establish adequately the relationships that hold among languages, so that, for instance, he will need to exclude similarities due to borrowing or due to universal tendencies in establishing genetic relationship.

Chance is, by definition, impossible to exclude as a potential factor, but we will assume that the languages in question show a sufficient range of logically independent similarities for the probability of this being due to chance to be minimal. This leaves the other three factors. Although historical-comparative linguists have generally been very careful, at least in principle, to distinguish between similarities due to common genetic origin and those due to borrowing, they have often been much less careful in distinguishing between either of these, especially common genetic origin, and similarities due to universals. One example of this will suffice as an illustration. In proposing the Uralo-Altaic family, which would include the Uralic, Turkic, Mongolian, and Tungusic families (each of which is in itself a well-established language family), early researchers often limited themselves to noting certain general structural similarities among languages of these families, for instance: the predominance of agglutinating, suffixing morphology, and the strong tendency towards verb-final, adjunct–head word order (with adjectives, relative clauses, and genitives preceding their head noun, and postpositions rather than prepositions). However, as we saw in chapter 4 on word order, there is a universal tendency for these parameters, in particular the word order parameters, to cooccur, so that the cooccurrence of these parameters within these four language families is not sufficient in itself to establish their genetic relatedness. The lesson of this example is that frequently recurring language types, whose cohesiveness is guaranteed by universal tendencies, cannot be used to establish genetic affiliation of languages.

In section 10.2 below, we return to the question of distinguishing genetic, areal, and typological factors, with particular reference to the second of these, in our discussion of areal typology.

Another way in which the study of language universals can be of relevance to diachronic linguistics is in setting limits to the potential for variation among languages. Clearly, if research on language universals suggests that a certain language type, though logically possible, is not in fact an actual possibility, then any reconstruction that sets up a language of this type as ancestor to attested languages must be rejected (or, of course, the universal must be rejected). Given the paucity of clearly established absolute universals, it is relatively rarely that this technique can be used in its strongest form, and what more frequently happens is as follows. Instead of absolute universals being used, universal tendencies are used in reconstruction, on the assumption that the reconstructed language is more likely to resemble one of the more frequently occurring types than to resemble some type which occurs only extremely rarely among the languages of the world. On this basis, for instance, one would be more likely to reconstruct a proto-language as SOV than as OVS, although both types are attested. This methodology brings with it the great danger that its reliability is only statistical, and the danger is particularly great with universal tendencies whose statistical validity is in itself relatively low. In section 10.3, we will illustrate some uses of this methodology, and also some of its dangers.

A more direct way in which one could tie in diachronic considerations to the study of language universals would be to look for universals of language change. For instance, it seems to be the case that there is only a relatively small number of possible diachronic origins for phonemic tone in a tone language, such as the influence of glottal properties of adjacent consonants, shift of stress (as in Serbo-Croatian), reassignment of syllable structure (as in some Scandinavian languages). If such generalizations can be established on the basis of a wide range of reliable data, then we can be reasonably sure that they can also be extended to the historical study of languages where there is no attested historical or comparative evidence for the origin of tone. So far, however, there are few, if any, reliable areas where universals of language change of this degree of strength have been established, and in section 10.3.2 we look critically at one suggestion that has been made in this area, concerning the possibility of reconstructing word order from morpheme order. Indeed, most of the work on reconstruction using results from universals and typology has been in the area of word order typology, testifying once again to the enormous influence, not always beneficial, that this particular area of typology has exercised recently.

In section 10.4, partly in order to end this chapter on a more positive note, we look at one area in particular where work from language universals and typology has proved useful in diachronic work, namely in providing an explanatory framework for diachronic changes involving grammatical relations, especially subjects (referring back to some of the material in chapter 5).

In discussing universal constraints on language change, there is one quite widespread myth that must be exploded, and this is the idea that the type of a language, however defined, is something mystical and immutable. This is sometimes expressed by saying that, while a language may and will undoubtedly change, both internally and as the result of contact with other languages, yet there are still certain basic aspects of its structure that will remain intact. There is undoubtedly no evidence in favour of this assertion, and numerous examples that go against it. The history of the English language, for instance, is a good example of a radical change in both morphological typology (drift from synthesis to analysis, with concomitant reduction in the degree of fusion), and in word order typology (establishment of subject – verb – object as virtually the only permitted word order): in terms of these parameters, it is hard to imagine two languages more different from one another than Anglo-Saxon and Modern English.

As a second example, this time clearly due to language contact, we may consider the introduction of the conjunction *ki*, borrowed from Persian (cf. Persian *ke* 'that') into Turkish. As we noted in chapter 7, with particular regard to relative clauses, Turkish in general does not have finite subordinate clauses, making use instead of various non-finite verb forms (verbal nouns, adjectives, and adverbs). Even though finite subordinate clauses are thus quite foreign to the basic type of Turkish, Turkish has nonetheless borrowed the conjunction *ki* from Persian and uses this conjunction in various subordinate constructions, competing with the native non-finite constructions, such as relative clauses (sentence (1)) and object complements (sentence (2)):

Bir zaman gelecek   ki, insanlar hür olacak.   (1)
a   time   will-come that people   free will-be
'There will come a time when people will be free.'

Herkes   bilir   ki,   dünya yuvarlak -tır.   (2)
everyone know that earth   round   is
'Everyone knows that the earth is round.'

This Turkish construction is an indispensable part of the modern
language. In many Turkic, Mongolian, Tungusic, Uralic, and Caucasian
languages of the USSR which until recently had only non-finite subordinate clauses, finite subordinate clauses are being used increasingly under
the influence of Russian and are even displacing the original constructions
in some instances. While purists may regret this infiltration, there is
apparently nothing they can do to stop it.

10.2   AREAL TYPOLOGY

It is well known that when languages come into contact, they tend to borrow
from one another, the most obvious instances of this being borrowed lexical
items. However, it sometimes happens that languages are in such intimate
contact that a wide range of similarities arise between them, often to the
extent that they seem to share more similarities with one another than with
languages to which they are genetically more closely related. In this section,
we will illustrate this phenomenon with two examples, the Balkan sprachbund, and Cushitic influence on the word order of the Semitic language
Amharic. Where we have a reasonably well-defined group of languages in
areal contact and sharing a number of common features that are not due to
common genetic origin, then it is obviously convenient to have a term to refer
to such a group, just as we have the term language family to refer to a group
whose similarities are due to common genetic origin. English, unfortunately,
does not have a convenient, accepted term for such a group, although
German linguists use the term *Sprachbund* (literally ' language-union '), and
this is often used as a technical term in English, as in speaking of the Balkan
sprachbund. In English, one could speak of the Balkan areal type, but it is
important to bear in mind that what is of interest here is not so much the
existence of a certain type, but rather of a geographically definable group of
languages that share this type : it is conceivable that one might discover some
language elsewhere in the world that, by chance, shared the characteristics of
the Balkan sprachbund; this language would adhere to the Balkan areal type,
but would not be a member of the Balkan sprachbund. For these reasons, we
retain the term sprachbund here.

Perhaps the initial impetus to areal typology came from the realization that languages spoken in the Balkan area, in particular Modern Greek, Bulgarian-Macedonian, Albanian, and Romanian, share a number of features in common which they do not share with other languages to which they are more closely related genetically, thus suggesting for the first time that there can be a reasonably well-defined geographically intact grouping of languages that share features in common that are not the result of common genetic origin, that are sufficiently unusual not to be the result of chance, and (though this we say with hindsight) that are sufficiently unusual typologically not to be a reflection of language universals.

The five languages mentioned above form the core of the Balkan sprachbund. Bulgarian and Macedonian are Slavonic languages, very close to one another, and we shall therefore often use the designation Bulgarian-Macedonian to refer to features common to both; exemplification here is from Bulgarian. The unravelling of genetic and areal factors in the case of Bulgarian-Macedonian is facilitated by the existence of the other Slavonic languages, and by the fact that we have texts in a Slavonic language, Old Church Slavonic, based on a dialect of the Bulgarian-Macedonian area from the end of the first millennium AD. Greek forms an independent branch of the Indo-European family, but given the existence of the widespread literary attestation of Ancient Greek, we can note those Balkan areal features of Modern Greek that are not found in the ancient language. Romanian is a Romance language, so we can compare it genetically with Latin and with the other attested Romance languages. Only for Albanian, another independent branch of Indo-European, do we lack any close basis for comparison, so that with Albanian we are not strictly in a position to determine which features are inherited or original innovations and which are due to contact with other Balkan languages. In Albanian there is, however, a major dialect split between the Geg (northern) and Tosk (southern) dialects, the former being somewhat less typically Balkan than the latter, so there is some basis for comparison. Some characteristics of the Balkan sprachbund also extend beyond this group of five languages, in particular to the Slavonic language Serbo-Croatian, especially in its Serbian (eastern) variety. All of the languages within the Balkan sprachbund are Indo-European, but they belong to different branches of Indo-European. Since, for most of these branches, we have historical and comparative evidence from other languages not within the Balkan sprachbund, we can establish that, indeed, we are dealing with similarities that exist within a group of languages that are in areal contact and which are not inherited from their common ancestor.

The Balkan languages share a number of features in common, including a wide range of lexical items, but for present purposes we will concentrate on a number of morphological and syntactic features, namely (a) the syncretism of genitive and dative cases, (b) the postposed article, and (c) the loss of the infinitive.

In each of the languages within the Balkan sprachbund (but not Serbo-Croatian), the same form is used to indicate both the indirect object (dative) of a verb and the genitive within a noun phrase. Thus in Romanian, both the genitive and dative of *fată* 'girl' are *fete*. In Albanian, *lum* 'river' has genitive-dative *lumi*. The adherence of Bulgarian-Macedonian to this type is particularly interesting. Whereas the other languages have case suffixes on a fusional basis, as in the older Indo-European languages, Bulgarian and Macedonian, uniquely among Slavonic languages, have replaced their case system by analytic means, in particular prepositions. However, the same preposition *na* (original Slavonic meaning: 'on, onto') is used in both dative and genitive functions, e.g. *na bəlgarija* 'to/of Bulgaria'. In Modern Greek, it is possible to use one form, etymologically deriving from the Ancient Greek genitive, in both functions, e.g. *tu anθrópu* 'of/to the man', although in dative function one can also use a distinct form, with the preposition *s(e)*, i.e. *s-ton ánθropo* 'to the man' (this preposition requires the accusative case).

The postposed definite article is found in each language of the Balkan sprachbund in the narrow sense except Modern Greek, which, like the ancient language, has a preposed definite article, e.g. *o ánθropos* 'the man'. In Bulgarian, we find *məž* 'man', *məž-ət* 'the man'. In Albanian, we have *lum* 'river', *lum-i* 'the river' (homophonous with the unarticled genitive-dative singular; for clearer comparison, note that the articled genitive-dative is *lumi-t*). In Romanian, we have *om* 'man', *om-ul* 'the man'. Serbo-Croatian again fails to share this phenomenon.

But perhaps the most striking phenomenon, from the viewpoint of most Indo-European languages of Europe, is the complete or widespread loss of the infinitive in the Balkan languages, as can be seen from the translation of 'give me (something) to drink': Romanian *dă-mi să beau*, Bulgarian *daj mi da pija*, Albanian (Tosk) *a-më të pi*, Modern Greek *dós mu na pjó*. The literal translation of each of these is 'give (to-)me that I-drink', i.e. in place of the infinitive we have a finite subordinate clause introduced by a conjunction. Loss of the infinitive is most thorough-going in Modern Greek, and almost as complete in Bulgarian-Macedonian. In Romanian, there is one verb, *a putea* 'to be able', which can still take the infinitive, though even here the alternative construction is more usual, giving rise to the alternants *pot bea* and *pot să beau* 'I can drink'. In Albanian, the Tosk dialects prefer finite subordinate clauses, while the Geg dialects prefer the infinitive, so that for 'if we wish to tell the truth', the Tosk would say *po të duajm neve të thëmi* (FINITE) *të vërtetën*, the Geg would say *me dashtë na me thânë* (INFINITIVE) *të vërtetën*. A similar distribution is found in Serbo-Croatian, where the eastern, Serbian, variety prefers the subordinate clause variant *želim da idem*, literally 'I-want that I-go', while the western, Croatian, variety prefers the infinitive variant, *želim ići* 'I want to go'.

These language-internal splits have a historical basis, easternYugoslavia and southern Albania being more closely linked culturally and historically to the Balkans than western Yugoslavia and northern Albania (for instance, eastern Yugoslavia is largely Orthodox in traditional religion, southern Albania is largely Muslim, while western Yugoslavia and northern Albania are largely Roman Catholic).

The introduction of the historical dimension in the last paragraph should remind us that the Balkan sprachbund, and indeed any other sprachbund, should not be regarded as something mystical which any language placed in the Balkans necessarily breathes in with the air: rather, these similarities do, presumably, have a historical basis, even if we are not at present able to ascertain this historical basis in all instances.The absence of historical documentation of Albanian is particularly unfortunate here, since it at least leaves open the possibility of attributing all Balkanisms to Albanian (explaining the unknown through the unknown). However, at least as a total solution, this suggestion can be rejected: it fails to account for the loss of the infinitive, since we know that Albanian, especially in its Geg variety, does have an infinitive, which at least suggests that the loss of the infinitive in Tosk is a more recent development, i.e. it is more likely that this phenomenon entered Albanian from neighbouring languages than vice versa.

With some of the Balkanisms, we can go some way to finding a historical explanation. The loss of the infinitive is one of the most promising here, since internally to the history of the Greek language this loss has a ready explanation. The Ancient Greek third person singular present and infinitive endings, in their Byzantine pronunciation, would have been -i and -in respectively, for the most widespread type of verb. However, loss of word-final -n would have merged these two forms as -i. In many instances, then, the infinitive would be formally identical with a finite verb form, and this identity, originally only in the third person singular, could have led to general replacement of the infinitive by finite forms in the other persons and numbers. Since Greek was widely used as a lingua franca during and after the Byzantine period in the Balkans, there was an ideal basis in widespread bilingualism for this feature to be borrowed into the other languages of the area.

Conversely, the merger of genitive and dative can hardly be a Greek innovation, since Ancient Greek had distinct genitive and dative cases, e.g. genitive *antʰrópou*, dative *antʰrópōi* 'man', and the modern language has replaced the latter by the preposition *s(e)*, which still exists as an alternative to the genitive-like indirect object. Conceivably, the impetus here could have been from Romanian, since in Vulgar Latin genitive and dative are identical in some declension types (cf. Classical Latin genitive-dative *mēnsae* ' of/to the table '), although this is more speculative. But in general, although we may not now be able to reconstruct all the historical stages leading to the emergence and spread of Balkanisms, it remains the case that the existence of these shared features is the result of development in one or other of the languages and spread as the result of bilingualism in the area.

Amharic is a Semitic language of Ethiopia, although it is spoken in an area which was once Cushitic-speaking. Although Semitic and Cushitic languages are ultimately related genetically, within the Afroasiatic family, this link is very distant, and Semitic and Cushitic languages are in many respects quite different typologically. One of these differences concerns word order. The Semitic languages, for the most part, adhere to the canonical VO (head–adjunct) type: their basic clause word order is either VSO (thus especially for the older languages, e.g. Classical Arabic) or SVO (as in many forms of vernacular Arabic); within the noun phrase, adjectives, genitives, and relative clauses follow the head noun; the languages have prepositions, and no postpositions. Cushitic languages show the precise inverse of this pattern, being canonical OV (adjunct–head) languages: basic clause order is SOV; adjectives, genitives, and relative clauses precede the head noun; the languages have postpositions rather than prepositions.

Presumably, the distant ancestor of Amharic, as a Semitic language, was of the head–adjunct type, like most Semitic languages, including many Semitic languages of Ethiopia (among them Ge'ez, also called Ethiopic, the church language of Ethiopia). However, modern Amharic has adapted almost entirely to the adjunct–head type, as can be seen in clause order:

ǝwru	*mɛṣaguwn*	*tɛšɛkkɛmɔw.*	(3)
blind-man	lame-man-ACCUSATIVE	carried	

' The blind man carried the lame man.'

Adjectives and genitives precede their head noun, as in *tɛnkolɛñña sɛw* ' cunning man ', *yɛmǝsalew tǝrgʷame* ' the parable's interpretation '. Although Amharic does still have prepositions, e.g. *bɛ Addis Abɛba* ' in Addis Ababa ' – one of the pieces of evidence for the earlier, more typically Semitic word order – it also has a wide range of postpositions, as in *Addis Abɛba lay* ' above Addis Ababa '.

The example of Amharic is important not only in its own right, as an illustration of a radical change in word order typology brought about by language contact, but also because it serves to re-emphasize the point made at the beginning of this chapter that the basic type of a language is not something mystical and immutable. Within a relatively short period of time, Amharic has completely reversed most of its basic word order patterns. To a native speaker of English, with its relatively consistent SVO word order, prenominal adjectives, postnominal relative clauses, etc., it might seem inconceivable that a language could so radically change its basic word order type. But this is viewed from the perspective of a language that is not, at least for the great majority of its speakers, undergoing any change as the result of contact with languages of a radically different type. The evidence from Amharic, and from many other contact situations, demonstrates just how unstable even canonical types are across the languages of the world.

In the light of the discussion of this section, where we showed how easy it is for a language to change in terms of basic typological parameters, and given also our knowledge that lexical borrowing is so easy when languages are in contact, the question might arise whether there is any constraint that can be placed on possibilities of language change, in particular when this change takes place as a result of contact: both principled word order correlations and arbitrary sound–meaning correspondences seem equally likely to undergo change.

One area where one might look for complete lack of susceptibility to language change is in the area of morphology, especially inflectional morphology, given that it might seem a priori unlikely that a language would borrow the inflectional system of another language, particularly if the two languages are not very closely related genetically, close enough to establish a point-by-point comparison between the old and the borrowed systems. However, this expectation, at least as an absolute expectation, is not borne out. One of the most discussed examples here is that of Ma'a (Mbugu), apparently originally a Cushitic language, but which, under contact with Bantu languages (it is spoken in a predominantly Bantu area in Tanzania), has adopted a Bantu inflectional system, in which both the forms of the affixes and their syntactic use (for instance, in concord) follow exactly that of neighbouring Bantu languages. In this particular case, the morphology of the donor language is basically agglutinating, so that at least segmentation is no great problem, which presumably facilitated the borrowing process. However, it is also possible for an inflectional system with widespread fusion to be borrowed, as when Yiddish, an off-shoot of German, incorporated many features of Semitic inflectional and derivational morphology in the process of borrowing a number of Hebrew–Aramaic lexical items with their various morphological forms, especially for nouns.

The remarks at the end of the previous paragraph, though in one sense apparently leaving the gate open for any kind of borrowing, do, however, also suggest an alternative method of constraining the possibilities for borrowing between languages. First, one could constrain this borrowing in terms of tendencies, e.g. by stating that although, in principle, anything can be borrowed, it is still more likely that lexical items will be borrowed than affixes, and more likely that clearly segmentable affixes will be borrowed than fusional morphology; and within the range of lexical items, one could go further, to say that nouns are more likely to be borrowed than other parts of speech. It seems, however, that we can tighten up these constraints somewhat, replacing these statements of tendencies by absolute (or almost absolute) implicational universals. Instead of saying that nouns are more likely to be borrowed than verbs, we can then say that a language will borrow non-nouns only if it also borrows nouns. Instead of saying that affixes are less likely to be borrowed than lexical items, we can say that a language will borrow affixes only if it also borrows lexical items from the same source. Indeed here we can probably be even more specific, and say that a language will only borrow an affix, as a segmentable unit in its own system, or a fusional morphological process as a productive process in its own system, if it has already borrowed forms of lexical items that contain the affix or fusional process in question. In Yiddish, for instance, Semitic morphology only entered the language as part of the general process of borrowing Hebrew-Aramaic lexical items, both singular and plural forms being borrowed into the language. In like manner, Yiddish borrowed the Slavonic suffix -*nik* by analysing previously borrowed lexical items with this suffix; and English in turn borrowed the suffix from Yiddish, cf. *beatnik*.

What this means is that, although the linguist interested in unravelling similarities due to common genetic origin and those due to contact will not be able to say, with respect to some individual phenomenon, that it must necessarily be due to one or other of these factors, where he has several different kinds of similarities and dissimilarities to work with, then he may be able to make firm or at least very reliable deductions concerning the distinction between common genetic origin and contact as the basis of language similarities.

10.3 TYPOLOGY AND RECONSTRUCTION

In this section, we will examine some of the ways in which results from universals and typology research, and more specifically from word order typology, have been used as the basis of new methods for reconstructing earlier stages of language families, in particular Proto-Indo-European, and to account for language change. The discussion of this section is, unfortunately, largely negative, in that the number of reservations that have to be made makes it questionable whether, to date, any solidly reliable results have been achieved in this area. However, the discussion is still valuable for two reasons. First, it indicates how one might in principle relate work on universals and typology to historical-comparative work, and hopefully ultimately some collaboration between these two disciplines will prove fruitful, even if not in the area of word order reconstruction. Secondly, applications of this methodology in word order reconstruction are so widespread that it would be unfair to close a chapter on typology and historical linguistics without discussing them, even if primarily to warn readers against too ready an acceptance of the results claimed in this area.

10.3.1   WORD ORDER TYPOLOGY

The major pieces of work attempting to relate word order typology and reconstruction of word order are by Lehmann and Vennemann. The two approaches share much in common, and for this reason we treat them together here, although where necessary differences between the two approaches will be outlined. The main applications of the methodology have been in the reconstruction of Proto-Indo-European word order, although in principle the methodology is applicable to any language family where sufficient historical or comparative material is available. In addition, the methodology has also been used to account for details of word order change in individual Indo-European branches and languages.

The basis of work in this area is the assumption of the two consistent (canonical) word order types, adjunct–head (operator–operand, OV) and head–adjunct (operand–operator, VO), which we outlined in chapter 4. It is assumed that these two types represent the most natural states for a language to be in, and that pressure to conform to these two ideal types is sufficient to initiate language change, i.e. if a language, for some reason, does not adhere to one of these two types, then change will be initiated to bring it into conformity with one or other of them. There is an initial problem here in that, although these two types are each more frequent (in terms of number of languages adhering to the type) than any other combination of parameter values, these two types do not in themselves exhaust or nearly exhaust the totality of the world's languages; indeed, it is probable, judging by Greenberg's original sample, that over half of the world's languages do not belong to either of these types. This makes questionable the extent of the alleged pressure to conform to one or other of the two ideal types: the pressure cannot be all that strong if over half of the world's languages do not conform to it. More specifically, there are some languages that appear to be quite stable in combinations that violate the canonical types, such as Persian, a head–adjunct language that nonetheless has stable verb-final order, and has been in this position for several centuries.

The fact that so many languages do not belong to the ideal types does of course have an explanation within this model: they are said to be in a process of drift from one of the ideal types to the other, i.e. any language that, synchronically, appears to be inconsistent is, diachronically, either changing from consistent adjunct–head to consistent head–adjunct or vice versa. The synchronic inconsistency stems from the fact that the various parameters are undergoing change at different rates. Again, we must note a number of conceptual problems with this aspect of the over-all model. First, the introduction of the notion of languages in drift between types means that the model no longer makes any predictions about the distribution of language types across the languages of the world. If all the languages of the world were inconsistent, then we would simply maintain that they are all in a process of drift. If they were all consistent, we would maintain that they have all achieved a state of equilibrium, or never departed from that state. Unless specific claims are made about the rate of drift, and the times at which the various drifts started in different languages or language groups, then we have no way of relating the observed distribution of language types to the predictions made by this theory. Secondly, this theory does provide an explanation for why, given the appearance of a typological inconsistency, the language should strive to drift back into consistency, but provides no explanation for why the inconsistency should have arisen in the first place – this is especially surprising given the alleged degree of pressure towards typological conformity. We return to this problem, which does have at least a partial solution, below.

Another assumption that underlies both Lehmann's and Vennemann's work is that Proto-Indo-European was a consistent language, in fact consistently adjunct–head. We return below to consideration of the factual basis for this assumption, for the time being concentrating on its validity as a methodological assumption. Presumably, it could be generalized to claim that any proto-language must necessarily be typologically consistent, although for present purposes we may restrict our attention to Proto-Indo-European. A priori, there is no reason to expect that Proto-Indo-European should have been typologically consistent, any more than we should expect this of any attested language. If over half of the languages at present spoken in the world are typologically inconsistent, then, other things being equal, we would actually expect a slightly greater possibility that Proto-Indo-European followed the majority, and was typologically inconsistent. One of the problems here is that of regarding Proto-Indo-European as the absolute starting-point of a developmental process. In one sense, it is of course, namely as the starting-point of the development of the various Indo-European languages. But given that language was spoken by man from long before the reconstructed date of Proto-Indo-European, this language must itself have been the end-product of a long period of development, and indeed we can gain some insight into developments before Proto-Indo-European by applying internal construction to the results of reconstruction by the comparative method. A proto-language, and specifically Proto-Indo-European, thus has no special claim to typological consistency, and there is no reason to suppose that Proto-Indo-European, whatever its cultural importance, was any more unique in this respect than any other language.

We may now return to the question of the impetus for departure from typological consistency, especially given our observation above that this impetus must have been very powerful, if it was to overcome the alleged strong pressure towards typological consistency. One possibility would be language contact, e.g. a language might borrow some word order feature from a neighbouring language, and then realign the rest of its word order parameters to match. This is a possibility – although it remains unclear, if typological consistency is so powerful, how a language could so readily abandon this consistency – but, as far as I am aware, this has not been suggested as the actual explanation of the shift from OV order in Indo-European. A second possibility would be that speakers of the language set themselves a target, the typological inconsistency simply being the intermediate stage in the achievement of this target. With respect to Proto-Indo-European, this would mean that, at some point, speakers of the language set a target of consistent head–adjunct typology, and over several millennia their descendants have been striving towards this target, although few of the daughter languages have in fact yet reached it: the Celtic languages are consistently head–adjunct, and the Romance languages close to being so, but most other branches, even with SVO word order in the clause, have inconsistencies elsewhere (e.g. English has prenominal adjectives, Lithuanian has prenominal adjectives and genitives). Although there are attested instances of drifts that take several generations to reach an apparent target, the length of time over which the putative adjunct–head to head–adjunct drift would have been operative in Indo-European languages would have to be measured in millennia. If a language can remain this long in an inconsistent state, then the pressure towards conformity cannot be that strong (and, incidentally, one would expect to find proportionately fewer consistent languages in the world).

A solution to this problem was proposed by Vennemann, who argues that the introduction of typological inconsistency arises through change in verb order, from sentence-final position to sentence-medial position, and that this change in verb order itself has an explanation. One of Greenberg's original universals, number 41, says that 'if in a language the verb follows the nominal subject and nominal object as the dominant order, the language almost always has a case system '. One specific instance of this tendency for SOV languages to have a case system is the frequent presence of a nominative–accusative distinction, correlating with that between S and O (or, in the terminology of chapter 5, in particular between A and P). Since many SOV languages actually have relatively free word order in relation to the order of nominal arguments of the verb, i.e. OSV is a frequent alternative word order for purposes of topicalizing the object or focusing the subject, the existence of a case marking system distinguishing subject from object clearly has a function, since word order is not itself sufficient. In addition to changes in word order due to pragmatic factors, it may also be possible to omit noun phrases that are recoverable from context, so that in the absence of a case marking system NP V would be ambiguous between subject or object before the verb.

Vennemann notes that over the history of the Indo-European languages, and perhaps more generally in language as a whole, there has been a tendency to erode the morphological system, so that by the time we get to modern English, French, or Welsh, there is no longer a nominative–accusative distinction for most noun phrases, and even in languages like German that preserve the distinction with some classes of noun it is lost with many others (in German, it is retained only for masculine singular noun phrases). The loss of the nominative–accusative distinction thus leads to increased ambiguity in a verb-final language, an ambiguity that can be circumvented if the verb, instead of being positioned sentence-finally, is positioned between subject and object, giving rise to SVO word order. Most SOV languages, even those that are often classified as rigidly verb-final (e.g. Turkish, Japanese), do in fact allow some leakage of noun phrases to the right of the verb, so all that would be required would be an increase in this possibility.

This scenario does, then, provide a mechanism whereby the typological inconsistency can be introduced in the first place. Thereafter, the pressure towards typological consistency leads to the other parameters being brought into line. However, there are still some problems, in particular data problems, that remain. First, there are some SOV languages that have no nominative–accusative distinction, and which therefore use word order as the basic carrier of grammatical relations, e.g. Ijo; indeed, it has been suggested that Proto-Niger-Congo, the ancestor of the family to which Ijo belongs, was an SOV language without case marking, so that under this theory the widespread drift to SVO in Niger-Congo languages would have no explanation. Secondly, when one looks at the occurrence of VO word order in modern Indo-European languages, this order is found in a number of languages that retain the nominative–accusative distinction, in roughly as many classes of noun phrases as Proto-Indo-European did: the

Baltic and Slavonic languages are particularly revealing here, especially Lithuanian, which has the most archaic case system of any contemporary Indo-European language. Thus even with this explanation for the initial departure from OV word order, however plausible it may be a priori, there are serious reservations about its validity in practice.

Finally, we may consider the factual question of whether or not Proto-Indo-European was a consistent adjunct–head language (or, conceivably, an adjunct–head language which was just beginning to drift towards head–adjunct). Unfortunately, the evidence is far from clear. Lehmann argues that Proto-Indo-European was adjunct–head, and draws on attested examples from the earliest recorded Indo-European languages to illustrate his claim. However, although such attestations can readily be found, it is also equally possible, for most of the early Indo-European languages, to find attestations of other word orders. All that the statistical facts indicate is that Proto-Indo-European probably had very free word order, as do most of the early Indo-European languages. In a critique of Lehmann's claims concerning Proto-Indo-European as an adjunct–head language, Friedrich argues, on the basis of actual statistical evidence from the early Indo-European languages, that there is at least as much evidence for basic VO order as for OV order, although he acknowledges that even posing this question makes a number of assumptions that may not be warranted, in particular that Proto-Indo-European had a basic word order. The differences in emphasis between Lehmann and Friedrich also stem in part from differences in importance attached to individual branches of Indo-European as more representative of the order of the proto-language, and here there is a great danger of circularity (e.g. one wants to show that Proto-Indo-European was SOV, so attaches more importance to early Indo-European languages where verb-final order predominates, like Sanskrit or Hittite, to the neglect of those where the evidence is less overwhelming, such as Homeric Greek). And Watkins, a third participant in the debate, argues that the question of Proto-Indo-European word order cannot be answered by statistical counting of word order patterns in early texts, especially given the freedom of word order in most of the early languages, but requires rather the identification of archaic, synchronically inexplicable, word order patterns, as the most likely source of evidence for the original word order: such evidence does favour OV.

An added problem is that, in addition to languages and branches which have gained head–adjunct (VO) characteristics over their attested history (such as the Germanic and Romance languages), there are also branches of Indo-European that have clearly increased the range of adjunct–head (OV) characteristics: in particular, a number of branches (Indic, Iranian, Armenian) have developed fairly rigid clause-final verb position during their attested history. While this can perhaps be explained as the result of contact (the Indic languages adopting this from Dravidian languages; the Iranian languages and Armenian from Turkic languages), it does undermine the empirical basis of the whole investigation.

In conclusion, we can say that investigation of Proto-Indo-European word order started out with the assumption that there has been a drift from adjunct–head (OV) to head–adjunct (VO), and sought an explanation for this drift. We now have an explanation, albeit subject to numerous qualifications that seriously compromise its validity – but the facts that the explanation is designed to explain tend to dissolve away as soon as they are subjected to further scrutiny.

10.3.2   WORD ORDER AND MORPHEME ORDER

In section 10.1, we noted that, if we could establish universals of diachronic change, then it would be possible to use these universals to constrain possibilities for reconstructing earlier stages of languages. In the present section, we will examine one particular suggestion that has been made in this respect, drawing mainly on work by Givón. As, unfortunately, throughout section 10.3, we will at almost every turn be counselling caution over the validity of the results obtained. However, the material of the present section does offer an insight into a potential manner of reconstructing word order that does not rely on the, to date, rather mystical notion of consistent word order type, but rather adheres more closely to the actual data.

The reconstruction process outlined in this section depends on three assumptions. The first is that verb agreement affixes invariably develop diachronically from pronouns. The second is that bound morphemes invariably derive from independent words. And the third is that, once a sequence of words becomes fused together as a sequence of morphemes within a single word, the order of the morphemes is thereafter not subject to change. If we make these assumptions, then it is possible to take synchronic evidence concerning the order of verb agreement affixes to reconstruct the word order of an earlier period. Let us assume that subject agreement affixes precede the verb stem. Then, by our first and second assumptions, these prefixes derive etymologically from subject pronouns. By our third assumption, the current order reflects the earlier word order, i.e. at the time when the subject pronoun was fused to the verb to give a subject prefix, the order must have been for the subject pronoun to precede. Generalizing the example, in a language which has agreement with subjects and objects, we can take the synchronic order of agreement affixes to reflect the original order of constituents. Thus, although most Bantu languages are synchronically SVO, the fact that agreement prefixes precede the verb stem in the order: subject, object, would indicate that the earlier order was subject – object – verb.

Unfortunately, none of the assumptions made above can be maintained as an absolute, and there is an equivocation in the term 'earlier word order' that seriously compromises the validity of the method. First, there are some instances where verb agreement affixes do not derive from pronouns. In Finnish, for instance, synchronically the third person plural suffix is -*vat*; etymologically, this is the plural of the present participle, and quite unrelated to any pronominal form. However, there are numerous instances where verb agreement affixes can be shown to derive from pronouns, so perhaps one could accept as a universal tendency that such affixes usually derive from pronouns: the generalization could then be applied, with a certain statistical reliability, to material where we are uncertain of the etymology of an affix.

Secondly, there are attested examples where bound morphemes do not derive from separate words. In comparing Estonian nominative singular *jalg* 'foot' and partitive singular *jalga*, it seems preferable, synchronically, to treat -*a* as the partitive singular suffix. Diachronically, however, this -*a* is part of the stem, which was lost in the nominative singular, but preserved in the partitive singular where it was originally non-final (see pages 47–8). Again, however, such examples are rare compared to those where the etymology of a morpheme can be reliably established as a separate word, so perhaps again we could accept this as a universal tendency.

Thirdly, there are known examples, albeit very rare, where the order of morphemes has changed after they became fused together, as when the etymologically expected morpheme order stem – superessive ('on') – possessive in Hungarian (cf. the frozen form *bennem* 'in me', for *bele-ne-m*, literally 'inside-at-my') was changed to stem – possessive – superessive, under the pressure of all the other cases (deriving etymologically from postpositions) with the order stem – possessive – case, to give, for instance *háza-m-on* 'on my house'. But again, we could accept that such inversions of morpheme order are rare, so that the methodology would retain a certain statistical validity.

The real problem, however, arises when we consider just what word order is being reconstructed. Rather than approaching the problem speculatively, we can illustrate the problem by looking at some actual data from Mongolian languages. Both Classical Mongolian and the modern languages are fairly rigid verb-final languages, at least as much so as Turkish or Japanese, the canonical examples of the verb-final type. The development of subject agreement in verbs is an ongoing process in the languages: some, such as Buryat, already have a fully-fledged set of subject agreement affixes, others, such as (Khalkha) Mongolian, do not. The subject agreement affixes clearly derive from the nominative pronouns. On Givón's hypothesis, since the almost invariable word order is for the subject to precede the verb, we would expect subject agreement prefixes to develop. In fact, subject agreement suffixes, and only suffixes, develop. This thus provides a clear counterexample to any absolute claim that one can reconstruct word order from morpheme order, even where it is known that the morphemes derive from words: from the subject suffixes one would reconstruct VS, and this is clearly not the basic word order of any Mongolian language.

However, we can make a further observation. In Mongolian languages (especially those without verb agreement), it is possible to place the subject, especially a pronoun, after the verb to de-emphasize that pronoun, thus giving rise to VS word order. It is precisely this word order that gave rise to the subject suffixes: if the subject were emphasized, then it would appear as a separate word, whether or not there is also verb agreement, so that it is natural that the verb agreement should derive from the de-emphasized subject pronouns in postverbal position. Thus, in a sense, the methodology is vindicated: the subject agreement suffixes do derive from subject pronouns placed after the verb. However, the significance of the methodology is almost totally vacuous as a result of this restriction: as originally proposed, it was supposed to enable us to reconstruct the basic word order of the ancestor language (e.g. that the ancestor of the Bantu languages was SOV), but in fact it only allows us to reconstruct a possible word order in the ancestor language, and the Mongolian data show that this may have been very much a minority pattern.

In this connection, similar reservations have to be expressed with regard to the oft repeated claim that the preverbal position of clitic pronouns in the Romance languages is evidence for earlier verb-final word order, i.e. (given that we know that Classical Latin was basically SOV) a relict of SOV word order. Detailed investigation of Medieval Latin and the early stages of the Romance languages shows that between the Classical Latin stage with basic SOV word order (including preverbal pronouns) and the stage represented by most (though not all) modern Romance languages with basic SVO word order but basically preverbal clitic pronouns, there intervened a complex of shifts including a stage with basic SVO word order whether the object was a noun phrase or a clitic pronoun. European Portuguese still positions clitic pronouns most frequently after the verb. Whatever the factors governing these various changes – and the problem can hardly be considered solved – the diachronic explanation for clitic pronoun positioning is more likely to be found in the stress rhythm properties of clitics, and certainly not as a relict of SOV word order.

10.4 TYPOLOGY AND DIACHRONIC EXPLANATION

One way of characterizing the methods proposed in section 10.3 is to say that they have attempted to set up a new all-embracing typological methodology in historical syntax. These attempts we believe have failed, for the reasons given above, i.e. primarily because of the large number of counterexamples which either falsify or reduce to vacuity the claims of the so-called typological method, and not because of any inherent contradictions within this methodology. There are, however, more modest claims that one might make concerning the relevance of typological studies to diachronic linguistics. In this section, we will show that results gained from typological studies can be of importance in understanding the mechanisms of syntactic change.

We have already indicated one way in which such relevance might be realized, in our discussion of animacy and definiteness in chapters 6 and 9. On the one hand, we have synchronic cross-linguistic generalizations, such as the observation that separate accusative marking and verb object agreement are more likely with noun phrases that are high in animacy or definiteness. This generalization can be taken further, however, since it also characterizes the diachronic acquisition or loss of accusative case marking or verb object agreement. When these rules enter a language, they often apply first to noun phrases highest in animacy, only subsequently spreading to less animate/definite noun phrases. Thus, in Slavonic, where the development of animacy as a morphological category is a spontaneous innovation vis-à-vis Indo-European, the separate accusative develops, first in the singular, for adult male healthy free-born humans only, spreading subsequently to all male humans, then to all male animates; in the plural, the rule first develops (and even then not in all languages, e.g. it is absent from Serbo-Croatian) with male humans, then extends to all humans, finally to all animates (as in Russian) (cf. page 189). In Eshtehardi, where verb object agreement is being lost, it is lost first with noun phrases of low animacy (inanimate noun phrases no longer show agreement), and the loss is now spreading to animate noun phrases (which typically show gender, but not number agreement) (cf. page 187).

For our detailed example in this section, however, we will examine a different example, namely the shift in subject properties (cf. chapter 5) in the possessive ('have') construction in Maltese. Maltese is, at least historically, a form of vernacular Arabic, and we can therefore compare the current Maltese construction with that of Classical Arabic (standing in here for Proto-Arabic). (Many other Arabic vernaculars have undergone changes similar to those described here for Maltese.)

The possessive construction in Maltese involves, in the present tense, the element *ghand*, which is identical to the preposition meaning 'at (the house of)'. In Maltese, prepositions take pronominal suffixes, e.g. *għandu* 'at his house', *għandha* 'at her house'. In strict locative use, this gives sentences like (4)–(9); note that there is no equivalent of 'be' in the present tense, and that verbs agree in person, number, and gender with their subject (*ktieb* 'book' is masculine, *ħobża* 'loaf' is feminine):

Il-ktieb għandu.   (4)
'The book is at his house.'

Il-ħobża għandu.   (5)
'The loaf is at his house.'

Il-ktieb kien għandu.   (6)
'The book was at his house.'

Il-ħobża kienet għandu.   (7)
'The loaf was at his house.'

Il-ktieb sa jkun għandu.   (8)
'The book will be at his house.'

Il-ħobża sa tkun għandu.   (9)
'The loaf will be at his house.'

At first sight, the possessive construction would seem to be identical to this, other than in word order:

Għandu ktieb.   (10)
'He has a book.'

Għandu ħobża.   (11)
'He has a loaf.'

However, as soon as one starts looking at the possessive construction in more detail, this superficial parallelism evaporates.

First, although this is not itself directly relevant to present concerns, for the possessive construction Maltese uses a different set of forms in other tenses, namely a form deriving etymologically from 'be' (cf. *kien* '(he) was', *sa jkun* '(he) will be') plus the prepositional suffix *-l* 'to' plus the pronominal suffixes:

Kellu ktieb.   (12)
'He had a book.'

Kellu ħobża.   (13)
'He had a loaf.'

> *Sa jkollu ktieb.*   (14)
> 'He will have a book.'

> *Sa jkollu ħobża.*   (15)
> 'He will have a loaf.'

Secondly, if we use a non-pronominal noun phrase in place of the pronoun in the locative construction, then the preposition *għand* simply governs the relevant noun phrase:

> *Il-ktieb għand Pawlu.*   (16)
> 'The book is at Pawlu's.'

> *Il-ktieb kien għand Pawlu.*   (17)
> 'The book was at Pawlu's.'

> *Il-ħobża kienet għand Pawlu.*   (18)
> 'The loaf was at Pawlu's.'

In the possessive construction, however, the possessor appears sentence-initially, and *għand* retains its pronominal suffix:

> *Pawlu għandu ktieb.*   (19)
> 'Pawlu has a book.'

> *Pawlu kellu ktieb.*   (20)
> 'Pawlu had a book.'

> *Pawlu sa jkollu ktieb.*   (21)
> 'Pawlu will have a book.'

> *Pawlu sa jkollu ħobża.*   (22)
> 'Pawlu will have a loaf.'

One cannot say, in this meaning, **għand Pawlu ktieb.*

Thirdly, in order to negate a sentence in Maltese, the preposed particle *ma* (*m'* before a vowel or silent consonant, e.g. *h* or *għ*) and the suffix *-x* are attached to the predicate-initial verb:

> *Il-ktieb ma kienx għandu/għand Pawlu.*   (23)
> 'The book wasn't at his house/at Pawlu's.'

If there is no finite verb predicate-initially, then the circumfix *ma* . . . *-x* is placed around a pronoun agreeing in person, gender, and number with the subject (e.g. *hu* 'third person singular masculine', *hi* 'third person singular feminine'):

Il-ktieb m'hux għandu.   (24)
'The book isn't at his house.'

Il-ħobża m'hix għandu.   (25)
'The loaf isn't at his house.'

The possessive construction, however, is negated by placing *ma* ... *-x* around the complex *għand-* (or, similarly, *kell-*) plus pronominal suffix:

M'għandux ktieb/ħobża.   (26)
'He doesn't have a book/loaf.'

Pawlu m'għandux ktieb/ħobża.   (27)
'Pawlu doesn't have a book/loaf.'

At first sight, the possessive construction *għandu ktieb* of (10) seemed to parallel exactly, apart from word order, the locative construction *il-ktieb għandu*. More detailed investigation showed a very different distribution of grammatical relations in the two constructions. In the locative construction, we have clearly a subject noun phrase ('the book/loaf'), either zero in the present tense or a finite verb agreeing with the subject noun phrase in other tenses, and a locative expression consisting of the preposition *għand* and its object (either a noun phrase or a pronominal suffix). In the possessive construction, the possessor – despite the locative form of, for instance, *għandu* – behaves as a subject: this is clearest when it is non-prominal, preceding *għand-/kell-/sa jkoll-* without any preposition. The possessive element (*għand-/kell-/sa jkoll-*) behaves like a verb, in particular in that it negates like a verb. Note, moreover, that it agrees with the possessor, although irregularly so: by means of prepositional object suffixes rather than by the usual subject agreement markers:

Pawlu għandu ktieb.   (28)
'Pawlu has a book.'

Marija għandha ktieb.   (29)
'Marija has a book.'

Finally, the possessive verb does not agree with the possessed noun phrase; this is clearest in the future tense, where one would expect **tkoll-* as the feminine of *jkoll-*, though in fact only *Pawlu sa jkollu ħobża* 'Pawlu will have a loaf' is possible, not **Pawlu sa tkollu ħobża*.

Summarizing the synchronic data of the Maltese possessive construction: the possessor noun phrase has nearly all subject properties, excepting only one morphological property, namely that it triggers prepositional object pronominal suffixes rather than subject verb agreement affixes; the possessed noun phrase has no subject properties. This is the converse of the locative construction, where the locative noun phrase has no subject properties, the located noun phrase all subject properties.

In Classical Arabic, the locative and possessive constructions are much closer to one another, the main difference being in preferred word order, and even here, arguably, the difference is determined by topic-comment structure rather than grammatical relations. The following are locative constructions:

> Ɂal-kitaabu ʕindahu.
> 'The book is at his house.'   30)

> Ɂal-xubzatu ʕindahu.   (31)
> 'The loaf is at his house.'

> Ɂal-kitaabu kaana (MASCULINE) ʕindahu.   (32)
> 'The book was at his house.'

> Ɂal-xubzatu kaanat (FEMININE) ʕindahu.   (33)
> 'The loaf was at his house.'

> Ɂal-xubzatu kaanat ʕinda Zaydin.   (34)
> 'The loaf was at Zayd's.'

The following are possessive constructions, using either ʕinda (the etymon of Maltese għand) or li (stem la-) (the etymon of Maltese -l):

> ʕindahu/lahu kitaabun.   (35)
> 'He has a book.'

> ʕindahu/lahu xubzatun.   (36)
> 'He has a loaf.'

> Kaana ʕindahu/lahu kitaabun.   (37)
> 'He had a book.'

> Kaanat ʕindahu/lahu xubzatun.   (38)
> 'He had a loaf.

> Kaanat ʕinda/li Zaydin xubzatun.   (39)
> 'Zaid had a loaf.'

(Note that nouns not accompanied by the definite article or other determiner take a final *-n*; the case ending *-u* on *kitaabu(n)*, *xubzatu(n)* is nominative, the case ending *-i(n)* on *Zaydin* is genitive, the regular case for a prepositional object). To see that word order is not a pure correlate of grammatical relations, note that the following is possible as a possessive construction:

> *Pal-xubzatu(kaanat) lahu/li Zaydin.* (40)
> 'The loaf is/was his/Zayd's.'

In Classical Arabic, then, in the possessive construction the possessor lacks virtually all subject properties, while the possessed noun phrase has subject properties, in particular triggering verb agreement (cf. masculine *kaana* versus feminine *kaanat*).

We can now characterize the historical development from Proto-Arabic (presumably the same, in these respects, as Classical Arabic) to Maltese as follows: in the possessive construction, subject properties have been transferred diachronically from the possessed noun phrase to the possessor, until finally the possessed noun phrase has no subject properties, while the possessor has all subject properties except the form of the verb agreement that it triggers. The seeds of this development are already present in Classical Arabic, which has, in addition to examples like (39), an alternative construction where the possessor is topicalized, standing sentence-initially in the nominative case:

> *Zaydun kaanat Ṣindahu/lahu xubzatun.* (41)
> 'Zayd had a loaf.'

While reanalysis of this topicalized construction as the basic construction is clearly at the root of the development of the current Maltese construction, note that in (41) little or no transfer of subject properties has yet taken place: in particular, the finite verb still agrees with the possessed noun phrase; in addition, type (39) exists as an alternative to (41) in Classical Arabic, thus allowing us to characterize the latter as an instance of topicalization, whereas in Maltese there is no such alternative to (19)–(22).

The discussion of this Maltese example illustrates three points. First, as already discussed in chapter 5, the notion of being a subject is not necessarily discrete, rather a noun phrase may have some subject properties while lacking others. Secondly, one possible (and, in fact, frequent) diachronic change is for subject properties to be transferred from one noun phrase to another, in many instances the transfer being gradual (some properties change before others) rather than all at once. Thirdly – and this is perhaps

the most important point – the change illustrated is motivated by a universal tendency of grammatical relations, not by the form of the construction.
We have already indicated how the apparent form of the construction, with
a locative preposition plus its object, is misleading for the later diachronic
stages, i.e. a reanalysis took place that went against the formal structure.
Note further that, in the possessive construction, the possessor is usually
high in animacy, while the possessed noun phrase is typically low. Given
the correlation between high animacy and topichood, and between topichood and subjecthood, this provides a promising base for the shift of
subject properties to the more animate noun phrase (i.e. the possessor) via
topicalization. The detailed historical development is thus in large measure explained by, and provides evidence for, a universal correlation among
grammatical relations, pragmatic roles, and inherent semantic features of
noun phrases.

NOTES AND REFERENCES

The most comprehensive account, with copious illustration, of languages
in contact is Weinreich (1953). A more concentrated introduction, with
special relevance to the present discussion, is Bynon (1978, chapter 6).

Standard works on the Balkan sprachbund are Sandfeld (1930) and
Schaller (1975). Ge'ez and Amharic word order are contrasted by Titov
(1959, 177–9). Ma'a (Mbugu) is discussed, with references, by Bynon
(1978, 253–5). Implicational universals of language contact are discussed
by Moravcsik (1978a).

Lehmann's approach to the reconstruction of Proto-Indo-European
word order can be seen in Lehmann (1974). The critiques referred to in the
text are Friedrich (1975) and Watkins (1976). For Vennemann's position,
see Vennemann (1974); for a critique, see Hawkins (1979). Word order in
Niger-Congo languages is discussed by Hyman (1975). Various problems
in and approaches to word order change are included in Li (1975).

Givón's views on the use of morpheme order to reconstruct word order,
with special reference to subject agreement, are contained in Givón (1976);
for a critique, see Comrie (1980). For a detailed consideration of clitic
pronoun positioning in early Romance, see Ramsden (1963).

The basic comprehensive discussion of acquisition of subjecthood is
Cole et al. (1980). The treatment of Maltese material is part of my own
ongoing research; for the data, reference may be made to the relevant
sections of such grammars as Aquilina (1965), Sutcliffe (1936).

11

CONCLUSIONS AND PROSPECTS

In this book, I have tried to illustrate some of the achievements of a method of studying language universals that uses data from a wide range of languages, and which tries to relate formal universal properties of languages to properties of language functioning in context. To drive this point home, I will mention a few of the more salient points, then turn to some problems and prospects for this particular approach to language universals.

There are several respects in which English is either atypical of the languages of the world as a whole, or in which English just represents one type among many others, and any approach which were to restrict itself primarily to analysis of English as a basis for uncovering language universals would be in danger of falling foul of these factors; it is my opinion that transformational-generative grammar, for instance, has indeed suffered in this way. Thus, English is a language with fairly fixed word order determined by grammatical relations, where moreover many syntactic processes can be described in terms of changes in linear order (whether or not this is in fact the best way of describing them). Other languages, as we saw in section 3.5, do not follow this type, and simple transference of a model that handles English syntax reasonably well often simply produces a distortion of the syntactic nature of those other languages. A universal syntactic theory – and I do not deny the possibility and desirability of such – must be sufficiently flexible to accommodate different syntactic types, without forcing the one into the mould of some other.

We can also find examples of a more superficial nature. In English, the only combination of person and number to have a distinct inflection in the present tense of regular verbs (and nearly all irregular verbs too) is the third person singular (in -s), which might lead one to conclude, on the basis of English data alone, that third person singular is the most marked combination of person and number. Yet consideration of a wider range of languages shows just how atypical English is here: the majority of languages with verb agreement show that third person singular is the least marked combination, and the situation found in English must be judged a historical accident. Another example of atypicality in English, which was noted in chapter 9, is the absence of a number distinction in the second person pronoun *you*, although all other pronouns and almost all other noun phrases do show this distinction. If one restricted one's attention to English, one might or might not consider this significant. Consideration of a range of languages shows clearly that it is not significant, and indeed it is no surprise that an individual isolated phenomenon in an individual language should go against an otherwise universal trend for number to be indicated more frequently in pronouns than in non-pronominal noun phrases. (Actually, even introduction of non-standard English would reveal a variety of attempts to create a distinct plural second person pronoun, e.g. *you-all*, *youse*, and even *unu*, a loan from Igbo, in Jamaican Creole.)

The importance of seeking explanations for language universals in terms of language in context can be seen by looking at examples where, from a formal viewpoint, two distributions would seem equally likely, but from the viewpoint of language in context only one is plausible, and this is precisely the one that is actually found. In section 6.2, for instance, we noted that many languages have a special accusative case used only for definite and/or animate Ps, all other Ps standing in the same case as A or S. From a formal viewpoint, it would be just as easy to write a rule that would assign a special case, distinct from that for A or S, for only indefinite and/or inanimate Ps, yet in fact we know of no language which has only the latter rule to the exclusion of the former, and very few languages which have the second rule in addition to the first. The explanation advanced in chapter 6 predicts precisely that we should expect the more frequently occurring distribution. Likewise, the pragmatic explanation given for the distribution of nominative–accusative and ergative–absolutive syntax in section 5.4 indicates that imperative addressee deletion should have a strong preference for nominative–accusative syntax, while resultative constructions should prefer ergative–absolutive syntax. Again, this distribution is borne out by the cross-linguistic distribution of data, although from a purely formal viewpoint it is as easy to write a rule based on ergative–absolutive syntax for one syntactic process as it is for the other.

While I believe that the achievements of this approach to language universals speak for themselves, there are also some problems inherent in this methodology. The linguist interested in language universals must, of course, when he is dealing with data from a wide range of languages, treat the data from each of these languages with respect, ensuring that they do in fact provide the evidence he claims they present, rather than forcing the data to fit the particular generalization he wishes to substantiate. Although this inter-relationship between the linguist interested in universals and individual languages imposes a duty on the universalist, I believe that equally it imposes a duty on those linguists whose primary interest is in the description of one or more individual languages. When a linguist publishes a grammar of a language, then he is making public the structure of that language, and while this may seem a truism, only too often do we find grammars of languages whose purpose is not so much to make data from the language available to the general linguistic public, but rather to try and make the language seem as mysterious and impenetrable to the outsider as possible. Work on linguistics, of whatever branch or whatever theoretical persuasion, requires reliable descriptions of languages, indeed reliable descriptions of a wide range of languages, if any progress is to be made by linguistics as the unified study of language as a general phenomenon.

In my final remarks, I want to indicate some ways in which the material used as data base in the present book is, perhaps unjustifiably, restricted, and also indicate some ways in which additional data might ultimately be incorporated into this discussion.

The discussion of the present book has been concerned exclusively with spoken languages (even if in their written form), and with languages as spoken by adults who have acquired these languages in childhood with native command. It is possible that data from languages other than these might provide insights into language universals and typology that could not be gained from the study of adult native spoken languages alone.

In seeking explanations for universals of spoken language, one obvious question that might arise is the extent to which these universals can be explained in terms of the medium employed. Thus, clearly many universals of phonetic structure are determined or facilitated by the structure of the human vocal tract and the nature of human auditory perception. It is conceivable that certain other universals of spoken languages might in turn correlate with properties of the medium, rather than, necessarily, with the human linguistic faculty at a more abstract level. Fortunately, we do here have a standard of comparison, namely various sign languages, which use a radically different medium. And there is at least some prima facie evidence that the difference in medium may condition some structural differences between spoken language and sign language, in particular American Sign Language: one such instance is the establishment of coreference relations (anaphora) between noun phrases (Friedman, 1976). In American Sign Language, if the sign relating to a given noun phrase is signed in a certain location within the over-all signing space, then making some other sign in, towards, or from that same location establishes coreference, so that one can indicate, for instance, that Bill, whose name last occurred some way back in the discourse, carried out a certain action by making the sign for the action in the same place where one previously signed *Bill*. In principle – and it remains an open question whether this possibility is utilized to the full in practice – this allows an indefinite number of entities to be kept track of in terms of their anaphoric relations, subject only to limitations on memory and discrimination of different locations within signing space. This is radically different from the usual means in spoken languages for keeping track of anaphoric relations, with a restricted set of pronouns.

One problem which I posed towards the very beginning of the discussion of language universals in chapter 1 is whether or not the set of attested human languages provides a potential representative sample of human language capability as a whole, or whether it has been too skewed by accidental historical circumstances. There is clearly no way in which we can ascertain this by observing actually spoken languages, no matter how many we take into our sample, but there is a possibility of studying this problem by looking at spontaneous innovation in language. One way of doing this was hinted at in chapter 6, where we saw that many languages, in the historical process of gaining or losing verb agreement or case marking, gain verb agreement first of all with nouns phrases of higher animacy, or gain accusative case marking first of all with noun high in animacy or definiteness, even where there is no language contact to account for this development.

Another area where one can study spontaneous innovation is in child language: if certain features recur regularly in child language which replicate language universals (tendencies or absolute universals) for which the adult language provides no evidence, then we can be reasonably sure that these are features of general language capacity that are not learned or acquired from the language environment. While this may seem to hark back to the orthodox transformational-generative view of innateness as the background to language universals, it does differ from this view in one crucial respect: it encourages the linguist who is interested in testing out this hypothesis to investigate child language and see how it differs from adult language, as opposed to the transformational-generative ploy of looking at features in adult language and arguing, or rather declaring by fiat, that these could not possibly have been learned by the child, while the actual child remains outside the purview of investigation.

Similarly, one could study the acquisition of a second language, to see if any universals are mirrored in its acquisition process, especially in cases where those universals are not the subject of direct evidence in either the native language or the target language. Recent studies of acquisition of relative clauses in English as a second language, for instance, suggest that students' order of acquisition follows the hierarchy described in section

7.3, even though English does not provide evidence for this differential accessibility (it allows relativization of all positions on the hierarchy), and even in instances where the native language also fails to provide the relevant evidence (Gass, 1980).

A final instance of nascent language is the development of pidgins. In some dialects of New Guinea Pidgin, for instance, a plural marker *ol* (deriving etymologically from English *all*) is beginning to be used obligatorily for certain classes of nouns. Since pronouns already have a number distinction, it is not surprising, given the universal that plural distinction is more likely higher up the animacy hierarchy, to learn that this marker is first made obligatory with human nouns (Mühlhäusler, 1977, 573) – even though there is no apparent motivation for this particular split in the indigenous languages of the area. In one sense, the inclusion of New Guinea Pidgin in this discussion is not a new kind of evidence: New Guinea Pidgin is a fully developed pidgin with a generally stable structure, so that acquisition of New Guinea Pidgin by speakers of other languages is more in the nature of second language acquisition than spontaneous creation of a new pidgin. Bickerton & Givón (1976), in reconstructing early stages in the development of Hawaiian Pidgin, give clearer independent evidence for the relevance of the development of pidgins to our present concern: in the development of Hawaiian Pidgin, participated in by speakers of an SOV language (Japanese) and several verb-initial Philippine languages, the topic-worthiness of noun phrases proves to be one of the main factors governing changes in word order, with greater probability of preposing of noun phrases that would be more likely to undergo marked topicalization.

All in all, the approach to language universals and language typology advocated in the present book is exciting not only because of the wealth of information it provides on principles of language structure, but also because of the wide range of implications for fruitful collaboration with a number of other disciplines, in particular those that study the context within which language structure functions.

LOCATION OF LANGUAGES CITED

Numbers identify approximate centre of area of traditional use of each language; geographical extent is not indicated. Numbers indicating extinct languages are in parentheses.

1 Eskimo, Siberian Yupik	22 German
2 Salishan languages	23 German, Zürich
3 Fox	(24) Latin
4 American Sign Language	25 Maltese
5 Navaho	26 Finnish
6 Tiwa, Southern	27 Estonian
7 Chickasaw	28 Lithuanian
8 Diegueño	29 Polish
9 Huichol	30 Yiddish
10 Jamaican Creole	31 Czech
11 Quechua, Imbabura	32 Hungarian
12 Hixkaryana	33 Serbo-Croatian
13 Irish	34 Romanian
14 Welsh	35 Albanian
15 English	36 Macedonian
(16) Anglo-Saxon	(37) Old Church Slavonic
17 Frisian, North	38 Bulgarian
18 French	39 Greek
19 Basque	40 Russian
20 Spanish	41 Georgian
21 Portuguese	42 Armenian

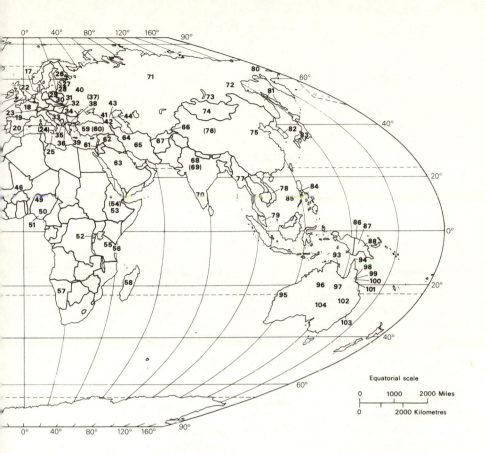

Equatorial scale

0   1000   2000 Miles

0   2000 Kilometres

3 Bats	64 Eshtehardi	85 Hanunoo
4 Lak	65 Persian	86 Arapesh
5 Wolof	66 Roshani	87 New Guinea Pidgin
6 Songhai	67 Burushaski	88 Hua
7 Bambara	68 Hindi	89 Hawaiian
8 Kpelle	(69) Sanskrit	90 Hawaiian Pidgin
9 Hausa	70 Kannada	91 Tongan
0 Igbo	71 Ket	92 Easter Island
1 Ijo	72 Tungusic languages	93 Ritharngu
2 Kinyarwanda	73 Buryat	94 Kalaw Lagaw Ya
3 Amharic	74 Mongolian	95 Thargari
4) Ge'ez	75 Chinese, Mandarin	96 Walbiri
5 Ma'a	(76) Tangut	97 Yalarnnga
6 Swahili	77 Burmese	98 Mbabaram
7 Khoisan languages	78 Vietnamese	99 Yidiny
8 Malagasy	79 Malay	100 Dyirbal
9 Turkish	80 Chukchi	101 Warungu
0) Hittite	81 Nivkh	102 Wanggumara
1 Hebrew	82 Korean	103 Gumbainggir
2 Aramaic	83 Japanese	104 Arabana
3 Arabic	84 Tagalog	105 Papago

REFERENCES

ALLEN, Barbara J. & FRANTZ, Donald G. 1978: Verb agreement in Southern Tiwa. *Proceedings of the Fourth Annual Meeting of the Berkeley Linguistics Society* (Berkeley: Department of Linguistics, University of California) 11–17.

ALTMANN, Gabriel & LEHFELDT, Werner 1973: *Allgemeine Sprachtypologie.* Uni-Taschenbücher 250. Munich: Wilhelm Fink.

AQUILINA, Joseph 1965: *Maltese.* Teach Yourself Books. London: English University Press.

Arbeiten des Kölner Universalien-Projekts (AKUP). Cologne: Institut für Sprachwissenschaft der Universität Köln.

BABBY, Leonard H. 1980: The syntax of surface case marking. *Cornell Working Papers in Linguistics* 1 (Department of Modern Languages and Linguistics, Cornell University) 1–32.

BACH, Emmon 1965: On some recurrent types of transformations. In Kreidler, Charles W., editor, *Georgetown University Monograph Series on Languages and Linguistics* 18 (Washington, D.C.: Georgetown University Press) 3–18.

BELL, Alan 1978: Language samples. In Greenberg *et al.* (1978), 1, 123–56.

BERLIN, Brent & KAY, Paul 1969: *Basic color terms: their universality and evolution.* Berkeley: University of California Press.

BICKERTON, Derek & GIVÓN, Talmy 1976: Pidginization and syntactic change: from SXV and VSX to SVX. In Steever, Sanford B., Walker, Carol A., & Mufwene, Salikoko S., editors, *Papers from the Parasession on Diachronic Syntax* (Chicago: Chicago Linguistic Society) 9–39.

BIRD, Charles 1968: Relative clauses in Bambara. *Journal of West African Languages* 5, 35–47.

BLAKE, Barry J. 1977: *Case marking in Australian languages.* Linguistic Series 23. Canberra: Australian Institute of Aboriginal Studies.

BROWNE, Wayles 1974: On the problem of enclitic placement in Serbo-Croatian. In Brecht, Richard D. & Chvany, Catherine V., editors, *Slavic transformational syntax.* Michigan Slavic Materials 10 (Ann Arbor: Department of Slavic Languages and Literatures of the University of Michigan) 36–52.

BYNON, Theodora 1978: *Historical linguistics,* corrected edition. Cambridge Textbooks in Linguistics. Cambridge: Cambridge University Press.

CHAFE, Wallace L. 1976: Giveness, contrastiveness, definiteness, subjects, topics, and point of view. In Li (1976) 25–55.

CHOMSKY, Noam 1965: *Aspects of the theory of syntax*. Cambridge, Mass.: MIT Press.

CHOMSKY, Noam & HALLE, Morris 1968: *The sound pattern of English*. Studies in Language. New York: Harper & Row.

CHOMSKY, Noam & HAMPSHIRE, Stuart 1968: Noam Chomsky and Stuart Hampshire discuss the study of language. *The Listener* (London: British Broadcasting Corporation) 79, no. 2044 (30 May 1968) 687–91.

COLE, Peter 1976: An apparent asymmetry in the formation of relative clauses in Modern Hebrew. In Cole, Peter, editor, *Studies in Modern Hebrew syntax and semantics*. North-Holland Linguistic Series 32. (Amsterdam: North-Holland) 231–47.

COLE, Peter 1982: *Imbabura Quechua*. Lingua Descriptive Studies 4. Amsterdam: North-Holland.

COLE, Peter, HARBERT, Wayne, HERMON, Gabriella, & SRIDHAR, S. N. 1980: The acquisition of subjecthood. *Language* 56, 719–43.

COLE, Peter & SADOCK, Jerrold M., editors 1977: *Grammatical relations*. Syntax and Semantics 8. New York: Academic Press.

COLE, Peter & SRIDHAR, S. N. 1977: Clause union and relational grammar: evidence from Hebrew and Kannada. *Linguistic Inquiry* 8, 700–13.

COMRIE, Bernard 1975: Causatives and universal grammar. *Transactions of the Philological Society 1974* (Oxford: Basil Blackwell) 1–32.

COMRIE, Bernard 1976: The syntax of causative constructions: cross-language similarities and divergences. In Shibatani (1976a) 261–312.

COMRIE, Bernard 1977a: In defense of spontaneous demotion: the impersonal passive. In Cole & Sadock (1977) 47–58.

COMRIE, Bernard 1977b: Subjects and direct objects in Uralic languages: a functional explanation of case-marking systems. *Études Finno-Ougriennes* 12 (Budapest: Akadémiai Kiadó) 5–17.

COMRIE, Bernard 1978a: Definite direct objects and referent identification. *Pragmatics Microfiche* (Oxford: Basil Blackwell) 3.1.D3.

COMRIE, Bernard 1978b: Ergativity. In Lehmann (1978b) 329–94.

COMRIE, Bernard 1978c: Genitive-accusatives in Slavic: the rules and their motivation. In Comrie, Bernard, editor, *Classification of grammatical categories. International Review of Slavic Linguistics* 3.1–2 (Edmonton, Alberta: Linguistic Research) 27–42.

COMRIE, Bernard 1978d: Linguistics is about languages. In Kachru, Braj B., editor, *Linguistics in the seventies: directions and prospects. Studies in the Linguistic Sciences*, Special issue (Urbana, Ill.: Department of Linguistics, University of Illinois) 221–36.

COMRIE, Bernard 1978e: Review of Dixon (1977). *Lingua* 46, 281–93.

COMRIE, Bernard 1979a: The animacy hierarchy in Chukchee. In Clyne, Paul R., Hanks, William F., & Hofbauer, Carol L., editors, *The elements: a parasession on linguistic units and levels, including papers from the Conference on Non-Slavic Languages of the USSR* (Chicago: Chicago Linguistic Society) 322–9.

COMRIE, Bernard 1979b: Definite and animate direct objects: a natural class. *Linguistica Silesiana* 3 (Katowice: University of Silesia) 13–21.

COMRIE, Bernard 1979c: Degrees of ergativity: some Chukchee evidence. In Plank (1979) 219–40.

COMRIE, Bernard 1979d: Russian. In Shopen (1979b) 91–151.

COMRIE, Bernard 1980: Morphology and word order reconstruction: problems and prospects. In Fisiak, Jacek, editor, *Historical morphology*. Trends in Linguistics, Studies and Monographs 17 (The Hague: Mouton) 83–96.

COMRIE, Bernard 1981a: Aspect and voice: some reflections on perfect and passive. In Tedeschi, Philip J. & Zaenen, Annie, editors, *Tense and aspect*. Syntax and Semantics 14 (New York: Academic Press) 65–78.

COMRIE, Bernard 1981b: Ergativity and grammatical relations in Kalaw Lagaw Ya (Saibai dialect). *Australian Journal of Linguistics* 1, 1–42.

COMRIE, Bernard 1982: Grammatical relations in Huichol. In Hopper, Paul J. & Thompson, Sandra A., editors, *Studies in transitivity*. Syntax and Semantics 15 (New York: Academic Press) 95–115.

COMRIE, Bernard Forthcoming, a: Causative verb formation and other verb-deriving morphology. In Shopen (forthcoming).

COMRIE, Bernard Forthcoming, b: On the morphological typology of Balto-Finnic: a reassessment. *Etudes Finno-Ougriennes* (Budapest: Akadémiai Kiadó).

COMRIE, Bernard & SMITH, Norval 1977: Lingua Descriptive Series: questionnaire. *Lingua* 42, 1–72.

CONKLIN, H. C. 1955: Hanunóo color categories. *Southwestern Journal of Anthropology* 11, 339–44.

CORBETT, G. G. 1978: Numerous squishes and squishy numerals in Slavonic. In Comrie, Bernard, editor, *Classification of grammatical categories*. *International Review of Slavic Linguistics* 3.1–2 (Edmonton, Alberta: Linguistic Research) 43–73.

DELANCEY, Scott 1981: An interpretation of split ergativity and related patterns. *Language* 57, 626–57.

DERBYSHIRE, Desmond C. 1977: Word order universals and the existence of OVS languages. *Linguistic Inquiry* 8, 590–9.

DERBYSHIRE, Desmond C. 1979: *Hixkaryana*. Lingua Descriptive Studies 1. Amsterdam: North-Holland.

DERBYSHIRE, Desmond C. & PULLUM, Geoffrey K. 1981: Object initial languages. *International Journal of American Linguistics* 47, 192–214.

DE RIJK, Rudolf P. G. 1972: Relative clauses in Basque: a guided tour. In Peranteau et al. (1972) 115–35.

DEŠERIEV, Ju. D. 1953: *Bacbijskij jazyk*. Moscow: Izdatel'stvo Akademii Nauk SSSR.

DIXON, R. M. W. 1972: *The Dyirbal language of North Queensland*. Cambridge Studies in Linguistics 9. Cambridge: Cambridge University Press.

DIXON, R. M. W. 1977: *A grammar of Yidiny*. Cambridge Studies in Linguistics 19. Cambridge: Cambridge University Press.

DIXON, R. M. W. 1979: Ergativity. *Language* 55, 59–138.

DIXON, R. M. W. 1980: *The languages of Australia*. Cambridge Language Surveys. Cambridge: Cambridge University Press.

FILLMORE, Charles J. 1968: The case for case. In Bach, Emmon & Harms, Robert T., editors, *Universals in linguistic theory* (New York: Holt, Rinehart & Winston) 1–88.

FRIEDMAN, Lynn A. 1976: The manifestation of subject, object, and topic in American Sign Language. In Li (1976) 125–48.

FRIEDRICH, Paul 1975: *Proto-Indo-European syntax: the order of meaningful elements*. *Journal of Indo-European Studies*, Monograph 1. Butte, Montana: Montana College of Mineral Science and Technology.

FRISHBERG, Nancy 1972: Navaho object markers and the great chain of being. In Kimball, John P., editor, *Syntax and Semantics* 1 (New York: Seminar Press) 259–66.

GARY, Judith Olmsted & KEENAN, Edward L. 1977: On collapsing grammatical relations in universal grammar. In Cole & Sadock (1977) 83–120.

GASS, S. 1980: An investigation of syntactic transfer in adult second language learners. In Scarcella, Robin C. & Krashen, Stephen D., editors, *Research in second language acquisition: selected papers of the Los Angeles Second Language Acquisition Research Forum*. Series on Issues in Second Language Research (Rowley, Mass.: Newbury House) 132–41.

GIVÓN, Talmy 1975a: Promotion, accessibility and case-marking: toward understanding grammars. *Working Papers on Language Universals* 19, 55–125.

GIVÓN, Talmy 1975b: Serial verbs and syntactic change: Niger-Congo. In Li (1975) 47–112.

GIVÓN, Talmy 1976: Topic, pronoun, and grammatical agreement. In Li (1976) 149–88.

GOODWIN, William W. 1894: *A Greek grammar*, new edition. London: Macmillan.

GREENBERG, Joseph H. 1960: A quantitative approach to the morphological typology of language. *International Journal of American Linguistics* 26, 178–94.

GREENBERG, Joseph H. 1966a: *Language universals, with special reference to feature hierarchies*. Janua Linguarum, Series Minor 59. The Hague: Mouton.

GREENBERG, Joseph H. 1966b: Some universals of grammar with particular reference to the order of meaningful elements. In Greenberg (1966c) 73–113.

GREENBERG, Joseph H., editor 1966c: *Universals of language*, second edition. Cambridge, Mass.: MIT Press.

GREENBERG, Joseph H. 1974: *Language typology: a historical and analytic overview*. Janua Linguarum, Series Minor 184. The Hague: Mouton.

GREENBERG, Joseph H., FERGUSON, Charles A., & MORAVCSIK, Edith A., editors 1978: *Universals of human language*, 4 volumes: 1, *Method and theory*, 2, *Phonology*, 3, *Word structure*, 4, Syntax. Stanford, Calif.: Stanford University Press.

HAIMAN, John. 1979: Hua: a Papuan language of New Guinea. In Shopen (1979b) 35–89.

HALE, Kenneth 1976: The adjoined relative clause in Australia. In Dixon, R. M. W., editor, *Grammatical categories in Australian languages*. Linguistic Series 22 (Canberra: Australian Institute of Aboriginal Studies) 78–105.

HAWKINS, John A. 1979: Implicational universals as predictors of word order change. *Language* 55, 618–48.

HAWKINS, John A. 1980: On implicational and distributional universals of word order. *Journal of Linguistics* 16, 193–235.

HAWKINSON, Annie K. & HYMAN, Larry M. 1974: Hierarchies of natural topic in Shona. *Studies in African Linguistics* 5, 147–70.

HEATH, Jeffrey. 1976: Substantival hierarchies: addendum to Silverstein. In Dixon, R. M. W., editor, *Grammatical categories in Australian languages*. Linguistic Series 22 (Canberra: Australian Institute of Aboriginal Studies) 172–90.

HETZRON, Robert. 1976: On the Hungarian causative verb and its syntax. In Shibatani (1976a) 371–98.

HOCKETT, Charles F. 1955: *A manual of phonology*. Indiana University Publications in Anthropology and Linguistics, Memoir 11. Bloomington: Indiana University. (Reprinted 1974, University of Chicago Press.)

HOCKETT, Charles F. 1966: The problem of universals in language. In Greenberg (1966c) 1–29.

HOPPER, Paul J. & THOMPSON, Sandra A. 1980: Transitivity in grammar and discourse. *Language* 56, 251–99.

HUMBOLDT, Wilhelm von 1836: *Über die Verschiedenheit des menschlichen Sprachbaues und ihren Einfluss auf die geistige Entwickelung des Menschengeschlechts.* Berlin: Königliche Akademie der Wissenschaften.

HYMAN, Larry M. 1975: On the change from SOV to SVO: evidence from Niger-Congo. In Li (1975) 113–47.

HYMAN, Larry M. & SCHUH, Russell G. 1974: Universals of tone rules: evidence from West Africa. *Linguistic Inquiry* 5, 81–115.

JACOBSON, Steven A. 1977: A grammatical sketch of Siberian Yupik Eskimo. Fairbanks: Alaska Native Languages Center, University of Alaska.

JAKOBSON, Roman, FANT, C. Gunnar M., & HALLE, Morris 1973: *Preliminaries to speech analysis: the distinctive features and their correlates.* Cambridge, Mass.: MIT Press.

JOHNSON, David E. 1974: On the role of grammatical relations in linguistic theory. *Papers from the Tenth Regional Meeting, Chicago Linguistic Society* 269–83.

JOHNSON, David E. 1977a: On Keenan's definition of 'subject-of'. *Linguistic Inquiry* 8, 673–92.

JOHNSON, David E. 1977b: On relational constraints on grammars. In Cole & Sadock (1977) 151–78.

JOHNSON, David E. & POSTAL, Paul M. 1980: *Arc pair grammar.* Princeton: Princeton University Press.

KAY, Paul & MCDANIEL, Chad K. 1978: The linguistic significance of the meanings of basic color terms. *Language* 54, 610–46.

KEENAN, Edward L. 1975: Logical expressive power and syntactic variation in natural language. In Keenan, Edward L., editor, *Formal semantics of natural language* (Cambridge: Cambridge University Press) 406–21.

KEENAN, Edward L. 1976a: Remarkable subjects in Malagasy. In Li (1976) 247–301.

KEENAN, Edward L. 1976b: Towards a universal definition of subject. In Li (1976) 303–33.

KEENAN, Edward L. 1978: Language variation and the logical structure of universal grammar. In Seiler, Hansjakob, editor, *Language universals.* Tübinger Beiträge zur Linguistik 111 (Tübingen: Gunter Narr) 89–123.

KEENAN, Edward L. & COMRIE, Bernard 1977: Noun phrase accessibility and universal grammar. *Linguistic Inquiry* 8, 63–99.

KEENAN, Edward L. & COMRIE, Bernard 1979: Data on the noun phrase accessibility hierarchy. *Language* 55, 333–51.

KEPPING, K. B. 1979: Elements of ergativity and nominativity in Tangut. In Plank (1979) 263–77.

KIEFER, Ferenc 1967: *On emphasis and word order in Hungarian.* Indiana University Publications, Uralic and Altaic Series 76. Bloomington: Indiana University.

KUNO, Susumu 1972: Functional sentence perspective: a case study from Japanese and English. *Linguistic Inquiry* 3, 269–320.

LAMBTON, A. K. S. 1957: *Persian grammar*, corrected edition. Cambridge: Cambridge University Press.

LEHMANN, Winfred P. 1973: A structural principle of language and its implications. *Language* 49, 47–66.

LEHMANN, Winfred P. 1974: *Proto-Indo-European syntax*. Austin: University of Texas Press.

LEHMANN, Winfred P. 1978a: Conclusion: toward an understanding of the profound unity underlying languages. In Lehmann (1978b) 395–432.

LEHMANN, Winfred P., editor 1978b: *Syntactic typology: studies in the phenomenology of language*. Austin: University of Texas Press.

LESOURD, Philip 1976: Verb agreement in Fox. In Hankamer, Jorge & Aissen, Judith, editors, *Harvard studies in syntax and semantics* 2 (Cambridge, Mass.: Department of Linguistics, Harvard University) 445–528.

LI, Charles N., editor 1975: Word order and word order change. Austin: University of Texas Press.

LI, Charles N., editor 1976: *Subject and topic*. New York: Academic Press.

LYONS, John 1977: *Semantics*, 2 volumes. Cambridge: Cambridge University Press.

MCCAWLEY, James D. 1978: Language universals in linguistic argumentation. In Kachru, Braj B., editor, *Linguistics in the seventies: directions and prospects. Studies in the Linguistic Sciences*, Special issue (Urbana, Ill.: Department of Linguistics, University of Illinois) 205–19.

MCCLOSKEY, Michael James 1978: *A fragment of a grammar of Modern Irish*. Texas Linguistic Forum 12. Austin: Department of Linguistics, University of Texas.

MAXWELL, Daniel N. 1979: Strategies of relativization and NP accessibility. *Language* 55, 352–71.

MEILLET, Antoine & COHEN, Marcel, editors 1952: *Les langues du monde*, second edition. Paris: Champion.

MORAVCSIK, Edith A. 1978a: Language contact. In Greenberg *et al.* (1978) 1, 93–122.

MORAVCSIK, Edith A. 1978b: On the distribution of ergative and accusative patterns. *Lingua* 45, 233–79.

MÜHLHÄUSLER, Peter 1977: Creolisation of New Guinea Pidgin. In Wurm, S. A., editor, *New Guinea area languages and language study*, 3, *Language, culture, society, and the modern world*. Pacific Linguistics, Series C 40 (Canberra: Department of Linguistics, Research School of Pacific Studies, Australian National University) 567–76.

MUNRO, Pamela & GORDON, Lynn 1982: Syntactic relations in Western Muskogean. *Language* 58, 81–115.

NEDJALKOV, V. P. 1979: Degrees of ergativity in Chukchee. In Plank (1979) 241–62.

NEDJALKOV, V. P., OTAINA, G. A., & XOLODOVIČ, A. A. 1969: Morfologičeskij i leksičeskij kauzativy v nivxskom jazyke. In Xolodovič (1969) 179–99.

NEDJALKOV, V. P., OTAINA, G. A., & XOLODOVIČ, A. A. 1974: Diatezy i zalogi v nivxskom jazyke. In Xolodovič, A. A., editor, *Tipologija passivnyx konstrukcij: diatezy i zalogi* (Leningrad: 'Nauka') 232–51.

NEDJALKOV, V. P. & SIL'NICKIJ, G. G. 1969a: Tipologija kauzativnyx konstrukcij. In Xolodovič (1969) 5–19. (German translation: Typologie der kausativen Konstruktionen, *Folia Linguistica* 6 (1973) 273–90.)

NEDJALKOV, V. P. & SIL'NICKIJ, G. G. 1969b: Tipologija morfologičeskogo i leksičeskogo kauzativov. In Xolodovič (1969) 20–50. (English translation: The typology of morphological and lexical causatives. In Kiefer, Ferenc, editor, *Trends in Soviet theoretical linguistics* (1973). *Foundations of Language*, Supplementary Series 18 (Dordrecht: Reidel) 1–32.)

NUSSBAUM, Loren V., GAGE, William W., & VARRE, Daniel 1970: *Dakar Wolof: a basic course*. Washington, D.C.: Center for Applied Linguistics.

PAYNE, J. R. 1979: Transitivity and intransitivity in the Iranian languages of the USSR. In Clyne, Paul R., Hanks, William F., & Hofbauer, Carol L., editors, *The elements: a parasession on linguistic units and levels, including papers from the Conference on the Non-Slavic Languages of the USSR* (Chicago: Chicago Linguistic Society) 436–47.

PERANTEAU, Paul M., LEVI, Judith N., & PHARES, Gloria C., editors 1972: *The Chicago which hunt: Papers from the Relative Clause Festival*. Chicago: Chicago Linguistic Society.

PERLMUTTER, David M. 1971: *Deep and surface structure constraints in syntax*. The Transatlantic Series in Linguistics. New York: Holt, Rinehart & Winston.

PERLMUTTER, David M. 1978: Impersonal passives and the unaccusative hypothesis. *Proceedings of the Fourth Annual Meeting of the Berkeley Linguistics Society* (Berkeley: Department of Linguistics, University of California) 157–89.

PERLMUTTER, David M., editor Forthcoming: *Studies in relational grammar*, 2 volumes.

PLANK, Frans, editor 1979: *Ergativity: towards a theory of grammatical relations*. London: Academic Press.

RAMSDEN, H. 1963: *Weak-pronoun position in the early Romance languages*. Publications of the Faculty of Arts of the University of Manchester 14. Manchester: Manchester University Press.

ROSS, John R. 1967: *Constraints on variables in syntax*. Bloomington: Indiana University Linguistics Club.

SAKSENA, Anuradha 1980: The affected agent. *Language* 56, 812–26.

SAMPSON, Geoffrey 1975: *The form of language*. London: Weidenfeld & Nicolson.

SANDFELD, Kr. 1930: *Linguistique balkanique: problèmes et résultats*. Collection Linguistique publiée par la Société Linguistique de Paris 31 Paris: Champion.

SAPIR, Edward 1921: *Language: an introduction to the study of speech*. New York: Harcourt, Brace & World.

SAXTON, Dean & SAXTON, Lucille 1969: *Papago and Pima to English/English to Papago and Pima dictionary*. Tucson: University of Arizona Press.

SCHACHTER, Paul 1976: The subject in Philippine languages: topic, actor, actor-topic, or none of the above. In Li (1976) 491–518.

SCHACHTER, Paul 1977: Reference-related and role-related properties of subjects. In Cole & Sadock (1977) 279–306.

SCHALLER, Helmut Wilhelm 1975: *Die Balkansprachen: eine Einführung in die Balkanphilologie*. Heidelberg: Carl Winter.

SHIBATANI, Masayoshi, editor 1976a: *The grammar of causative constructions*. Syntax and Semantics 6. New York: Academic Press.

SHIBATANI, Masayoshi 1976b: The grammar of causative constructions: a conspectus. In Shibatani (1976a) 1–40.

SHIBATANI, Masayoshi 1977: Grammatical relations and surface cases. *Language* 53, 789–809.

SHOPEN, Timothy, editor 1979a: *Languages and their speakers*. Cambridge, Mass.: Winthrop.

SHOPEN, Timothy, editor 1979b: *Languages and their status*. Cambridge, Mass.: Winthrop.

SHOPEN, Timothy, editor Forthcoming: *Syntactic typology and linguistic fieldwork*, 3 volumes.

SHOPEN, Timothy, and KONARÉ, Mamadou 1970: Sonrai causatives and passives: transformational versus lexical derivations for propositional heads. *Studies in African Linguistics* 1, 211-54.

SILVERSTEIN, Michael 1976: Hierarchy of features and ergativity. In Dixon, R. M. W., editor, *Grammatical categories in Australian languages*. Linguistic Series 22 (Canberra: Australian Institute of Aboriginal Studies) 112–71.

SKORIK, P. Ja 1961: *Grammatika čukotskogo jazyka*, I, *Fonetika i morfologija imennyx častej reči*. Moscow-Leningrad: Izdatel'stvo Akademii Nauk SSSR.

SMITH, N. V. 1980: Review of Lehmann (1978b). *Journal of Linguistics* 16, 150–64.

SRIDHAR, S. N. 1976: Dative subjects, rule government, and relational grammar. *Studies in the Linguistic Sciences* 6 (Urbana, Ill.: Department of Linguistics, University of Illinois) 130–51.

SUTCLIFFE, Edmund F. 1936: *A grammar of the Maltese language, with chrestomathy and vocabulary*. London: Oxford University Press.

TAGASHIRA, Yoshiko 1972: Relative clauses in Korean. In Peranteau *et al.* (1972) 215–29.

THOMPSON, Sandra A. 1978: Modern English from a typological point of view: some implications of the function of word order. *Linguistische Berichte* 54, 19–35.

TIMBERLAKE, Alan. 1977: Reanalysis and actualization in syntactic change. In Li, Charles N., editor, *Mechanisms of syntactic change* (Austin: University of Texas Press) 169–83.

TITOV, E. G. 1959: Ob osobennostjax amxarskogo jazyka v sravnenii s nekotorymi drugimi semitskimi jazykami. In Ol'derogge, D. A., editor, *Afrikanskij etnografičeskij sbornik*, 3, *Jazykoznanie* (Moscow-Leningrad: Izdatel'stvo Akademii Nauk SSSR) 169–83.

VENNEMANN, Theo. 1972: Analogy in generative grammar, the origin of word order. In Heilmann, Luigi, editor, *Proceedings of the Eleventh International Congress of Linguists*, 2 volumes (Bologna: Il Mulino) 2, 79–83.

VENNEMANN, Theo. 1974: Topics, subjects, and word order: from SXV to SVX via TVX. In Anderson, John M. & Jones, Charles, editors, *Historical linguistics*. North-Holland Linguistic Series 12 (Amsterdam: North-Holland) 339–76.

VOEGELIN, C. F. & VOEGELIN, F. M. 1977: *Classification and index of the world's languages*. New York: Elsevier.

WACHTEL, Tom 1979: The demotion analysis of initially unaccusative impersonal passives. *Papers from the Fifteenth Regional Meeting, Chicago Linguistic Society* 321–30.

WATKINS, Calvert 1976: Towards Proto-Indo-European syntax: problems and pseudo-problems. In Steever, Sanford B., Walker, Carol A., & Mufwene, Salikoko S., editors, *Papers from the parasession on diachronic syntax* (Chicago: Chicago Linguistic Society) 305–26.

WEINREICH, Uriel. 1953: *Languages in contact: findings and problems*. Publications of the Linguistic Circle of New York 1. (Reprinted by Mouton, The Hague.)

Working Papers on Language Universals 1969–76: 20 volumes and bibliography. Stanford, Calif.: Linguistics Department, Stanford University.

XOLODOVIČ, A. A., editor 1969: *Tipologija kauzativnyx konstrukcij: morfologičeskij kauzativ*. Leningrad: 'Nauka'.

YAR-SHATER, Ehsan 1969: *A grammar of southern Tati dialects*. Median Dialect Studies 1. Publications in Near and Middle East Studies, Columbia University, Series B 3. The Hague: Mouton.

YEOH, Chiang Kee 1979: *Interaction of rules in Bahasa Malaysia*. Ph.D. dissertation, University of Illinois at Urbana-Champaign.

ŽIRKOV, L. I. 1955: *Lakskij jazyk: fonetika i morfologija*. Moscow: Izdatel'stvo Akademii Nauk SSSR.

INDEX OF LANGUAGES

Languages and language families given in italics within an entry are also to be found as separate entries in this index. Controversial genetic groupings are so described (e.g. as putative language families), and no stand is taken on their validity.

235

INDEX OF PROPER NAMES

Where the occurrence of a name is subsumed in the text under *et al.*, this index gives in parentheses after the page reference the co-author mentioned by name in the text. See also the list of references (pages 226–34).

INDEX OF TOPICS